THE
FAMILY
MANAGER
TAKES
CHARGE

KATHY PEEL

Perigee Books

THE
FAMILY
MANAGER
TAKES
CHARGE

*Getting on the Fast Track
to a Happy, Organized Home*

While the author and publisher have no reason to believe that the methods and instructions set forth in this book are not safe and effective they do not make any warranties or representation with respect to such methods and instructions, and shall not be liable for any loss or damage to persons or property arising from the use thereof.

A Perigee Book
Published by The Berkley Publishing Group
A division of Penguin Group (USA) Inc.
375 Hudson Street
New York, New York 10014

Copyright © 2003 by Kathy Peel
Text design by Tiffany Estreicher
Cover design by Wendy Bass
Illustrations by Laura Cornell

ISBN: 0-399-52913-6

First edition: September 2003

Peel, Kathy, 1951–
    The family manager takes charge : getting on the fast track to a happy, organized home / Kathy Peel—1st ed.
        p. cm
Includes index.
        1. Home economics. I. Title.

TX147.P343 2003
640—dc21

2003057200

Printed in the United States of America

10   9   8   7   6   5   4   3

Contents

CONTENTS

PART II:

Taking Charge of Meals and Entertaining 197

You don't need to be a gourmet cook!

PART III:

Taking Charge of Your Family's Money 261

You don't have to be a Wall Street wizard!

Acknowledgments

Any good manager—whether she runs a home, company or book project—doesn't try to do it alone. Building a good team is what it's about: everyone working together doing what they do best. I am deeply grateful to my family team, Bill, John, Joel and James Peel; my good friend and agent, Patti DeMatteo; publisher of Perigee Books, John Duff; editorial assistant, Kathryn McHugh; my team of contributing editors and editorial assistants; and the experts in various fields who have helped make sure this is a book that will help you be the best family manager you can be. The management of this project has been a delightful experience because of the hard work and commitment to excellence of the following people:

CONTRIBUTING EDITORS:
Rosemary Black
Maureen Connolly
Holly Halverson
Doug Mackay
Ann Matturro

EDITORIAL ASSISTANTS:
Sally Grammar
Catherine Ray
Audra Sullins
Michal Sullivan

THE FAMILY MANAGER'S CREED

I oversee the most important organization in the world—

Where hundreds of decisions are made daily

Where property and resources are managed

Where health and nutritional needs are determined

Where finances and futures are discussed and debated

Where projects are planned and events are arranged

Where transportation and scheduling are critical

Where team-building is a priority

Where careers begin and end

I am a Family Manager.

Introduction

This is a true story. I never did a load of laundry in my life until I went away to college. I was seventeen years old and doing well in school, but to save my life, I couldn't figure out how to start the washing machine and I was far too embarrassed to admit that to anyone. So, the first time I "washed" clothes, I put the detergent and the dirty clothes in the dryer. Not a good move. The heat from the dryer melted the soap. My socks stuck to my nightshirt. My bras and panties stuck to . . . well, never mind. Let's just say it wasn't a pretty sight.

When I got married the summer before my senior year and began my role as the Peel Family Manager, I was domestically challenged—very. In addition to my laundry room woes, I struggled with keeping the house clean and organized, preparing meals, balancing the checkbook plus completing many other household jobs other women seemed to excel at—and even enjoy—instinctively. I wondered what was wrong with me.

You see, my mother was a businesswoman. She owned several dress shops and had help at home by way of a cook and housekeeper. So, I never learned to sew, clean house, or prepare food. Clearly, domestic issues were a challenge for me, but putting myself down wasn't going to change that. To make myself feel better I decided to face the fact that I had a lot to learn, and I headed for the library. I wanted to know how to create a smoothly functioning, warm, and welcoming home, so I hit the books. I read countless how-to manuals, looking for information about how to do housework faster and more efficiently. I collected piles of magazine articles that promised to help me get dinner on the table at a decent hour and the kitchen clean in record time. I devoured dozens of money management books, trying to gain insights from the experts. And I interviewed many successful Family Managers. Whenever I found myself admiring someone else's family, I'd track down the mom and seek advice. How did she do it, I wanted to know. Why were she and her kids always smiling? How could I get to that same calm, happy place?

After a while their answers started sounding the same. These women spoke of setting priorities, making plans, having a vision, sharing responsibility and taking one day at a time. They sounded like managers. In fact, running a home and raising a family sounded a little like running a business. That's when it dawned on me. Why not apply some fundamental business strategies—managing by department, team-building, delegating, establishing routines—to the business of running a home?

Mom may not have taught me how to make a meatloaf but I did know a lot about running a business. I was good at problem-solving, team-building, goal-setting, delegating, budgeting money and innovating. What if I applied these skills to my family? Perhaps if I thought more like a manager my home would run more smoothly.

To prove my theory, I started reading again, this time picking up book after book on business management and leadership, and I found that my hunch was correct. The same principles and procedures that make companies operate productively can benefit families, too.

I call it The Family Manager System and the way I see it, we are nurturing the most important organization in the world: the family. I believe it is our job to ensure that our home becomes a greenhouse where each of the human lives within it can flourish.

As Family Managers we have enormous influence on our children and spouses. So, the next time the countless, mundane tasks you and I perform on a daily basis start getting you down, consider this: making lunches, folding laundry and creating a college savings plan for our children are as critically important as reaching a sales quota or winning a case in court.

I sincerely believe that strong families build strong communities. Strong communities build a strong culture, and a strong culture builds a strong country. Who can tell what might result if we all began to find a haven of peace, sanity and happiness at home? Yes, our role as Family Managers is very important, because behind every great person, you usually find a great family.

A Well-Run Family Is a Happy Family

Good family management has more benefits than just increasing efficiency. Knowing your life is in some order reduces stress, quells frustration and boosts confidence. In short, establishing your own method of surviving and thriving means that you, the Family Manager, have a more enjoyable job, too. And everyone feels the effects of that.

But please understand! The point of this book is not to turn you into something you're not. I'm not recommending that you alphabetize your soup cans or rotate your shoes so they wear out evenly—unless that makes sense to you and your family.

The goal for all of us is to run our homes more efficiently—not run them, or ourselves, into the ground. Countless women feel desperate for help but, like I was, are too embarrassed to ask a friend or family member for basic home-management information. If you're one of those women, I hope you'll let me be that big sister or close girlfriend you can come to. Thirty-two years of marriage and twenty-nine years of motherhood has afforded me a lot of practical experience. I know a whole lot about running a home and family—and I'm here for you.

The goal of this book is to provide you with the means for being a great success as a Family Manager. You will find a comprehensive guide, organized by the many jobs every mom undertakes. Each section includes hundreds of practical strategies, tips and lists. Plus, in the first chapter, "You're the CEO," you'll find a quick overview of the management course we all needed before we married. This is the book I needed when I married my husband and had children: the how-to for every aspect of family life.

Ah! There is nothing like staying at home, for real comfort.
—Jane Austen

Putting up the school lunch for the children or cooking a good meal for the family may seem very insignificant tasks as compared with giving a lecture, writing a book, or doing other things that have a larger audience; but I doubt very much if, in the ultimate reckoning, they will count for as much.
—Laura Ingalls Wilder, Little House in the Ozarks

Benefits of the Family Manager System

The Family Manager System will help you:

1. Create order out of chaos.

2. Focus your time and energy.

3. Spend less time on the have-to's; have more time for the want-to's.

4. Make selective decisions when you are overloaded with options.

5. Live a balanced life.

6. Stay motivated.

7. Establish and stick to priorities.

8. Plan memorable events and occasions that strengthen family ties.

9. Affect the quality of your life for the better.

10. Improve the quality of your family's life.

The book is divided into three parts that correspond to the three biggest departments under your care: Taking Charge Around the House, Taking Charge of Meals and Entertaining, and Taking Charge of Money. You'll find that by managing these areas smarter, you'll accomplish many of the mundane maintenance chores you dread faster. The end result? Your home and your life will be happier, schedules will run more smoothly and you'll mitigate that nagging I'll-never-catch-up feeling.

Keep the End Goal in Mind

All good home and family management is about nurturing human lives—including your own—by creating a home where family members feel good about where they live. It's about helping family members love themselves and others. It's about helping them feel a sense of responsibility to be the best they can be and to share their skills, resources and love with family, friends and strangers. It's about giving each other—and yourself—room and time to grow, getting and giving the mental, physical, spiritual and emotional nourishment you all need. All in all, it's about creating a happy home.

If all of this sounds too lofty, too noble, *relax.* Think of yourself as a Family Manager on the road to becoming a *better* Family Manager. Don't get down on yourself when you make mistakes. No one has ever been or ever will be a perfect mom. What's important is that we keep learning and trying.

May this book inspire, guide and encourage you every step of the way.

PART I

Taking Charge Around the House

It has been said that home is where the heart is. But it's also where the furniture, appliances, clothing, electronic gadgetry, sports equipment, tools and toys are, too. Many homes also come with garages, basements, attics and yards. All of this needs cleaning, maintaining and decluttering—a huge task.

Don't worry. There is a sane way to do it, and do it you must, or be robbed of the ability to relax and enjoy your nest. Not being able to put your hands on something when you need it or finally finding what you're looking for, only to discover it's not working, is annoying, stressful and a huge waste of time. A home that runs smoothly—one that is attractive, yet functional, and most of all fun—is just what the doctor (who makes house calls) ordered!

As Family Managers, we are the sculptors of our homes and families. Managing our home and property is about much more than having orderly closets. It's important work. Whenever I'm dreading an onerous chore I think of Winston Churchill's lovely image of home. He said, "We shape our houses, then our houses shape us." This place where we eat, sleep, play and recuperate from the day's stresses is something *we* create. That, my fellow Family Managers, is an awesome responsibility.

Of course, I can't tell you exactly how to manage every detail of your home and property. A lot of it has to do with the uniqueness of your family—the age of your children, how much laundry you do, the kind of furniture you have, the size of your home and yard, how much clutter you can tolerate and the amount of time you're willing to devote to the task. But I can tell you this: whether you live in a cottage or a castle, the time you spend thinking about the type of home in which you are raising your children is time well spent.

Getting organized and attending to the seemingly endless details of home and property may not be much fun but being organized will save you time, money, energy and stress. Fortunately, the ideas and strategies in this book will help you meet these goals and send you on your way to creating the well-run home of your dreams.

CHAPTER 1

You're the CEO

In my continuing pursuit to become a better manager of my home and family, I've read a lot about corporate management, effective leadership and the habits and philosophies of renowned CEOs. I found that many of the skills required for success—in business or in the family—are the same. Here are some of the words that inspired me most:

- Peter Drucker, the father of modern management, taught me **the value of time**: "Time is the scarcest resource, and unless it is managed, nothing else can be managed."
- Tom Landry, legendary coach of the Dallas Cowboys, explained **the importance of team-building**: "I don't believe you can effectively manage people without helping them understand where they fit into the goals of the organization. So individual goal-setting becomes an important means of communicating with a player and involving him in the team."
- Henry Ford showed me how to **break big tasks into little pieces**: "Nothing is particularly hard if you divide it into small jobs."
- Theodore Roosevelt's words gave me much-needed **perspective**: "Do what you can, with what you have, where you are."

- Tom Peters, author and management guru, inspired me to **think outside the box** and look for creative solutions when faced with obstacles, with his book *The Circle of Innovation*.
- And lastly, former Chrysler Chairman Lee Iacocca's wise observation helped me understand **the importance of managing myself first**: "I'm constantly amazed by the number of people who can't seem to control their own schedules. Over the years, I've had many executives say with pride: 'Boy, last year I worked so hard that I didn't take any vacation.' It's actually nothing to brag about and I always feel like responding, 'You dummy. You mean to tell me you can take responsibility for an 80 million dollar project and you can't plan two weeks off with your family to have some fun?'"

Thinking like a CEO and seeing myself as the person in charge of an important organization—my family—is how I have realized my dream of a happy home. The following eleven essential strategies are the culmination of thirty-two years of research, experience and thinking about a concept in which I truly believe. No matter what the makeup of your family, I believe the Family Manager method of running a home can work as well for you as it has for us.

Family Management: A Primer

I. SEE YOURSELF AS A TRUE "MANAGER."

Being a mom means more than being a parent. You oversee an economic institution that includes such services as meal preparation, housecleaning, transporting people, shopping, lawn maintenance, car and house repairs and banking.

The following list may be a stunning look at all the jobs you likely manage. Check the jobs that apply to you:

☐ Accountant/Bookkeeper ☐ Building Supervisor
☐ Auto Maintenance Supervisor ☐ Chauffeur
☐ Baby-sitter/Day-care Worker ☐ Cheerleader

> *By and large, mothers and housewives are the only workers who do not have regular time off. They are the great vacationless class.*
>
> —Anne Morrow Lindbergh

☐ Chef

☐ Coach/Team-builder

☐ Counselor

☐ Dean of Education

☐ Entertainment Chairman

☐ Fashion Coordinator

☐ Filing Clerk

☐ Fitness Trainer

☐ Gardener

☐ Gift Coordinator

☐ Health-care Practitioner

☐ Historian and Curator

☐ Hotel Manager

☐ Interior Designer

☐ Laundress

☐ Maid

☐ Manager of Food Services

☐ Purchasing Agent

☐ Referee

☐ Seamstress

☐ Secretary

☐ Short-order Cook

☐ Travel Agent

☐ Veterinarian

As you can see, being a Family Manager is no small task. To keep things running smoothly, you need to function as a manager.

2. MANAGE BY DEPARTMENTS.

While none of us performs all of the jobs listed above in any one day, we do most of them regularly. We need a way to approach and attack our never-ending responsibilities—lest we end up in a home for the terminally overwhelmed. It was the salvation of my sanity and revolutionary to my family when I realized that all the chores and responsibilities of running a home and family—whether they have to do with the house, clothing, children, relatives, bank accounts, pantry, schools, vacations, furniture, holidays and so on—fall into seven distinct departments. Compartmentalizing my duties made a lot of sense. These departments are:

1. **Home and Property**. Overseeing the maintenance and care of all tangible assets, including personal belongings, the house and its surroundings.
2. **Food**. Meeting the daily food and nutrition needs of the family economically and creatively.
3. **Money**. Budgeting, investing, paying bills, saving and handling a host of other monetary issues.

4. **Family and Friends**. Dealing with family life and relationships, including child-rearing, education, marriage, friends, neighbors and aging parents.

5. **Special Events**. Coordinating large and small projects—birthdays, holidays, vacations, garage sales, family reunions—that fall outside the normal family routine.

6. **Time and Scheduling**. Acting as the facilitator so the household runs smoothly and family members get to the right places at the right time, with the right equipment.

7. **Self-Management**. Taking care of yourself physically, emotionally, intellectually and spiritually.

This book focuses on the first three (and biggest) departments. Taking control of these areas will get you well on your way to creating a smoothly run, well-organized home.

3. HAVE A BASE OF OPERATION.

Every manager needs a Control Central, be it a desk, countertop or office. In a company, it's the place from which he or she calls the shots. In a home, it's the place from which the Family Manager organizes, tracks the family's schedule, notes changes, responds to messages, makes lists and keeps all those important papers in their places. By setting up your own Control Central, you can better oversee your family's comings and goings and manage the countless tasks, responsibilities and decisions that are made every day. If the CEO is calm and organized, everyone else is too.

4. KNOW YOUR MISSION.

Successful businesses have a mission. They know where they are going. It's not a big leap to see that if successful companies have a mission statement, we as Family Managers should, too.

When I tried my hand at writing a mission statement, here's what I wrote:

My mission is to create a home that my family (me included) would describe as a great place to be; a home where family members know they are valued, where they feel loved for who they are as individuals, where they know they belong yet can grow in their separate interests; a home that is comfortable and relaxed enough for those of us who can stand clutter, and orderly enough for those of us who like everything in its place.

Over the years, I've simplified my mission statement to read:

To create a home full of love and comfort, order and flexibility, stimulation and relaxation.

As you think about your mission for your home, also think about what you *don't* want it to be, such as a fast-food drive-thru where family members rush in, grab a bite to eat and clean clothes, ask for money, exchange a few words and rush out again. In large part it's up to you and me, the Family Managers, to prevent whatever we don't want from happening.

5. DREAM BIG.

Successful companies don't get that way because the leaders believe in resting on their laurels and settling for past accomplishments. No, admired leaders dream of change for the better, envision positive development and hope for the improvement of something—whether it be a product, service, neighborhood, city or country.

If we aspire to be successful Family Managers, we need to share that visionary quality. We must spend time dreaming, picturing what our home, family and life would look like at their best. (Keep in mind that this means *your* family's best—not another families' best.) To improve anything, we have to start with an honest evaluation of how it is now. Place an X by the following words you feel describe your home today. Then place a ✓ by the words that you would like to describe your home.

☐ Welcoming	☐ Uncomfortable	☐ Messy
☐ Stressful	☐ Light	☐ Cluttered
☐ Warm	☐ Dark	☐ Unpleasant
☐ Drab	☐ Dirty	☐ Happy

Take Note

Think about what's truly important to you. What do you want to see happen in your home and in your life? Unless you know what's most important, your life will be tyrannized by the urgent.

To be happy at home is the ultimate result of all ambition, the end to which every enterprise and labour tends.
—Samuel Johnson

7

☐ User-friendly	☐ Quiet	☐ Energizing
☐ Perfect	☐ Fun	☐ Homey
☐ Neat	☐ Calm and	☐ Convenient
☐ Noisy	soothing	☐ Joyful
☐ Chaotic	☐ Confusing	☐ Tacky
☐ Unorganized	☐ Rigid	☐ Intense
☐ Tidy	☐ Unsanitary	☐ Imaginative
☐ Shiny	☐ Disheveled	☐ Fragrant
☐ Sloppy	☐ Grand	☐ Purposeful
☐ Organized	☐ Creative	☐ Simple
☐ Orderly	☐ Chaotic	☐ Appropriate
☐ Attractive	☐ Fun	☐ Immaculate
☐ Formal	☐ Coordinated	☐ Functional
☐ Dusty	☐ Large	☐ Fresh
☐ Smelly	☐ Cozy	☐ Bright
☐ Beautiful	☐ Different	☐ Spacious
☐ Charming	☐ Unique	☐ Cold
☐ Positive	☐ Spirited	☐ Expensive
☐ Well-arranged	☐ Balanced	☐ Relaxed
☐ Tense	☐ Eclectic	☐ Sunny

Congratulations, you have begun to dream big! Now you can begin realizing that dream.

6. WORK SMARTER.

It occurred to me one day that I could be working smarter—spending less time on the things I *have* to do and more time on the things I *want* to do. Maybe it was all the time I wasted scrubbing pans until I figured out that if I coated it first with nonstick vegetable spray, whether the recipe called for it or not, I could cut down on cleanup time. Or, perhaps it was when I finally realized that by grocery shopping during off-peak hours I'd spend a lot less time in the check-out line.

A good manager is always learning from her mistakes and scheming, if you will, for a better way to do things. It's important—no, essential—to get into the habit of thinking about how you can make your job more

"Whoever lives is always learning."
—Giovanni Battista Gelli

efficient and—dare I say it?—more enjoyable. Working smarter primarily means spending a little extra time on something now to make more time for fun later.

7. MAXIMIZE YOUR STRENGTHS.

Let's face it: none of us does everything equally well. And you know what, that's okay! There are many ways to fill in the gaps. For example, if you hate to cook, but have a good eye for style and color, when you entertain, you can serve simple, but nicely presented food or plan parties when you know your husband can give you a lot of support in the kitchen. Or, if you have the money, you might hire a caterer. No matter how the food gets on the table, I bet you like to have fresh-cut flowers arranged in various containers, your table usually looks great and your house is decorated according to the season or occasion.

Our weaknesses can actually have unexpected and delightful consequences. For example, I had the idea to install a valance above our bedroom window but I realized I had two choices: I could put myself down because I couldn't make it myself or I could pick out the fabric, set up the sewing machine and supplies and ask my husband, Bill, for help. Since he's a detail person, he's terrific at measuring and stitching. As a result of my inability to sew, we spent time working on a project together *and* made our bedroom look better.

8. BUILD A TEAM AND DELEGATE.

Family management, like all good management, is not about autocratic rulers imposing arbitrary standards from on high. It is not about inventing and engraving in stone a family bureaucracy that will give you headaches, make your children want to join a union, and have your husband filling out forms in triplicate just to get a Friday-night movie date with you. Modern management provides peace, fun and a sense of satisfaction—for *everyone* in the family. By functioning like a team, rather than a group of individuals, you'll have a better time and increase your ability to get things done. Activities that aren't particularly enjoyable, such as weekly cleaning chores, take less time and take on new meaning when everyone shares in the burden.

Take Note

Good family management demands a set of skills that no one person has. There will always be jobs we hate. The trick is learning to work with our strengths, work around areas where we are not gifted and work through people who are.

To build your team, focus on the "in" list.

What's In	What's Out
Do it together	Do it yourself
Collaborate	Legislate
Brainstorming	Fretting
Cooperation	Do your own thing
Convictions	Convenience
Best effort	Perfection
Accept	Reject
Be good at a few things	Be mediocre at a lot of things
Mergers	Competition
Encouragement	Criticism
Flexibility	Rigidity
Faith	Distrust
Distributive authority	Dictators
Everyone has something to contribute	Mother knows best
Serving	Servitude
Trying different approaches	Sticking to the way you've always done it

A good manager assumes responsibility for initiating projects and provides needed assistance toward their completion, yet will delegate tasks as needed. In a family, this means sharing responsibility. If a twelve-year-old girl can master the computer to stay in touch with her friends over the Internet, she can certainly learn basic laundry skills. Any man who can program a VCR so he won't miss game four of the World Series can learn how to start the washing machine. Even a preschool-age child can help dust baseboards and fold towels and, at that age, kids love to help. The home belongs to the entire family, so all of its members should contribute to its care.

9. KNOW YOUR MANAGING STYLE.

All of us have energy boosters and drainers in our lives. There are some things we love to do that actually energize us. Sometimes I can work on a project for hours at a time—through meals and late into the night—and feel invigorated. Other activities drain me, five minutes seems like five hours.

It's important for every Family Manager to discover her unique—I repeat *unique*—style. To do this, you need to know yourself, the ways you like to work and the atmosphere in which you work best in, so you can better develop your strengths, compensate for your weaknesses, choose your priorities and delegate wisely.

Ponder the following questions to come to a greater understanding of how you work best.

- What makes me feel energetic?
- What drains my energy?
- What time of day do I feel I'm at my best?
- What motivates me?
- What frustrates me?
- Do I like focusing on one thing or doing multiple things at once?

Remember, your answers to these questions will be unique to you. That's exactly what I mean by "your style," you're looking here to discover what works best for *you*, not your best friend, your mother, or another Family Manager you admire.

10. BE PREPARED.

Be prepared is the scout's motto but it could also be the Family Manager's motto. If you have a shelf stocked with office and school supplies, you won't have to run to the store at 10 P.M. in search of index cards and a folder for a child's report that's due the next day. If you have a list of quick menus and always keep the food supplies on hand, when you get a call from an out-of-town friend at dinnertime, pulling a nice meal together becomes much easier. If you're already operating by a budget you created, when you have a financial setback, it will be easier to identify areas where you can save on expenses. Being prepared is the number-one family-stress reducer. Spending time organizing your day or your week is time well spent.

So there you have it. The top 10 ways to be an effective Family Manager. Get ready to experience life as the CEO of a happy family. Being a mom never felt so good.

Building Your Team

One of the strategies that helps companies run smoother can also help your family run smoother: team-building. A good manager delegates tasks to others, assuming responsibility for initiating projects and providing needed assistance toward completion. A good Family Manager is always learning how better to get her family to work as a team.

There are a number of ways to involve your family in the process of becoming a one-for-all, all-for-one team. Many of the principles company managers use to motivate employees, improve productivity and boost morale work for Family Managers as well.

1. **Schedule a family meeting.** A few days before, post the time for the meeting on the refrigerator or somewhere everyone will see it often. Unless you have an unusual family, don't expect them to jump for joy over the fact that you're having a family meeting. Just make sure that each member knows that attendance is mandatory. Fix their favorite snack or dessert. Good food has a way of fostering goodwill and cooperation.

2. **Before the meeting, discuss the agenda with your spouse.** Explain that you want your home to be less stressful, more organized and a good place to be for all of you.

3. **"Market" your cause.** Family members won't buy into the cause of working as a team on household chores just because Mom says so or the Joneses do it that way. If your family understands how and why it will better their lives, they will be more likely to pitch in. For example:

   • If the house is cleaner, you can have sleepovers more often.
   • If we have a regular laundry plan, mornings will be less stressful because we'll always have clean clothes.

- If we all pitch in, it will get done sooner and we'll have more time for fun.
- If we all help out, Mom will be in a better mood. (This has great value.)

4. **Clearly state your motivation.** Make sure your spouse and kids know you're not trying to make them miserable or burden them with extra responsibilities; you're simply trying to make everyone's life a little easier by spreading out the work more evenly. Talk together about how if everyone benefits from your home, then everyone should contribute to its care.

5. **Take the high road.** No one will jump at the chance to be on your team if you're negative, critical, or playing chief nag. Don't say things like, "I'm sick and tired of living in a pigpen," "If you ever did anything around here . . ." or "I've told you that a thousand times . . ."

6. **Get input from the team.** Ask each family member what would make home a good place to be for him or her. Ask them to be as specific as possible. It's going to mean a lot to them that you care about what they think. Once everyone's had his or her say, review the suggestions and decide which ones are most important and do-able. What can you all agree on? What are bottom-liners for Mom and Dad?

7. **Come up with a *family* definition of "clean and organized."** The definition of clean and orderly to one person may be filthy and disorganized to another. For example, maybe your husband's mother kept a hospital-clean home so he thinks the kitchen should be cleaned three times a day, while you really see the need for that only once daily and your teenage son thinks it should be cleaned when there aren't any more clean dishes. Bear in mind that everyone will have to compromise on some things.

   If you're a neatnik, realize that attempts to reform the packrats in your family won't work. Instead, allow packrats some space of their own—preferably a confined space with a door—and make common areas clutter-free zones.

13

8. **Assign tasks specifically and set realistic goals.** "Just do your best" instructions can lead to frustrating results because you haven't set a measurable goal. Let each assignee know what the end result should look like. Perhaps your idea of cleaning the living room is making sure that everything is put away, pillows are fluffed, carpets are vacuumed, magazines are stacked nicely and there's no cat hair on the sofa. Maybe your ten year old's idea is that he spends an hour cleaning underneath the sofa pillows (looking for coins and treasures) and vacuuming the center of the room, tending to ignore the fur balls under the coffee table and all the rest of the mess. Devise a master chore list, and post it in a place where everyone can see it.

Creating Your Control Central

To most effectively corral and administrate the myriad details of family management, including the countless pieces of paper that come into your life every day, set up a home base of operation—a place where you run the show, so to speak.

SETTING UP SHOP

- Choose a smart location. A desk or countertop by the phone in the kitchen or family room is ideal, but the corner of a bedroom or hallway will work, too. My first Control Central was in a centrally located closet. I had a phone jack installed, created a desk from an old door and two filing cabinets and made a giant bulletin board to hang on the wall above the desk.
- It's ideal if your filing cabinet is easily accessible.
- Hang a family calendar on the wall, and record each person's appointments, activities and important dates. A bulletin board with plenty of pushpins is a good idea, too.
- Post a daily hit list, grouped according to the seven Family Manager departments, so it's easy to refer to when you're home. Don't forget to carry it with you if you're out running errands.

- Stock Control Central with pens, pencils, highlighters and some notepads for jotting down ideas and recording phone messages.
- Put a copy of your local phone directory there, as well as a list of the numbers your family regularly calls.
- Keep an ongoing grocery and personal-needs list here so family members will always know where to add items you're running low on.
- Have an easy-access file for take-out menus.
- Create a system for dealing with kids' school papers—permission forms, schedules, tests to be signed and so on. One way to do this is to set up in-boxes for your kids. (I like the stackable kind you can buy at office-supply stores, or use a stand-up tickler file.) Designate one in-box per child and label the front of it with his or her name. Have your children unload their backpacks first thing after school and put important papers in their in-boxes. Whichever method you use, it's Mom's or Dad's responsibility to go through the in-boxes at night.
- Keep a trash can close by.
- Create a "To Be Filed" box for important papers you need to save. When you have a five-minute block of time, file a few of the papers from the box into your filing system.
- Designate an envelope to store library and due date cards. When you come home from the library with children's books, take out the due date cards and put them and your child's library card in the envelope at Control Central for safekeeping. (Make a note on your calendar of the date they're due.) When it's time to return the books, you'll know how many to look for.

CONTROL CENTRAL DOS AND DON'TS FOR FAMILY MEMBERS

Have a family meeting to inaugurate and explain Control Central, what it's for, what it's not for and how to use it.

Do:
- Write all of your commitments—including sports events/practices, parties, appointments—on the family calendar.

Kids Can . . .

At about age six or seven, children can learn to answer the phone politely and take messages efficiently. Make sure they understand the following:

- How to answer politely.

- How to say "May I ask who's calling?" or "Just a moment, please."

- How to write down a message and phone number.

- What to do if it's a wrong number, prank call or solicitation call.

- How to give an honest reply without revealing too much information. They should never agree to buy anything or tell a caller, "Nobody's home" or "My Mom's in the bathroom."

15

Bright Idea

Keep a highlighter handy
to highlight numbers you
look up in the phone
book.

- Tack personal information and invitations on the bulletin board.
- Keep all phone messages here.
- Put your important papers in your in-box or folder.
- Tell the Family Manager if you're in need of school supplies, toiletries, groceries and so on. Write them on the ongoing list.

Don't:
- Take supplies from this area.
- Toss any papers or messages unless you know it's old information.
- Don't commit anyone's time to anything without asking Mom or Dad.
- Don't forget to tell Mom or Dad if you need a ride to an event, must bring a gift or pick up someone else.

CREATE A FAMILY YELLOW PAGES

On your computer or notebook paper (one page for each letter) record alphabetically the numbers you're always looking up. This way you can store and easily update the information. On some of the entries, such as the library, dry cleaner or post office, it's helpful to include the hours of operation. At the top or on the first page of the notebook, have emergency numbers. Then include any of the following categories that apply to your family:

- Accountant
- Air-conditioning service
- Alarm company
- Appliance repair
- Attorney
- Auto parts store
- Auto repair
- Baby-sitters
- Bakery
- Bank
- Cable company
- Carpenter
- Carpet-cleaning service
- Charity organizations
- Child-care
- Church
- Community center
- Congressman or Congresswoman
- Decorator
- Dentist
- Drugstore
- Dry cleaners
- Electric company
- Electrician
- Exercise class
- Exterminator
- Firewood supplier
- Florist
- Furnace maintenance and repair

- Gas company
- Golf club
- Grocery store
- Hairdresser
- Handyman
- Hardware store
- Health club
- Hospitals
- Housekeeper
- Kennel
- Landscape contractor
- Library
- Nail salon
- Neighbors
- Newspaper delivery
- Orthodontist
- Painter
- Photographer
- Physicians
- Plumber
- Police
- Pool cleaner
- Post office
- Printer
- Real estate agent
- Restaurants (for home delivery, reservations)
- Schools
- Shoe repair
- State Representative/ Senator
- Stockbroker
- Synagogue
- Tax consultant
- Telephone company
- Town Hall
- Travel agent
- TV repair
- Veterinarian

AN OFFICE FOR THE MANAGER

If you're a family manager who is blessed with enough space for a home office, consider these issues when arranging your setup:

- What view do you want from your chair? Out the window or into the room? Can you work with your back to the door or do you like to see the door?
- Where will you put the telephone? Will you need to reach into a file cabinet or bookcase while you're on the phone?
- How many phone lines will you need? How will you connect to the Internet? Dial-up cable or DSL? Do you need a dedicated fax line?
- Do you have enough electrical outlets and surge protectors?
- Is there enough space to store all the equipment and supplies you'll need? (It's easy to overlook all the machines you're accustomed to using at the office.)
- Is there space for family members to help out?

Equipment Checklist

When getting a home office arranged, use this equipment checklist to
make sure you are fully stocked and ready for business:

Furniture

- ☐ Desk with drawers
- ☐ Filing cabinet
- ☐ Ergonomic chair
- ☐ Overhead and desk lighting
- ☐ Filing cabinet
- ☐ Bookshelves
- ☐ Work table

Equipment

- ☐ Computer (with modem)
- ☐ Power surge protector
- ☐ Laser printer
- ☐ Copier
- ☐ Answering machine (if you don't have voicemail)
- ☐ Fax machine
- ☐ Telephone
- ☐ Headset for hands-free talking
- ☐ Calculator
- ☐ Tickler file holder
- ☐ Bulletin board
- ☐ Wastebasket
- ☐ Clock
- ☐ Dictionary and thesaurus
- ☐ Pencil sharpener
- ☐ Stapler and staples
- ☐ Staple remover
- ☐ Scissors
- ☐ Stackable trays
- ☐ Letter opener
- ☐ Postage scale/meter
- ☐ In/Out-boxes

Supplies

- ☐ Envelopes (letter and legal size)
- ☐ Stationery
- ☐ Large manila envelopes
- ☐ Stamps
- ☐ Paper for printer, fax, copier
- ☐ Notepads
- ☐ Sticky notes
- ☐ Pens, pencils and highlighters
- ☐ Eraser
- ☐ Ruler
- ☐ Transparent tape
- ☐ Shipping tape
- ☐ Shipping labels
- ☐ Felt-tip pens
- ☐ Paper clips, large and small
- ☐ Binder clips
- ☐ Colored file folders
- ☐ Hanging file folders
- ☐ Pushpins
- ☐ Business card organizer
- ☐ CDs or floppy disks
- ☐ Tissues

TIPS FROM THE PROS: HOME OFFICE ORGANIZATION

- Place only the most frequently used items in your desk drawers, grouping similar items together.
- Keep a "desk junk" drawer or basket for miscellaneous things that always accumulate. Empty and organize it at least once a month.
- Store empty file folders nearby to create new files as soon as you have paperwork or items related to a new subject.
- Don't overload electrical outlets. Set computers on a stable surface, out of direct sunlight, with plenty of ventilation around them.
- Avoid the nightmare of losing your work by regularly backing up your files on your hard drive. Keep a zip drive, CDs or floppies with your backed-up computer content at an alternate site, or consider subscribing to a service that automatically backs up your hard drive every time you log on to the Internet.
- Consider purchasing a computer program to organize your calendar, to-do lists and address book all in one handy format.

FILING: A SYSTEM THAT MAKES SENSE

A logical way to store papers is to categorize them by the seven Family Manager departments. These suggestions can help get you started.

1. **Home and Property.** This department would include decorating ideas, sanitation and recycling information, auto information, dream house pictures and plans, gardening information, household inventory, appraisals and receipts for all home improvements, additions and repairs.
2. **Food.** This department would include nutritional information, takeout menus, party menus, caterers, centerpiece inspirations and recipes.
3. **Money.** This department would include banking (checking and savings) records, spare checks, loan papers, insurance records, receipts for purchases, mortgage or rental papers, tax information, investment records, paperwork for organizations to which you pay annual dues, retirement information and health insurance information.

Bright Idea

Buy a label maker. You can label shelves, notebooks, kids' belongings, plus lots more. They are available at office supply stores and are not expensive.

4. **Family and Friends.** Assign each family member a file folder in a different color and store in it: birth certificates, immunization records, school history/report cards, résumés, hobby and sports information and prescriptions for eyeglasses and contacts. If you have young children, the Missing Children Center in Tampa, Florida, recommends keeping a home identification file on each child to assist law enforcement officials in the event of a child abduction. The file should include a complete set of fingerprints as well as dental information. If you have any pets, you can set up a separate folder to contain their pet records.

5. **Special Events.** This department would include travel information, vacation research, maps and tourist information, garage-sale records (what worked and what didn't work last time you held one), birthday party and your holiday ideas, your holiday greeting card list, family reunion research and rental company brochures.

6. **Time and Scheduling.** This department would include tips/articles on time management, last year's calendar and public transportation schedules.

7. **Self-management.** This department would include personal interests and hobbies, personal medical records, weight loss information, beauty and wardrobe information and information for your community or church volunteer work.

KEEP ONLY THE ESSENTIALS

Use these tips to help you sort and toss.

- Keep bank statements and corresponding cancelled checks for three years. You may need them for proof of payment on a bill, a mortgage application (to prove the down-payment money is not borrowed) or a tax audit. For more information on current guidelines for keeping tax-related information, see IRS publication 552, "Recordkeeping for Individuals," at www.irs.gov.

- Save paycheck stubs, deposit slips, ATM withdrawal slips and debit charge receipts to verify amounts on your next bank statement. After that, toss all but any debit receipts you need to hold onto for proof of purchase or tax-deductible expenses.

Hard work is often the easy work you did not do at the proper time.
—Bernard Meltzer

- Keep home-improvement receipts for work done on your home or rental property for as long as you own it. These can affect your capital gains/losses computation.
- Keep only this month's investment summary statements if the information is cumulative.
- Keep warranties, guarantees and bills of sale in their own file so you can find them quickly.
- Keep receipts and sales slips to check against your monthly bills, and to use in case you need to return or get something repaired during the warranty period.
- Keep all owner's manuals in an accordion folder, or store them in a ring binder. (Throw away instruction manuals to simple appliances like can openers or coffee makers unless you honestly think you'll forget how to use them.)
- Shred any personal documents before discarding.

Like any CEO, you need a way to organize your head, your team and the myriad details you deal with daily. As you apply these smart management routines and strategies, the amount of stress and chaos will diminish and you'll feel a great deal of satisfaction as your family enjoys each other, and your home and life together.

Man's best friend, aside from the dog, is the wastebasket.
—*Business Week*

21

CHAPTER 2

You're the All-Purpose Maid

Some people actually enjoy cleaning. They have fun turning gray grout white; shiny wood floors make them happy; dusting furniture takes away their worries—well, at least temporarily. While you'll never see me dashing for the dust rag the moment I hear bad news, I do love having a clean house.

My philosophy about cleaning is since everyone in the family contributes to the dirt, everyone in the family should help clean it up. Having said that, I firmly believe that if there's a choice between cleaning the dirty bathroom that's been gnawing away at you and playing a game with your child, the bathroom can wait. Cleaning is just not as important. When your kids are grown they won't remember the dust bunnies that drive you crazy, but you can bet your life they'll remember passing the time with you.

Fortunately, there is more than one way to clean a house, which is a good thing since certain phases of kids' lives—the toddler and teenager phases, for instance—are messier than others. When my sons were little, cleaning took a lot of time and effort. The reality of having all my rooms clean at the same time just wasn't in the cards for a while. So I lowered my standards a bit. I decided what I could and couldn't live with (dusty furniture, yes; a dirty kitchen, definitely no) and figured out a cleaning plan that made that happen.

As the kids got older and could help out more, cleaning became a family activity. Each week every family member had specific responsibilities and it was up to him to accomplish them by the end of the week. Besides basic housecleaning, the boys learned a little about budgeting time, too.

Now that it's just Bill, our youngest son, James, and me at home, we don't devote nearly as much energy to the task. But we still take turns with cooking, laundry, vacuuming, and other routine chores. That way, no one feels unduly burdened.

The following section offers a smorgasbord of cleaning plans, strategies and plain old tips. Pick one to help you get the job done in less time.

> *Housework is what a woman does that nobody notices unless she hasn't done it.*
> —Evan Esar

The Truth About Cleaning

UNIVERSAL CLEANING TRUTH #1

We won't do a major cleaning more than once or twice a year, because it's a lot of hard work and the demands of daily life mean we probably don't have time to. This is just one of those facts of life we're going to feel better about if we accept. No Family Manager ever earned a gold crown because she washed her walls monthly.

UNIVERSAL CLEANING TRUTH #2

We can't clean until we declutter. Just like you've got to mow before you rake, or cut before you sew, you've got to clear out the debris so you can find the surface you want to scrub. So before tackling a major housecleaning, schedule some time to declutter. (See Chapter 3.)

UNIVERSAL CLEANING TRUTH #3

We can't clean without a team. Well, we can, but it's both overwhelming physically and demoralizing emotionally. It's worth repeating: your home belongs to everyone who lives in it. Everyone who lives in it benefits from its use, so everyone should and can contribute to its livability.

Don't fall for the guilt-inducing voice that suggests a great Family Manager can and should do it all. Every manager knows that isn't true. Do your family the favor of having them learn how to invest in their common ground—for their mutual enjoyment.

23

UNIVERSAL CLEANING TRUTH #4

No cleaning day will be time-effective without preparation. Set aside the day or weekend, make sure family members are committed to participating and have all supplies ready and out. Expect a thorough cleaning—depending on how many able helpers you have—to take four to five hours. If it's just you and your spouse, or you and an older child, you may need to spread out these chores over a two-day period. If your budget and priorities allow, you can cut back on your time by hiring some things out—for example, window washing or carpet cleaning—or having a cleaning service come in and do the big jobs, so you can concentrate on details like polishing silver and brass, organizing bookcases and so forth.

UNIVERSAL CLEANING TRUTH #5

Any big cleaning day is more approachable if there are rewards at the end—maybe dinner out or pizza and a movie in. Offer something to celebrate everyone's efforts.

Motivating Your Team

Unfortunately, no one in my family was born with a natural love for housework, so over the years I've had to be creative in motivating my family, as well as myself. Here are some ways to get your team moving:

- Make a simple "Laundry Man" cape and mask for a younger child who's in charge of folding laundry.
- Give older kids a "Cash and Carry" incentive for large jobs. Offer a small cash reward for carrying all the boxes to the attic, or hauling the mounds of garbage outside.
- Have a "White Glove Contest" between siblings to see who can do a better job of cleaning his or her room.
- Play "Beat the Clock" while working on a particular job. Set the kitchen timer and see who can finish his or her task before the buzzer rings.

Who's Responsible for What?

In every successful organization, team members know their responsibilities.
Take some time to discuss this list with your spouse.

——————— Picking up the house

——————— Cleaning the kitchen

——————— Cleaning the bathrooms

——————— Cleaning the family room

——————— Sweeping/mopping/waxing floors

——————— Dusting

——————— Vacuuming

——————— Making beds

——————— Changing sheets

——————— Doing laundry

——————— Taking clothes to the dry cleaners

——————— Mending

——————— Shopping for clothes and other items

——————— Organizing closets and drawers

——————— Collecting and taking out trash

——————— Recycling

——————— Doing household repairs and maintenance

——————— Contacting repair services

——————— Decorating

——————— Doing yard work

——————— Maintaining outdoor furniture and equipment

——————— Maintaining the car

——————— Watering plants

——————— Cleaning carpets

——————— Washing windows

- Station laundry baskets, boxes, clothes hampers and trash cans in strategic locations around the house. Label each receptacle according to what you want to end up in it, and let the kids gently toss in clothes they've outgrown, unbreakable items and trash into their respective containers.

- Designate one person to be in charge of sorting through and folding the clothing that will be stored or given away. Unusable clothing can be cut up for rags, and the buttons can be cut off for crafts.

- Wear comfy clothes, eliminate all distractions (turn off the television and let the answering machine get the phone) and put on some peppy music to keep everybody moving and energized.

- Go out for a treat or fun activity together after you finish all your chores.

Delegating: What Kids Can Do to Help

Preschoolers can...
- Make beds (a comforter is easier for them to handle)
- Fold towels and wash cloths
- Put away clothes in drawers
- Hang clothes on hooks
- Put dirty clothes in hampers or laundry baskets
- Help feed animals
- Pick up toys
- Wipe off baseboards, windowsills and wooden shutters wearing an old pair of socks on their hands
- Empty light wastebaskets
- Wipe off the front of large appliances using a spray bottle of water and a sponge
- Help wipe up spills
- Dry unbreakable dishes
- Sweep with a child-size broom
- Bring in the newspaper
- Pick up litter in the yard

Kindergarteners can...
- Vacuum small areas with a lightweight, handheld vacuum
- Sweep the porch or other small areas with a dustpan and broom
- Clean bathroom sinks
- Hang up the towel after a bath
- Store bath toys
- Help in the kitchen—stirring, tearing lettuce and putting refrigerated rolls on pans
- Set the table with napkins and silverware
- Clear dishes from the table
- Help load the dishwasher
- Straighten plastic dishes in a lower cabinet
- Straighten pots and pans

- Sort family members' clean laundry
- Put away their own laundry
- Dust furniture
- Shine windows that you've washed with a clean blackboard eraser
- Strip linens from beds
- Straighten books on a bookshelf
- Put game and puzzle pieces in correct storage containers
- Brush upholstered furniture with a lint remover to pick up pet hair
- Be responsible for having a tidy room

Younger elementary school kids can...
- Make beds
- Take out the garbage
- Sweep stairs and walks
- Clean out the car
- Vacuum their own room
- Sort and straighten toys
- Fold and put away laundry
- Empty the dishwasher
- Feed and care for pets
- Set and clean the table (if using plastic dishes and nonbreakable drinking cups)
- Sort clothes for washing
- Clean off outdoor furniture
- Wash outside toys and equipment
- Help wash the car

Older elementary school kids can...
- Clean bathroom mirrors
- Vacuum
- Clean toilets
- Clean countertops and the kitchen sink
- Mop small-area floors
- Use the washer and dryer
- Wash, dry and put away dishes

- Fold laundry and put it away
- Clean pet areas
- Take out the trash
- Clean cobwebs and dust in high places with a cobweb pole. (Put one thick cotton sock inside another and slip them over the end of a yardstick, securing with a rubber band.)
- Help straighten the garage
- Sweep the garage

Teenagers can . . .

- Wash the windows
- Mend clothes
- Wash the car
- Change linens
- Do their own laundry
- Iron
- Clean the bathtub/shower stall
- Polish furniture and dust lampshades
- Empty the vacuum the cleaner bag
- Straighten and organize linens
- Clean tiles and toilet with disinfectant
- Clean out the refrigerator
- Defrost the freezer
- Clean the stove and oven
- Polish silverware
- Clean out and organize the attic, basement and garage
- Clean light fixtures
- Change lightbulbs
- Wax the car

Down 'n' Dirty Cleaning Plans

THE 1-2-3 TEAM CLEANING PLAN

When our boys were old enough to help carry the load, Bill and I came up with a manageable way to get the job done. At first, the kids protested, but we explained how privileges and responsibilities go hand in hand—you help fold laundry then you can go outside and play. It didn't take long for them to figure out that they didn't want to do without some toys, television and treehouse time. Plus, when everyone helps with chores they get done a lot faster. They liked the idea of having more time for family fun and, when necessary, we'd reward them with a visit to their favorite ice cream parlor.

This plan works with three chore lists. List one has the weekly speed-cleaning jobs that require less than an hour to complete. The chores on the second list require a little more time and should be done at least once a month if possible. The same holds true for the third list. These are the heavy-duty jobs that can be done on a Saturday morning a couple of times a year. I organized our efforts on a separate cleaning calendar to keep track of the larger cleaning jobs and make sure the work was divided evenly.

Each week assign capable family members a certain area of the house to speed clean. Make copies of the list for each person so they can stay on track.

LIST ONE
Weekly Speed-Cleaning Chores

Living areas
- ☐ Pick up clutter
- ☐ Clean glass, mirrors, TV or computer screens and tabletops
- ☐ Dust furniture, lamps, windowsills, pictures and mantle
- ☐ Empty wastebaskets
- ☐ Toss or recycle newspapers
- ☐ Plump sofa cushions and throw pillows
- ☐ Vacuum carpets and mop floors

> It is my belief that no one (except infants and individuals who are ill or physically disabled) should have a free ride when it comes to the work of the house. This does not mean that everyone should share equally; circumstances may dictate otherwise. But neither does it mean that one person should become the sacrificial household lamb.
>
> —Marjorie Hansen Shaevitz

29

Bedrooms

- ☐ Pick up clutter
- ☐ Straighten closet and hang clothes
- ☐ Sort laundry for mending and dry-cleaning
- ☐ Clean mirrors, glass and tabletops
- ☐ Dust furniture, windowsills and pictures
- ☐ Empty wastebaskets
- ☐ Vacuum carpets or mop floors
- ☐ Strip beds and wash and change linens (depending on your family, you may only change sheets every two weeks)

Bathrooms

- ☐ Pick up clutter
- ☐ Collect dirty towels and take to the laundry area
- ☐ Spray and wipe mirror with glass cleaner
- ☐ Clean the sink
- ☐ Use glass cleaner on faucets and chrome
- ☐ Spray the tub/shower walls with a heavy-duty cleaner
- ☐ Squirt cleaner in toilet and swish around bowl; wipe outside of bowl
- ☐ Wipe off windowsills and scale
- ☐ Empty wastebasket
- ☐ Sweep, mop or vacuum floor

Kitchen

- ☐ Pick up clutter
- ☐ Clean outside of large appliances with a glass cleaner
- ☐ Shine outside of small appliances with a glass cleaner
- ☐ Wipe out inside of microwave
- ☐ Wipe off windowsills
- ☐ Wipe off countertops
- ☐ Wash and disinfect trash can; replace liner
- ☐ Sweep, mop or vacuum floor

LIST TWO

Once-a-Month Chores

- ☐ Polish wood furniture
- ☐ Vacuum upholstered furniture
- ☐ Vacuum baseboards, moldings, stairways, lamp shades and behind furniture
- ☐ Dust ceiling fans
- ☐ Toss or recycle magazines
- ☐ Dust knickknacks
- ☐ Wash throw rugs
- ☐ Scrub tile and grout
- ☐ Clean the inside of the medicine cabinet and other concealed storage areas; toss expired medications; take inventory and restock linen closet shelves if necessary
- ☐ Wash shower curtain and/or liner
- ☐ Scrub kitchen and bathroom floors
- ☐ Clean the inside of the microwave

LIST THREE

Three- to Four-Times-a-Year Chores

- ☐ Clean stovetop and replace burner bibs
- ☐ Vacuum vent hood and coils
- ☐ Clean the inside of the oven; wash the stove knobs with mild soap, warm water and a toothbrush
- ☐ Wash woodwork
- ☐ Polish silver
- ☐ Polish chrome (rubbing alcohol does a terrific job)
- ☐ Clean out kitchen pantry and cabinets
- ☐ Wipe out drawers and clean silverware holders
- ☐ Declutter kitchen junk drawers
- ☐ Scrub and wax the floor
- ☐ Clean out the refrigerator. Wipe off interior walls and shelves. Clean the door seals with a mix of baking soda and water (an old toothbrush makes this job easy). It's a good idea to keep an open box of baking soda in your refrigerator to absorb smells. When it's time to

Women, for hormonal reasons, can see individual dirt molecules, whereas men tend not to notice them until they join together into clumps large enough to support commercial agriculture.

—Dave Barry

clean, use that same box as a cleaning agent, then replace it with a new box to quell odors.

☐ Remove the grill from the condenser at the bottom of your refrigerator and vacuum out the dust. Dusty coils make the motor work harder.

☐ Empty the refrigerator drip pan

☐ Defrost or clean out freezer and take inventory

☐ Clean light fixtures and door knobs. Carefully remove plastic panels from fluorescent light boxes. Clean them with warm soapy water.

☐ Wash your walls at least once a year. (Cleaning expert Don Aslett has a simple two-bucket technique for removing serious dirt from painted walls. Fill one bucket halfway with a warm water and ammonia solution. Leave the other bucket empty for now. Apply the solution to the wall with a sponge. Squeeze the dirty sponge into the empty bucket and continue cleaning by rewetting the sponge with the clean water from the first bucket. Then wipe the wall with a clean cloth.)

THE POWER-OF-TEN-MINUTES METHOD

Like many women, I seldom have large chunks of time to devote to cleaning my whole house, so I developed the Power-of-Ten-Minutes method. Here's how it works: I clean something every day for ten minutes. On some days I can carve out two or three ten-minute cleaning slots. By the end of the week, the dirt that really needs to be kept after is pretty well gone.

In ten minutes, you can . . .

- Wipe down the inside of the microwave oven, sponge the front of the refrigerator and unload the dishwasher
- Clean the TV and computer screens as well as the mirrors in your bathrooms
- Dust part of your bedroom, or at least get the dust bunnies under the bed and spot clean picture frames
- Clean quite a few switch plates and door knobs with an all-purpose cleaner and rag in hand

- Clean the top of the refrigerator
- Clean the track of a sliding glass door (use a screwdriver wrapped in a thin towel to pry stubborn dirt)
- Clean kitchen countertops; wipe off canisters and small appliances
- Vacuum the staircase
- Clean one cabinet or drawer at a time, and watch your dream of having tidy, clean storage spaces materialize before your very eyes
- Straighten a shelf or two in the linen closet
- Remove the books from one shelf on a bookcase, dust the books and shelf off and replace them
- Vacuum two or three pieces of upholstered furniture
- Sweep, vacuum or mop the kitchen or bathroom floor
- Spray the inside of your microwave with a plant mister, then turn on high for a few seconds. Allow it to sit for a minute or two, then wipe with a clean cloth. (You can also clean the microwave by nuking a few tablespoons of baking soda in a cup of water and then wiping up the mist with a paper towel.) Use a toothbrush to scrub stubborn stains. It shouldn't take more than ten minutes.

THE CLEAN-WHILE-YOU-SLEEP PLAN

There are some cleaning tasks you can start before bed, and they'll be done the next morning. Here are a few ideas to try some night before turning in:

- Line a white bathroom sink with paper towels soaked in laundry bleach. In the morning, toss them out and admire your white sink. (Do not use bleach on colored porcelain sinks. It will fade the color.)
- For a white kitchen sink, pour enough bleach in the sink to cover the bottom, then fill the sink with cold water. If you have hard-water stains on rubber-coated or plastic dish drainers, put them in the sink, too. Let them soak overnight.
- Treat your toilet to an overnight soaking of white vinegar on a weekly basis. By morning, it will be completely disinfected. Just flush clean.

Every minute is a golden one for him who has the vision to recognize it as such.
—Henry Miller

33

- Clean out clogged drains. Pour a half cup each of baking soda and salt down the drain. Follow with a cup of boiling water and let sit overnight. Flush with hot tap water the next morning.

- Put dishwasher detergent and hot water in crusty casserole dishes and let them soak overnight. They will be much easier to clean in the morning.

- Spray your oven with cleaner the night before and let it do its job. You can also put automatic dishwasher soap or baking soda on the bottom of your oven and cover it with wet paper towels. Wipe clean the next day.

- Fill your teakettle with equal parts vinegar and water. Bring to a boil, turn off the heat and let it stand overnight. This will remove the lime deposits left behind by hard water.

- Got a broiler pan or burner trays caked with grease? Put them in a plastic bag along with some ammonia. Seal the bag, put it outside overnight and let the fumes clean off the grease. Just wash with soap and water the next morning.

- Start a load of laundry before you go to bed (some utility companies will reward homeowners with lower rates for using electricity during nonpeak hours). Put in the dryer in the morning.

- Clean oil stains on cement floors overnight. Make a paste of automatic dishwasher detergent and hot water. Scrub it onto the spot and let it work overnight. Rinse with water. Repeat process if necessary. Or sprinkle oil spots with cat litter. Leave overnight, and sweep away the next morning.

- Clean stubborn residue from flower vases and thermoses. Mix 2 tablespoons of oxygen bleach with 1 gallon of warm water. Let the bubbles work while you sleep. Rinse clean the next morning.

- Mix baking soda with a few cloves and sprinkle on carpeting for the night to absorb musty odors; vacuum in the morning.

THE PREVENTION PLAN: STOPPING DIRT BEFORE IT STARTS

Preventing dirt and mess is the first line of cleaning defense. Spend a little time now and save a lot of time later by using these tips.

In the Kitchen

- Clean up drips from pots and cookware right away; wipe up countertop spills as soon as they occur.
- Keep fresh vegetables in plastic bags with holes that allow air to circulate. If the vegetables go bad, you can lift them out of the fridge with a lot less mess.
- Line crisper drawers with paper towels so you don't have to clean the drawer; just toss the dirty paper towel and replace with a clean one every two weeks or so.
- Cover the top of the refrigerator with plastic wrap you can pull off and throw away when it's dirty. Moisten the surface slightly so the plastic wrap will stay put. (Clean the top of your refrigerator one last time before applying the wrap. If grease and dirt have built up, spray a solution of one part ammonia and ten parts water and let the grime marinate for an hour or so. Wipe clean with paper towels.)
- Spray the egg compartments in your refrigerator with cooking spray. No more stuck, broken eggs.
- Slip plastic lids from coffee cans under sticky items (like jam, jelly or honey) in your refrigerator or pantry.
- Before putting muffins or a cake into the oven, wipe off drips from the rim of the pan so they won't get baked on and require extra elbow grease to remove.
- Wash dirty dishes, high-chair trays and greasy pans before food dries on them.
- Use powdered cleanser in the sink bowl only so you won't have to spend a lot of time rinsing off the residue. Use all-purpose cleaner on the rim and faucet.
- Always turn on your oven exhaust fan when cooking.
- Before working with messy foods—for example dipping fish or chicken in bread crumbs or peeling potatoes—cover the countertop or sink with waxed paper or a ripped-open brown grocery bag to catch the mess. When finished, wad up the paper and throw it away.
- Use aluminum foil with abandon (just be sure to stock up on it when it goes on sale). Line the bottom of your oven, roasting pans and cookie sheets.

35

- Before you grill, clean the rack with a wire brush dipped in warm, sudsy water. Rinse and dry, then spray with nonstick spray made especially made for grills. It will be faster and easier to clean after the meal.
- Spray nonstick spray on plastic storage containers before filling with tomato-based sauces.
- Place a piece of waxed paper in the bottom of your microwave to catch spills.
- When coating a baking pan with flour, use an empty spice jar (the kind with holes in the lid) to shake it neatly into the pan.
- When putting down a new kitchen floor, avoid indented or embossed tile or linoleum. They're real dirt catchers and hard to keep clean.

All Around the House

- Spray fabric guard on anything prone to stains—sofas, chairs, kids' comforters, tablecloths, tennis shoes.
- Before vacuuming, always check to be sure the disposable vacuum cleaner bag is secured tightly into the base of the vacuum. If it's not, the vacuum will likely throw out as much dust as it takes up.
- Never allow the vacuum cleaner bag to reach the bursting point. It could weaken the suction and cause the bag to leak dust.
- Change or clean both the furnace and the air-conditioning filters regularly. A clean filter will prevent fried or frozen dirt from being blasted around the house.
- Be sure doors and windows fit snugly in their frames. If they don't, add weather stripping to keep dirt and allergens at bay.
- Paint basement and garage floors with a concrete sealer to keep concrete dust down.
- Put low-pile floor mats in front of every door to catch outside dirt.
- Use dark-colored throw rugs inside entryways to your house, at the kitchen sink or on heavy-trafficked areas. They show less dirt and won't need to be washed as often as light-colored ones.
- Use drawer dividers to corral various items. Make sure the dividers are at least half as deep as the drawer or they'll add to the confusion.

- The next time you paint interior walls select a finish that is durable and easy to clean such as semi-gloss.
- Put pet dishes on vinyl place mats.
- Confine art projects, involving crayons, finger paints, glue and other messy media, to a plastic craft table. Use an old shower curtain as a drop cloth beneath the table to protect your floor.
- Wipe your TV screen with a fabric softener sheet. This will help cut down on static electricity, which attracts dust.
- Don't allow children to consume red fruit drinks or frozen treats near the carpet. Better yet, restrict all eating to the kitchen.
- Train your kids to take off their shoes as soon as they come in from the outside. If your house has an entryway or mud room with space for a shoe rack, purchase one. Store indoor shoes or slippers on one side of the rack and leave the other side available for street shoes.
- When buying new furniture, carpeting or rugs, remember that texture and subtle patterns show less dirt than smooth, solid-color fabrics.
- Use pump soap dispensers instead of bar soap to wash hands. You don't have to deal with cleaning up built-up scum in soap dishes.
- Keep your pets well groomed, so you'll have less pet hair to deal with.
- To prevent tarnishing, store sterling silver in zip-top plastic bags. Put a little bit of baking soda in the bottom of the bag before releasing the air and sealing tightly.
- Prevent soap-scum buildup in the bathroom by coating tiles with a solution of automatic dishwasher detergent or oil soap (like Murphy's) mixed with water.
- Apply car wax to glass shower doors every two to three months for easier cleaning.

TACKLING HEAVY-DUTY CLEANING JOBS

According to one statistic I came across, each year 40 pounds of dust sneaks into the average home. Where does it go? In all the nooks and crannies found in every room. It's the invisible particles that turn clear water muddy as you mop floors you didn't think looked that bad. This uninvited resident rests in the woodwork. It loves the top of the refrigerator. You can find it behind the couch, in the back of the toilet, under the beds, in the closets and beneath your carpeting. While some of your regular housecleaning gets rid of it, most dust lives in the less obvious spaces. To remove it, you'll need to do heavy cleaning two times a year. My mother-in-law used to devote an entire weekend to it each March and September—she called it spring and fall cleaning. Today's families are more likely to tackle one or two jobs over the course of several weeks—or at least, find someone to do the windows! Here's a list of chores to get you on your way:

- Wash windows inside and out and clean windowsills. Don't forget to remove debris from window wells while you're at it.
- Clean window screens outside with a hose and stiff brush.
- Launder or dry clean drapes, or vacuum them using the upholstery attachment.
- Wash (with bleach, water and a bath towel) or replace all shower curtain liners; wash shower curtains according to directions on tag.
- Whiten grout and bathroom tile.
- Clean out the medicine cabinet. Wash shelves and toss expired medication.
- Clean and straighten the linen closet.
- Wash walls and woodwork.
- Shampoo carpets.
- Have upholstered furniture professionally cleaned.
- Clean out clothes closets and while you're in there, prune the wardrobe (donate seldom-worn or out-grown items).
- Clean out kitchen cabinets. Toss expired food and wipe down shelves and doors.
- Clean the refrigerator inside and out.
- Remove the splash guard from the garbage disposer and clean off formerly hidden food particles.
- Clean the oven, stovetop and burners.
- Clean the exhaust fan filter in the dishwasher, or soak it in a heavy-duty cleaner.

- Move large appliances and clean beneath them with a vacuum. Pay particular attention to the coils.
- Clean the fireplace hearth and remove ashes.
- Flip mattresses.

How to Work a Room

LIVING AREA TIPS

Ten Tips for Treating Your Carpet Well

1. Buy a good vacuum cleaner, but be wise about it. You don't need dozens of extra attachments. You need a round brush, a crevice tool and a 4-inch upholstery brush. Test the weight of the vacuum cleaner and how hard it is to push before you buy it.

2. Vacuum at least twice a week. Once dirt is allowed to sink deep into the fibers it can cause the carpet to wear our more quickly. Vacuum high-traffic areas more often.

3. Clean up spills immediately. The longer they sit, the better the chance of a permanent stain.

4. When cleaning up spilled liquid, use only a white cloth, because colors can bleed and make the stain worse.

5. Spritz the spot with a little cold water to help dilute it, then blot again. Repeat this process until the stain is gone.

6. Keep stains wet. If you can't remove a stain yourself, douse it with club soda or keep it moist by misting with cold water until it can be professionally cleaned. A dry stain is harder to get out.

7. Rent a rug shampooer and do it yourself, or have your carpet professionally cleaned at least one a year. Be wary of carpet-cleaning specials. Ask if they charge for extras, like spot removal and other basics that should come in the package deal. (Be sure your professional carpet cleaner is experienced, as well as bonded or insured, before you agree to the service.)

8. Before shampooing, give the room a good vacuuming. Slip a sandwich bag under each leg of the furniture to prevent water damage when shampooing the carpet. Be careful not to overwet the carpet

*Here lies a poor woman who always was tired,
For she lived in a place where help wasn't hired.
Her last words on earth were, Dear friends I am going
Where washing ain't done nor sweeping nor sewing,
And everything there is exact to my wishes,
For there they don't eat and there's no washing of dishes . . .
Don't mourn for me now, don't mourn for me never,
For I'm going to do nothing forever and ever.*

—Anonymous epitaph in churchyard, pre-1860

as this can separate the backing and seams, or cause shrinkage and discoloration.

9. To remove dents in carpet made by heavy furniture, place ice cubes on the marks and vacuum when dry.

10. If the carpet thread is loose, snip it level with the pile. If you try to pull out the thread, you risk unraveling part of the carpet.

Lighten Up the Living Room

- Consider life as a minimalist and cut down on tchotchkes. They are too time-consuming to clean. A few favorite keepsakes add warmth and personality, a collection gone wild never looks nice. If you find it impossible to part with your treasures, display them in a curio cabinet so you won't have to dust them as often.

- Don't dry-dust. It stirs up dust and sends it someplace else. Spray dust cloths with a product such as Endust to capture dust particles, or use pretreated dust cloths. At the very least, use a damp rag.

- Clean the dust off of broadleaf plants by putting damp socks on your hands.

- To remove dust from the pleats in a lampshade, use a wide, soft-bristled paintbrush. It's much gentler than a vacuum cleaner attachment and does a more thorough job.

- Keep a masking-tape lint roller easily accessible to quickly pick up pet hair from furniture.

- Using a long extension cord when vacuuming will save you extra steps and reduce time spent plugging and replugging.

- Windows are less likely to streak if you clean them on a cloudy day. Direct sunshine causes them to dry faster and unevenly. Many cleaning professionals recommend cleaning windows using newspaper (instead of paper towels). They say the newsprint really makes glass sparkle. Another way to deal with window-washing streaks is to wipe windows horizontally on the inside and vertically on the outside. This method will allow you to see streaks instantly.

- Think gravity when cleaning: work from the top down. Do ceilings first, floors and baseboards last. Except when washing walls. Wash them from the bottom up. Drips are easier to clean from already-washed walls.

- Keep a package of pretreated dust cloths in the closet of each bedroom. Dust whenever you have a spare minute or two.
- Glue felt pads on the bottoms of vases, table lamps and other heavy metal accessories to prevent scratching wood furniture.
- Apply spot remover from the edge of stain to the center so you won't spread the stain.
- Never spray glass cleaner directly on framed paintings or prints. The liquid can leak through the frame at the edges and damage the artwork. Instead spray the cleaner on a cloth and rub glass gently using a circular motion. Avoid cleaning mirrors with water, which can trickle down behind the glass and damage the silvering. Instead, use a commercial glass cleaner, then buff the mirror well.
- Don't ever go from one level of the house to the next empty handed.
- Be alert for natural housework opportunities. If the kids splash water all over the bathroom floor, go on and mop it. On a rainy day, take your houseplants outside, pull off dead leaves and let the rain water them.

SMARTER KITCHEN CLEANUP

- Your first step in cooking or baking should always be to fill the sink with warm, soapy water. Toss bowls and utensils in the water as you finish using them.
- Use less elbow grease. Soak grimy pans in warm, soapy water while you eat. After the meal, messy pots and pans will be much easier to clean. For really greasy cookware, use dishwashing detergent instead of regular dish soap.
- Limit extra dishes as much as possible. Grate cheese on a paper towel or a piece of waxed paper. Mix dressing directly in the salad bowl. Put casseroles together in the pan you plan to bake them in. Marinate chicken or steaks in zip-top plastic bags instead of bowls or pans.

- After using your blender, partly fill it with warm water, give it a squirt of dishwashing liquid and run it for a few seconds. Rinse it out, then turn it over and allow it to dry on a towel.
- Keep a plastic windshield ice scraper in the kitchen to pry dried-on foods from the floor and countertop.
- To avoid chipping precious china and crystal, place a kitchen towel or a rubber pad in the bottom of the sink before hand-washing them.
- Alka Seltzer tablets in water will clean stains from the bottom of vases and thermos bottles. Give them at least an hour to do their job.
- Use mild, soapy water to clean stove knobs, all-purpose cleaner can remove the words and numbers on the dials.
- Clean out your refrigerator every week the night before trash pickup.
- Keep a clean trash liner at the bottom of your kitchen garbage pail. When it's time to empty the bin, a fresh liner is readily available.

BATHROOM TIME SAVERS

- The best time to clean the bathroom is right after taking a shower, when the steam has loosened the dirt.
- Take bubble baths or use water softeners instead of bath oil, which leaves a ring. Encourage kids to swish their hands and feet around the water line to loosen a bathtub ring before they let the water out.
- Clean your tub without scrubbing. Fill it with hot water and add 2 to 3 cups liquid bleach. Allow the solution to sit for twenty minutes or so. Drain the tub and rinse clean. Voila!
- If you have a fiberglass tub or shower, a cleaner made to clean the fiberglass on boats works really well.
- Install a handheld showerhead so you can rinse the tub when you're finished.
- Turn on the exhaust fan when taking a shower to draw out excess moisture. You'll have less mildew.
- Keep a toilet brush in a caddy next to the toilet. Train family members to give it a frequent swish.

Cleanliness is not next to godliness. It isn't even in the same neighborhood. No one has ever gotten a religious experience out of removing burned-on cheese from the grill of a toaster oven.

—Erma Bombeck

- Keep a box of disposable rubber gloves underneath the bathroom sink for unpleasant cleaning tasks.

- Allow cleansers a chance to work. Instead of rushing to wipe up tile cleaner as soon as you apply it, wait a few minutes. The surface will be cleaner, and you won't have to work as hard to get it that way.

- Wrap a terrycloth rag around a screwdriver to clean out shower door tracks. Spray generously with an all-purpose cleaner and make several passes along the track.

- Before mopping the bathroom floor, vacuum around a dry tub, toilet and sink to remove lint and hair.

- Use a clean sponge mop to wash the tub and wall tiles in the bathroom. No more back strain.

- To remove mold from bathroom tile, soak a cotton ball in bleach. Press it into the yucky area and allow it to sit for a few minutes.

- Clean a rubber or vinyl bathtub mat by tossing it in the washer with two or three bath towels. Wash a vinyl shower curtain liner the same way.

Take Note

When using heavy-duty cleaners in the bathroom be sure to open a window or turn on the exhaust fan.

Special-Care Items

CRYSTAL AND CHINA

Some simple steps will help you preserve your shiniest pieces for many meals to come. It's best to hand-wash your fine glassware.

1. Remove jewelry (rings, watch, bracelets) so they won't scratch items.

2. Use a plastic dishpan, or line sink with a rubber pad or folded heavy towel. If you're using a divided sink, cover the ridge between sinks with a towel or pad as well.

3. Before washing, use a soft, all-cotton cloth (like a diaper) to dust each piece of glass. Handle stemware by the bowl, not the stem.

4. Fill sink with lukewarm water and a little mild (hand) dishwashing liquid. Avoid extra suds. (Never wash in hot water and rinse in cold water. This can cause fine glass to crack.)

5. Don't load the sink; wash one piece at a time, underwater, using a small cotton cloth. Move the faucet head away from where you're working to avoid accidentally knocking glass against it.

6. On stubborn spots, rub gently with a soft toothbrush and baking soda. For cloudy glassware, fill with water and dissolve a denture-cleaning tablet in it. Let stand until "clouds" clear up! Or try soaking in water with a penny in it. The chemical reaction will lift dirt from crevices.

7. Rinse twice, first in a sink or pan filled with lukewarm water and a capful of ammonia or white vinegar, then give the glass a long final rinse using your sink's spray attachment. Well-rinsed glass will dry without spots. If spots appear, though, dry with a soft cloth dipped in lemon juice.

8. Drain on towel-lined counter or on rack. If glass needs more shine, dry with a clean, lint-free cloth.

HOW TO CLEAN SILVER

Hand-washing and drying are best for a glowing patina. Silver washed in dishwashers stands longer in water and is exposed to excess heat and detergent. New sterling sometimes develops brown spots from dishwasher cleaning.

Using warm, sudsy water, wash, then rinse well. *Don't soak.* Dry quickly. If you'd rather use the dishwasher, use these tips to safeguard your silver:

- Do not spill dry dishwasher detergent on flatware; it may cause dark spots.
- Don't wash stainless steel or aluminum and silver in the same load. (Or if you must, make sure the items don't touch. The other metals will blacken the silver.)
- Use the automatic rinse dispenser. These products helps keep droplets from forming. If your machine doesn't have a dispenser, use the solid kind that hangs on the rack.
- For the first few washes, after the last rinse cycle, take out new silverware immediately and towel dry.

Sometimes after cleaning silver, you'll notice a purplish stain. This is actually oxidized copper that is called a "firestain," found on many colonial through nineteenth-century pieces. It is *not* tarnish, so don't try to remove it. If you do, you will harm your heirloom!

Silver does not like acids. If you are wrapping silver, use acid-proof material, not acidic papers like newspaper. Don't store silver objects in the drawers of oak cabinets, or place them directly on top of oak for prolonged periods. Oak contains acids that silver doesn't like. The best way to store silver is to keep it in a closed chest or drawer lined with silver cloth.

Silver utensils and containers can obviously be used for eating, but make sure you wash them soon after using. Many foods contain ingredients including salt and acids that lead to tarnish and other damage. It's best to use salt shakers made of other materials instead, and preserve your silver ones for display. Wash tomato products off of silver soon after using. Don't store fruit in silver bowls or trays for a long time, and wash the silver afterward.

Laundry and Sewing Made Simple

LAUNDRY BASICS

Before you start . . .

- Stock your laundry area with detergent, bleach, a stain remover, presoak, fabric softener, soap for hand-washables, starch, a zipper mesh bag for delicates, a measuring cup, an old toothbrush for stubborn stains, hangers, laundry baskets and ironing supplies.

- Store stain-removal spray or stick in the bathroom so family members can apply it to stains before throwing clothes in the hamper. Or dab a little club soda on a stain to temporarily keep it from setting.

- For the benefit of all family members, write down and post directions near your washing machine on how to wash different types of clothing.

Sorting . . .

- Separate whites that can take chlorine bleach (sheets, towels, children's socks) from delicate whites (lingerie, permanent press) that need nonchlorine bleach. Separate noncolorfast colors (jeans, dark towels) from the rest of the laundry. Separate slightly dirty articles from heavily soiled ones. Separate lint-givers (chenille, towels, throw rugs) from lint-receivers (corduroy, permanent press, socks).
- Empty all pockets before washing clothes. Stick a small plastic basket on the side of your washer to hold pocket treasures—coins, candy, crayons, and so on. (Baskets are available at home stores that have magnets on the back.)
- Turn knits inside-out to avoid snags and pilling.
- Attach a large safety pin to drawstrings on sweat pants and shorts, and hooded sweatshirts so they won't snake back into the garment.

Washing . . .

- Use suggested amounts of detergent recommended by manufacturer. Too much detergent can weaken fibers; too little won't get out stains.
- Dissolve detergent and additives before adding clothes to washing machine.
- Be careful not to spill laundry products on the exterior of your washer or dryer. Wipe up any spills at once. The enamel and plastic control panel used on most exteriors can be damaged by solvents or other chemicals often used in laundering and stain removal.
- Rinse clothes in cold water. This not only saves energy, it cuts down on wrinkles.
- Don't use fabric softener every time you wash towels. They'll lose their absorbency.
- Wash all pieces of an outfit at the same time. If they fade, they'll do so evenly.

Drying . . .

- For minimum wrinkles, only load dryer one-third to one-half full.
- For more even drying, dry fabrics of similar weights together. Size of items does not matter.

- Don't over-dry clothes. Too much heat can weaken fabrics.
- Bring clothes in from the clothesline when dry. The sun fades clothes.
- Clean the lint filter after each load. Built-up lint can start a fire. If a load is extra linty, clean the filter partway through drying cycle. Use a vacuum hose to clean out the exhaust vent system at least once a year, and be sure it is not clogged at any time. Never vent a dryer into your house.
- Never put items in the dryer that have been in contact with flammables, such as gasoline, paint or machine oil. The fumes could ignite. Line dry instead. When all traces of flammables are gone, you can dry as usual.

BLEACHING BASICS

- Use bleach only on white and colorfast washables; always read fabric and bleach labels. Never use chlorine bleach on silk, wool, spandex or fabrics treated with flame-resistant finishes. You can use all-fabric/oxygen bleach, which comes in dry and liquid form, with most washable silks and woolens: unless the garment manufacturer's label says no bleach.
- Never apply undiluted bleach directly onto fabrics.
- If machine-washing, add chlorine bleach manually or by bleach dispenser (if your machine has one) after the wash cycle has begun. If hand-washing, add it to either the wash or rinse water, or both.
- Wear rubber gloves when hand-washing with bleach.
- Test bleach before use. For chlorine bleach, mix 1 tablespoon bleach with ¼ cup cold water. Place a drop on a hidden area, and leave it on for one minute; blot to see if there is any color change. For all-fabric/oxygen bleach, mix one teaspoon bleach with 1 cup hot water. Place a drop on a hidden area, and leave it on for ten minutes. Blot to see if there is any color change. Thoroughly rinse out bleach.
- Use only the amount of bleach recommended on the package or bottle label.

Kids Can . . .

Children can learn to help with laundry at an early age.

- *Age 3:* Can fold tea towels and washcloths.

- *Age 4–5:* Can bring dirty clothes to the laundry room, and put away some clean laundry.

- *Age 6–9:* Most kids this age can sort laundry, empty pockets and fold and put away their laundry.

- *Age 10–12:* In addition to the above, by this age can learn to operate the washing machine.

- *Age 13 and up:* Can be responsible for all their laundry—sorting, washing, drying and putting away.

- Be careful using chlorine bleach if your household water supply has a high iron content; it can draw out the iron and deposit it as spots on clothes.
- Never use bleach and ammonia in the same wash. The combination can create hazardous fumes.
- Keep bleach away from children.

HAND-WASH OR DRY CLEAN?

The dyes and fabric finishes used by manufacturers give clothes luster and sheen, minimize wrinkles and shrinkage, repel stains and create softness or stiffness. However, it can also make it difficult to generalize about which fabrics can stand up to hand-washing and which can't. Even if a garment tag says dry clean, you still may be able to launder it. If it says dry clean only, take it to the cleaners.

- As a general rule, fabrics made of a mixture of natural and synthetic fibers tend to be stronger than natural fibers alone and stand up to hand-washing better. In addition, many woolen and linen garments, some rayon and even a few silks can be hand-washed. However, be extra careful with silk, which is delicate and discolors easily. Never use water on cotton or silk velvet.
- Test any garment labeled dry clean for colorfastness before washing. Put the edge of an inner seam or hem on a paper towel, then saturate a cotton swab with cool water and press it firmly down on the fabric. If no color bleeds onto the paper towel, you don't need to have it dry-cleaned.
- Use the gentle cycle of your washing machine whenever you can. It will clean just as well, but without the "intense agitation" that can shorten the lifespan of your clothes.

DRY-CLEANING DISPUTES

If your favorite sweater comes back shrunken, or your silk blouse is damaged, what are your rights? Here's a start, from the International Fabricare Institute:

Take Note

Time it takes to do laundry:

- **5 minutes to sort**
- **25 to 25 minutes to wash**
- **30 to 60 minutes to dry**
- **5 to 10 minutes to fold or hang, depending on items**

1. **Explain it.** If you have a problem with a dry-cleaning, return the item immediately to the cleaner and explain the problem. If you and the cleaner can't agree, call the Better Business Bureau (BBB).

   If the cleaner is a member of the International Fabricare Institute, you can request that the item be sent to a lab for evaluation. There, the item will be analyzed for the specific complaint, and a report will be issued stating the cause. The lab won't accept the item directly from you; the cleaner or BBB will have to send it. The fee is $16.50 plus $8.50 return shipping, and you'll have to reach an agreement with the cleaner on who pays it.

2. **Find a Remedy.** If the dry cleaner gives you money for the damaged item, it's industry practice that he'll keep the item. If only a partial settlement is made, though, you might get the item back. There is a guide, *The American National Standard Fair Claims Guide for Consumer Textile Products*, which can help the dry cleaner decide fair compensation. But you don't have to accept whatever he offers. You—or your attorney—can negotiate.

3. **Know a Cleaner's Limits.** If you've got a very heavy stain, dry cleaners might ask for extra money to remove it. Dry-cleaning solvents won't remove stains such as ink, blood, food or beverages. Stains such as these will need to be pretreated at the dry cleaners and may require large amounts of chemicals and a lot of time. Dry cleaners usually carry insurance for fire and theft, but not for damaged clothes or improper cleaning procedures that contribute to damage.

4. **Let Dry-Cleaned Garments Breathe.** Un-bag garments when you hang them. These bags are only meant to protect the garment until you get back home. Leaving the bags on can promote the growth of mold and will not protect garments from light. If you want to store items covered, use fabric garment bags.

SMART IRONING

- Use a full-size ironing board. Small ones require lots of turning and time.

Bright Idea

If you get a pink load from a dye transfer, don't dry it. Immediately rewash the load with a little bleach. It may take three to five washings, but most dye-bleeding will come clean if you haven't put the items in the dryer.

> *I've buried a lot of ironing in my backyard.*
> —*Phyllis Diller*

- Use a thick, cotton pad under the ironing board cover. This keeps the board from overheating and helps reduce wrinkles. Nonstick-coating covers are easier to clean.
- If ironing with steam, use only distilled water to avoid stains.
- If clothes have sat in the dryer, try tossing in a damp cloth and drying for another five minutes to release more wrinkles.
- Sort your clothes by ironing temperatures. Start with those requiring a cool temperature, and work your way up. You'll save time! Also, do all of your ironing at once, rather than making frequent trips to get the board out and heat up the iron.
- Iron along the grain of the fabric. Circular or diagonal strokes can stretch fabric.
- No need to push the iron down on the fabric. Heat, not weight, erases wrinkles.
- Never iron silks on the right side.
- You can avoid shine on wools and dark colors by ironing on the wrong side, or using a pressing cloth or ironing shield.
- To avoid crushing a fabric's nap, place a thick towel underneath the garment and press the wrong side.
- Cut down on ironing time by drying clothes loosely and taking them out of the dryer immediately after the cycle is done. Air-dry cotton clothes on plastic hangers, smoothing them with your hands.
- If you spot a stain, don't iron the garment. Heat will make the stain permanent.
- Use steam to your advantage: hang a wrinkled skirt or shirt in the bathroom while you shower. The wrinkles may disappear, or at least make fabric ready for swift ironing.
- Add a drop of your favorite fragrance to your water-misting bottle.
- Use spray starch in moderation to prevent build up on your iron and residue on your clothes.
- Clean your iron regularly.

EXTEND THE LIFE OF YOUR WARDROBE

Clothing will last longer and look nicer if it's cared for properly. Here are some simple strategies to lengthen your wardrobe's life:

- Repair tears promptly so they don't get worse.
- Sew on loose buttons before they fall off.
- Fix unraveling hems promptly.
- Hang up or fold your clothing as soon as you take it off, rather than piling it on a chair.
- Avoid hanging clothing where the sun might fade it.
- Keep clothing in your closet from becoming dusty.
- Hang clothing on wooden or plastic hangers instead of wire hangers.
- Use suit hangers contoured for coats, jackets and suits.
- Avoid leaving sharp or staining objects (like nails and pens) in your pockets.
- Watch what you sit on or lean against to avoid stains, fabric pulls and so on.
- Use the coolest temperature setting possible when drying clothes.
- Treat stains promptly, before they set.
- Wash delicate clothing by hand instead of by machine, or place delicate items into a mesh bag and select the gentle cycle.
- Keep an umbrella in your car so you can protect clothing when it rains.
- Wear old clothing to do work around the house.
- Give clothes and shoes at least one day of rest between wearings, even if they're the most comfortable, high-quality items you own.
- Brush suits with a natural-bristle clothes brush and then hang them out overnight to air to stretch time between dry-cleanings.

KIDS' CLOTHES: MAKE THEM LAST LONGER

- Save wear and tear on kids' school clothes by having them change into play clothes after school.
- Iron heavy-duty patches inside the knees of new jeans to prevent worn knees.
- Have kids wear slippers around the house. Going sock-footed will wear out socks faster and wearing shoes inside will track more dirt.
- Persuade younger children to wear a smock or apron when eating to protect clothes from food stains.

Bright Idea

If your laundry has really piled up or if you've just come home from vacation with a lot of dirty clothes, go to a laundromat and get it all done at once. If you've got eight loads to do, you can fill up eight washers and dryers and do all eight loads in the time it takes to do two loads at home. Go at off-peak hours so there are plenty of free machines.

51

Sewing Basket Basics

- Package of needles in assorted sizes.
- Thread in basic colors like white, black, beige, red, yellow, navy, plus spools of other colors you keep in your wardrobe, such as pastels.
- Thimble.
- Needle threader. These inexpensive tools make needle-threading easy. It's a flexible steel wire with a diamond-shaped opening that's easy to thread; it collapses when you push it through the needle's eye.
- Sharp scissors for cutting thread.
- Straight pins and various sizes of safety pins.
- Velcro, hooks and eyes and some white shirt buttons.
- Mending and hemming tape. This iron-on adhesive tape is great for quickly mending a tear or drooping hem.

■ Make craft smocks available for messy projects. (Easy smocks: cut off the sleeves from men's shirts and have kids wear them backward.)

■ Purchase good sneakers for school, and inexpensive ones for home.

■ Buy over-the-shoe rain boots to preserve shoes when it's wet or muddy outside.

■ Insist your child use a napkin instead of wiping his hands or mouth on shirt sleeves or pant legs.

■ Fix rips, split seams and missing buttons as soon as possible to prevent worse damage.

■ Check the fabric content label before you buy an article of clothing. Synthetic fabrics, such as acrylic, tend to pill and look shabby after several washings. All cotton garments will last longer.

■ Buy outfits one size larger than your child's size. Even if it's prewashed, the item will shrink.

■ For girls, buy leggings and bike shorts. Both can be worn alone or layered under skirts and shorts.

■ To get maximum wear out of a dress, choose a baby-doll style that has no defined waistline. When it gets a little short, you can layer it with leggings or bike shorts, as noted above.

- Don't buy baby clothes with built-in feet. Infants grow quickly, so it's better to dress them in nonfooted clothes and add booties or socks.

NINE QUICK TIPS FOR FAST FIXES

1. Keep two needles threaded and knotted—one with white thread, one with dark thread—ready to go.

2. Designate a special place for to-be-mended clothing. (See Work Centers, page 72.) Then, once a month, load your sewing machine with transparent nylon thread for mending split seams quickly. It works on all colors, plus it's strong.

3. Cut down on time-consuming hemming jobs. When making a hem, knot the thread every few inches. When a small tear occurs, you won't have to re-hem the entire garment.

4. A bar of soap, still in the wrapper, makes a great pincushion. It not only stores pins, it makes them slide more smoothly.

5. Get a little longer wear from children's clothes by sewing waistband buttons with elastic thread.

6. Help buttons stay on longer by coating the center of each one with clear nail polish. Use dental floss, instead of thread, to secure buttons onto overcoats.

7. Use iron-on patches to close small tears in clothing and linens.

8. For easy-view and dust-free storage, place needles, bobbins, thread and other sewing supplies in empty baby food jars.

9. Have a zip-top plastic bag where you keep your sewing supplies to hold all the little packages of extra buttons and thread that come with clothing items.

A stitch in time saves nine.

—*Proverb*

Home Sweet (Smelling) Home

Several years ago a magazine ran a contest, asking readers to create a new type of game show. One of the winning entries was "Oooo, What Smells." You can only imagine how that game was played. There are, of course, good smells and bad smells, and most people have strong reactions to both. Here are ways to encourage the good and eliminate the bad.

Smells are surer than sounds and sights to make heartstrings crack.
—Rudyard Kipling

IN-HOME FRAGRANCES

When selecting fragrances for your house, choose softer, more neutral scents in the living areas. Guests who are sensitive or allergic to fragrances appreciate this courtesy, and it prevents an overpowering first impression of your home. Reserve any stronger aromas for your bedroom, bathroom, dresser drawers and closets. For kitchen and bathrooms, make sure the fragrance isn't covering up an odor that requires prompt attention.

POTPOURRI AND SACHET ESSENTIALS

Collect leaves, small pine cones, pieces of bark, acorns and flower petals and seed heads. You can also add cinnamon sticks, whole cloves, whole nutmeg and orange peel. Dry the potpourri by spreading it one layer deep on a cookie sheet and warm in a 100-degree oven, leaving the oven door slightly ajar. Roasting time depends upon the quantity, and can be anywhere from just a few minutes to several hours. You'll only know when it's ready by checking it often. Place the potpourri on top of radiators, near wood burning stoves and in bathrooms. Pretty baskets and decorative bowls are perfect containers.

You can also air-dry potpourri on a window screen or on newspaper, placing it in a cool, dry place for several days, depending upon the humidity and temperature of your home. Do make sure the potpourri dries completely so it won't mildew. When dry, put the potpourri in a self-locking plastic bag with a few drops of fragrant oil and shake gently. Leave the bag in the freezer for two days to set the scent.

To create a sachet, place a small handful of potpourri in an 8-inch square of lace or netting. Tie the ends of the square with ribbon and stash it in your linen closet or lingerie drawer. Give it a squeeze to refresh the scent when adding clean items to the drawer. Or toss a securely tied sachet in the clothes dryer for nice-smelling sheets and towels.

To revive potpourri, stir with a wooden spoon or, for more intense revitalization, add a drop of essential oil and gently turn. You can also add drops of brandy, olive oil, liqueurs, lemon juice or a favorite perfume, depending upon what you like and the location of the potpourri. If you're leaving on vacation or business for an extended period, then cover the mixture or place it in a plastic bag to stay fresh.

Revive a sachet by emptying the bundle, adding a few drops of your favorite potion and curing it in a brown paper bag lined with wax paper for a few days before refilling the sachet.

SWEET-SMELLING TIPS FROM THE PROS

- Place the stopper from an empty perfume bottle in the bottom of a drawer until the smell fades away.
- For a comforting smell in the kitchen, boil a pot of water, turn off the heat and add cinnamon sticks or cloves. The steam carries the aroma around the house.
- Make your own fragrance rings to place on top of lightbulbs, using small-size canning jar rings. With pliers, slightly bend the inside rim up to create a shallow trough. Place two or three drops of fragrance inside. The heat of the light bulb then releases the scent.
- Spray index cards with your favorite scent and place them in your desk drawer, stationery box or bookshelf. Department store samples and scent strips from fashion magazines work well, too.
- Keep vases of fresh flowers around the house, such as lilies, roses and hyacinths. Grow fragrant bulbs, like narcissus, indoors in wintertime. Near your outside doors, grow fragrant shrubs like boxwoods or containers of aromatic herbs and flowers.
- Throw pieces of dried citrus peel into a fire and clear the air of any smoky smells.
- Fragrant bars of soap create a nice, long-lasting scent for drawers. You can even leave wrapped bars in the drawer until you're ready to use them. Scented drawer paper is another option.
- For scenting wooden drawers, dot essential oil on a cotton ball and rub the side of the drawers. This method also works on storage trunks, wooden blanket chests and even the underside of a table in the family room.
- Use a cotton swab to apply a few drops of fragrant oil to heating and cooling system filters, spreading a nice aroma through the house.

ELIMINATING UNPLEASANT ODORS

- Eradicate bad smells immediately by checking all the likely places: bottoms of trash cans, athletic shoes and equipment, the laundry hamper, the litter box, the dog bed or that mildewy shower stall in the basement. Be vigilant.

- Eliminate odors from garbage disposals by grinding chopped-up citrus rinds and flushing the disposal with hot water.

- Always drain any liquids from cans, containers and serving pieces to keep the garbage bag relatively dry. Empty the bag often.

- Always line garbage cans with a plastic bag. Spray the can with a pleasant-smelling disinfectant each time you empty it, or put a couple of fabric-softener sheets in the bottom before you replace the bag. Twice a month wash the can with a disinfectant cleaner and hot, sudsy water, then let air-dry before placing a bag inside.

- Prevent trash compactor odors by rinsing smelly cans, like tuna fish, before throwing away. Clean the compactor's ram weekly. Unplug the unit, then open the drawer and lift it off its tracks. Wash the bottom of the ram with disinfectant and hot water.

- Boil a few slices of lemon for twenty minutes in a pan of water to clear the air of any burned food odors.

- When frying foods, place a small bowl of white vinegar next to the stove to combat any smells.

- Ban smoking from your house always, without exception.

- Keep the bathroom door closed, but open a window for fresh air. In windowless bathrooms find a bathroom spray that is effective but not overpowering.

- Banish anyone's really smelly shoes to the great outdoors, the farther away the better.

- Transfer washed clothes promptly to the drier. If clothes sit overnight, then run a rinse cycle before drying to eliminate any possibility of mold.

- Run sponges through the dishwasher to clean and also change dishtowels every day or two.

AND DON'T FORGET THE BAKING SODA!

- For neutralizing carpet odors, sprinkle baking soda over your carpet. Wait fifteen minutes, then vacuum thoroughly.
- If scented detergents and dryer sheets are too strong for your nose, toss a tablespoon of baking soda into the laundry machine for clean-smelling, but not overly scented clothes.
- Keep drains odor-free by pouring 3 tablespoons of baking soda into the drain once a week and running very hot tap water over it for one minute.
- Sprinkle baking soda liberally into smelly shoes. Let stand overnight, and then shake them out before wearing.
- Freshen your dishwasher by sprinkling baking soda under the bottom rack in between loads.
- Keep an open box in the refrigerator to absorb smells. (Write the date on the box; replace it every two to three months.)
- Always buy two boxes at the supermarket, as something this good gets used up quickly.

No mom likes to think of herself as a maid, but cleaning comes with the job of Family Manager. Remember, good housekeeping means keeping in mind your own family's age, stage and definition of cleanliness—not mine, your mother's, or the latest cleaning guru's. Fortunately, you've got a family cleaning team to help get your house into shape quickly and effectively. So take heart! You're on the road to making your home a good place to be.

CHAPTER 3

You're the Home Organizer

I know a couple who never entertain. It's not that they don't have any friends or don't enjoy hosting parties, it's just that . . . well, there's no place to sit. This predicament isn't due to a lack of furniture. But every sofa, chair and tabletop is covered with clutter.

Clutter suffocates. It robs you of counter space, closet space, storage space, even thinking space. And it can be disguised in many forms—clothes, paper, toys, over-wrought collections, handed-down furniture that doesn't look right in any room, old linens, broken appliances, the china you inherited from your great aunt that just isn't you.

If the clutter around you is causing anxiety or interfering with the joy you get from your home, you have a problem. But not an unsolvable problem!

Clutter accumulates for several reasons. Some of us are just plain indecisive. We find it easier to stash an item than to figure out where and how best to store it. We hang on to things thinking they will come in handy back in style someday or. We reason that an old chair, toy or wooden bowl may be worth something in the future, or the kids may want it. Others mistakenly think dealing with clutter takes huge amounts of time, and the rest of us blame the problem on a lack of storage space.

Where I live in Texas, homes don't have basements, so my family has gotten really good at culling. We have no choice; there just isn't a place to put it all. Although inconvenient at times, it forces us to be more selective, and that's what conquering clutter is all about.

In this section you'll learn how to part with clutter whether you have a ten-minute block of time or a free weekend. Once you've decluttered, you'll find ideas for what's left over—clever storage tricks for small spaces and tips on how to organize drawers, rooms and closets, and for involving your family in the process. After all, it's their junk, too! So, read on and send clutter packing for good.

Six Bad Excuses for Clutter

For some of us—pack rats in particular—parting with almost anything is such sweet sorrow. So we don't. We find hanging on to clutter easier than deciding what to do with it. If this behavior is familiar to you, overcome these excuses and make a dent in a nearby pile today.

1. **Everyone has one, so I must need one, too.** Or the opposite, It's so unique, I've got to have (or keep) it. I know of a family who nearly broke up over a suit of armor. She wanted to buy it from a restaurant that was going out of business. He wanted to know where she was going to put it, since they didn't live in a castle and he rarely went out to slay dragons.

2. **It may come in handy someday.** I have a friend who held or to a down coat ten years after she moved from Minnesota to Florida.

3. **I'll keep it until I find someone to give it to.** And when you finally meet that person, how are you going to find it?

4. **I don't have time to sort through my stuff.** How much time do you spend taking care of things you don't use? Cleaning around them? Looking for things you really do need amid the clutter?

5. **If I get rid of things, I'm throwing money away.** Maybe you can't afford *not* to get rid of some stuff. Plus it's a well-known fact that one person's castoffs are another person's treasure. Have a garage sale or take your stuff to a consignment store.

The Case Against Clutter

- **Clutter is not just a space-taker, it's a stress-raiser.**

- **Clutter wastes time.** Who among us hasn't spent valuable minutes/hours searching for something we need right now (car keys, sunglasses, Tums)?

- **Clutter wastes money.** When any item is buried in an abyss, you may find yourself buying a duplicate, even though you know you already own one.

- **Clutter wastes energy.** You have to clean it, work around it or move it to get behind or under it.

- **Clutter is ugly.** Coming home to a space-choked house invites anxiety and grumpiness.

- **Clutter is dangerous.** It can cause household accidents.

The Verdict

■ **Clutter control requires just two things:** *elimination* and *concentration*. Eliminate what you don't need, and concentrate on taking care of what you do.

■ Clutter is not defeated in a day; it's an ongoing process. Exercise your decluttering muscle on a daily basis and clutter will never take up residence in your home again.

How many things I can do without!

—*Socrates*

6. **I don't know where to start.** Start by decluttering one small area. See how you feel. Be careful: once you get the hang of it, decluttering is fun and can be habit-forming.

Motivating Your Team

For family members who protest that getting organized is someone else's domain, remind them that since they live in the house, they contribute to its care.

■ **Help team members buy into the cause.** Family members won't buy into the idea of getting rid of clutter and getting organized just because Mom or Dad says it's time to do it. If they understand how and why getting organized will better their lives, they will be more likely to cooperate. For example you might say, "If the videos and CDs are in order, you'll be able to quickly find what you want to watch or listen to," or "If we know where things are, Dad won't get cranky because he can't find something."

■ **Seize the high ground.** No one will jump at the chance to be on your team if you're negative or critical. A team has to be inspired, and that means aiming for improvement with a positive attitude.

■ **Offer fair rewards.** You might suggest, "When the kitchen cabinets are organized and your closet is neat, we as a family will . . . (and offer a mutually agreed upon treat)," or, "If you help clean out the attic and basement for the garage sale, you can keep part of the profit."

Delegating to Your Team

A DOZEN WAYS KIDS CAN CONTROL CLUTTER

1. When your children get a new game or toy, help them decide where its storage place will be. Involving them in the where-it-goes decision also helps remind them to put it there when they're not using it.
2. Limit the number of toys that can be out at one time.

3. Have designated toy pickup and put away times.

4. Put a small-size laundry basket in each child's closet for dirty clothes.

5. Mount hooks at a child's level so they can hang hats, jackets, pajamas and so on.

6. Buy assorted sizes of clear plastic boxes for kids to categorize and store their belongings.

7. Avoid toy boxes and trunks. Small items sift to the bottom and you have to empty the whole box or trunk to find them.

8. Paint young children's shelves different colors to encourage sorting things like puzzles, games and books. Label drawers and storage containers; paste on appropriate pictures for small children.

9. Keep a clean plastic dustpan in your child's room to scoop up multipiece toys.

10. Establish specific food and nonfood places in your house. Restrict eating to the kitchen and possibly the TV or family room. Forbid food in the bedrooms.

11. Create an after-school unloading routine. Designate a place to put coats, mittens, hats and backpacks.

12. Encourage the regular weeding out of toys your kids have outgrown. Let your kids go with you to take them to a mission or shelter so they can see how their contributions help other people.

Clutter Battle Plans

WEEKEND BATTLE PLAN: CONQUERING CLUTTER ON A SATURDAY

Before you can enjoy the benefits of life without clutter, you'll need to do a whole-house clutter sweep. Then, you can get serious about storing and organizing the rest. This Ten-Step Plan makes it a snap. No free morning? No sweat. See "Ten-Minutes-a-Day Battle Plan" on page 64 for tips on taking on clutter one room at a time.

1. If possible, arrange your schedule to do clutter battle during one large block of time, like a Saturday. This way you'll save on start-

Bright Idea

An oversize fishing-tackle box that has two or three levels of compartments is perfect for storing rubber balls, action figures, miniature cars and other small treasures.

The Ten Clutter Commandments

1. Thou shalt ask yourself the following questions before acquiring something new:
   - Do I/we really need it?
   - How often will I/we use it?
   - How much space will it take up?
   - How much care does it require?
   - Do its design and quality meet my standards?
   - Is the price right?

2. Thou shalt buy something because it is truly useful, not because an advertisement promises it will be.

3. Thou shalt show an old item the door every time a new item comes into the house.

4. Thou shalt develop a habit of regularly giving things away to relatives, family or a charitable organization.

5. Thou shalt learn to enjoy things without having to own them.

6. Thou shalt put things where they belong when you're finished with them; don't take them halfway to their destination.

7. Thou shalt clean up the kitchen every night. Starting the day with a sink full of dirty, hard-to-clean dishes makes working in the kitchen difficult and inefficient.

8. Thou shalt save photos, not objects. Take a picture of your son in his Cub Scout uniform. Keep the photo; give away the uniform. It's the memory you want to hold on to.

9. Thou shalt resist the temptation to drape clothing on a piece of bedroom furniture. Undress near your closet and either hang up, put away or toss clothing into a laundry basket as you remove it.

10. Thou shalt flex your clutter control muscle every day. Maintaining a clutter-free environment requires a daily commitment, but it takes just minutes.

up/knock-down time, you'll be more serious and you'll do a more thorough job. As you see the results, you'll gain the momentum you need to keep going.

2. Arrange for the Salvation Army or another charity to come to your house. This gives you a deadline. (I keep the phone number in our

Family Yellow Pages and have them come four or five times a year.)

3. Dress so you can put all your energy into the job. Wear comfortable clothes and tennis shoes.

4. Go into battle prepared. You'll need several types of containers: boxes labeled Give Away, Garage Sale and Store; plastic storage bins (the see-through kind are best) and a large plastic garbage bag for every room. If you think you'll be distracted by things you don't know what to do with, put them in a box, too. Label the box Questionable and give yourself a deadline for deciding where those difficult items will end up. Don't forget a small box to collect safety pins and buttons, a shoe-size box for random photos you find and another box or a piggy bank for coins.

5. Start with the most cluttered room in your house. Work your way methodically around the room. Remove clutter from shelves, bookcases, drawers, tabletops, floors and walls. When you pick up an item, ask yourself these questions:

   • When is the last time it was used? Worn? Played with?
   • Does it deserve space in our home? If it wasn't here, what would be here instead?
   • Are there memories attached to it?
   • What will I do with it? Fix it, sell it, store it, toss it or donate it?

6. Toss or give away as much as possible. Be ruthless with things like gift boxes, grocery sacks, old magazines and catalogs and craft materials you saved to use but haven't used. Weed out games. You don't need Chutes and Ladders if your youngest child is a teenager. Classics such as Monopoly are probably worth holding on to, but be sure to check for missing pieces.

7. Broken objects are also clutter; they're not useful and not decorative. (The one exception: antiques that can often be restored for less than the cost of a new piece.) Either get them fixed or give them away to a charity that repairs donated items. Don't feel obligated to hold on to gifts. If you don't like, need or use them, treat them as clutter.

Clutter Combat Rules for Kids

1. Do not take food into the bedroom.

2. All dirty clothes go in the basket or hamper.

3. Do not leave dangerous items—balls, sharp plastic building pieces, roller skates—on the floor.

4. Put away the toys you're finished playing with before taking out something new.

5. Clean up the room every night before going to bed.

Bright Idea

Many toy and baby-equipment manufacturers will replace lost pieces for free or for a small fee. Hasbro (888-836-7025), for example, will replace up to ten Scrabble tiles for free or sell you a whole set for $5.50, less than half the price of the boxed game. The same phone number takes calls for Tonka, Playskool, Kenner, Nerf, Milton Bradley and Parker Brothers. For Fisher-Price, call 800-432-5437 in the United States or 800-567-7724 in Canada.

8. Use strict criteria in your closet. Get rid of anything permanently stained or badly worn. Clothes you haven't put on in the last three years and trendy items that aren't well made should also go.

9. Don't allow nonemergencies to interrupt your clutter-clearing time. Eliminate all distractions. Turn on your answering machine, turn off the TV and put on some peppy music. When you find the umbrella your friend left three months ago, don't call her now to tell her about it. Or the book that's been missing. Don't take a break now to crack it open.

10. If it's hard for you to toss things, organize a clutter-clearing party with a friend. In exchange for her helping you, you help her declutter another day.

TEN-MINUTES-A-DAY BATTLE PLAN: CONQUERING CLUTTER DURING FREE TIME

For those who can't see a free Saturday in the next five years, try getting into the free-minutes mindset. You'd be surprised how much you can accomplish in five, ten or fifteen minutes, and how many "free" small blocks of time you can grab here and there. No, you won't finish tasks like unloading the basement of a five-year stash of magazines you saved for articles on how to get organized, but you'll make progress, which will make you feel better about yourself, and eventually finish the chore.

- Take a few minutes to make a list of clutter hot spots in your house. Post the list where you'll see it and be reminded to declutter on a regular basis.

- Purge your pantry of food you never use but have somehow acquired. Give it to a shelter. Do one shelf at a time in five-minute segments.

- Sort through a junk drawer. Just toss items you don't need or use. You can organize it later.

- Clean out odds and ends from your refrigerator and freezer.

- Remove duplicates from kitchen drawers, again, one drawer at a time. How many cheese slicers do you really need? Even the messiest of drawers probably won't take more than ten minutes.

■ Reorganize your dish cupboards one shelf at a time. Ask yourself if you need that pan you find in the back corner of the bottom shelf. Be honest. If you're not sure *what* it's for, let alone the last time you used it, don't keep it.

■ Clean out your medicine cabinet a few shelves at a time. Check expiration dates and toss old bottles.

■ Cull children's clothing one drawer or shelf at a time. Save outgrown clothing for younger siblings in labeled boxes; trade with friends for clothes your kids can use now; give them to charity or a neighbor/relative who can use them. Repeat this exercise three times a year. (I always did it in the fall before school started, after Christmas and at the end of the school year.) Involve your kids in the process, and by the time they're teenagers they'll be able to do it on their own. Go through your own clothing and accessories twice a year, in the same way.

■ Declutter your linen closet one shelf at a time. Count the beds in your house and keep two sets of linens for each bed. Give away the leftovers or turn them into rags.

■ Put a bookshelf or basket in every room of the house—including your children's rooms—where you read or collect books, papers or magazines. Make a daily practice of putting the books, magazines or papers on the shelf or in the basket instead of on the floor, on the dining room table or wherever such clutter accumulates. When the shelf or the basket is full, cull, cull, cull. (Again, you can do this one shelf or basket at a time, probably in five minutes or less.)

■ Make it a game. Walk through your house with a plastic garbage bag and see how much junk you can gather in a set amount of time. Set your kitchen timer. Toss out expired coupons or packages of food no one will eat, single or worn-out socks (save a few for cleaning), old travel brochures, expired medicines, makeup that's more than a year old, extra grocery bags (keep 5 to 10 on hand), things that are broken, rusted tools and utensils and games with missing pieces. Do this the night before garbage pickup so you won't be tempted to retrieve anything.

CLUTTER PREVENTION BATTLE PLAN: STOP IT BEFORE IT STARTS

Got a clutter hot spot? You know, those stubborn places that you just can't seem to unearth? Here's how to prevent clutter buildup and get ready to take back your valuable space!

1. **The home office.** Collect your mail in a basket or contained area, then deal with it every day. Toss the junk mail, file whatever needs to be kept and circulate the rest to the appropriate family member. Put bills in a separate basket with everything you need to pay them: a letter opener, pen, stapler, envelopes and stamps. If you must hang on to back issues of magazines, keep them neatly stacked on a bookcase shelf in inexpensive cardboard magazine holders. Vow not to let newspapers and catalogues pile up. Yesterday's news is old, so toss it. If you haven't read Sunday's paper by Tuesday, get rid of that, too. An old catalogue should be thrown out when the new one arrives, if not sooner.

2. **Flat surfaces.** Kitchen countertops, the dining room table, your desk and side tables throughout the house are magnets for clutter. The best strategy is to give everything a place and train family members to put things where they belong now, not later. I keep my counter-tops clear with inexpensive plastic baskets. They're terrific for organizing junk drawers and for containing small or oddly shaped items such as taco or gravy mixes and salad dressing. You can claim even more space by hanging produce (potatoes, onions and the like) from the ceiling in wire baskets. A brightly colored wall grid is a good way to remove cooking utensils from drawers and countertops.

   To keep other areas clear of clutter, each family member should have a box or a folder for their mail or other papers. The folders are stored in a plastic desktop shelf unit. The kids unload their back-packs of important papers that need parental attention, and they check their shelf for mail or phone messages I may have left them.

3. **The foyer.** For safety as well as cosmetic reasons, the main entryway into (and out of your home) should be kept free and clear. Unless something is on its way out the door soon—such as overdue library books gathered in a bag—don't use the foyer as a depository.

4. **The kitchen.** A bulletin board and a large family calendar will do a lot to reduce the clutter in your kitchen. To keep loose papers organized, divide the bulletin board into sections; for example, put phone numbers and messages in one section, shopping lists in another, school papers and reminders in the third and takeout menus in the last. If your children bring home a lot of artwork (and your refrigerator is already covered in it), you may want to designate a second bulletin board to display their creations.

Post the family calendar in a central location. Be sure the daily blocks are large enough for kids to post their activities. Assign each child a different colored marker so it's easy to distinguish their schedules.

5. **Bedrooms.** Because bedrooms are private places that nonfamily members rarely see, it's easy to stash clutter there behind closed doors. To combat a child's natural tendency to drop clothing on the floor, lower the rods in her closet to make them easier to reach and show her how to group like items together. Shirts go with other shirts but short-sleeved attire should be separated from long-sleeved attire. Pants and skirts should each have their own areas.

Make use of under-the-bed storage space. Put off-season clothing and outdoor wear in low, wide plastic containers. To keep desktops clear for homework consider a small filing cabinet and chest of plastic drawers for pencils, paper and other school supplies. A small bookshelf can hold books as well as toys and other keepsakes.

6. **The family room.** This general living area often gets cluttered with day-to-day activities and projects. One idea is to ask your local pizza restaurant for a few clean boxes. Then have the kids decorate the covers and store their artwork in them. The boxes fit nicely beneath beds, too. Keep an attractive basket with a lid in the family room to kccp toys out of sight when not in used. High-tech entertainment is a lot of fun but the countless components can make you crazy. There are many practical and inexpensive products for organizing and storing videos, DVDs, CDs, video games and the like. Check out your local mass-merchandise store for options.

Bright Idea

Spend a few minutes each day decluttering a problem area. Keep at it, little by little, day by day, until it's done.

67

Bright Idea

Start a family game:
every time you bring one
new item into the house,
get rid of five others.
Keep a To-Be-Donated
box in an out-of-sight but
easily accessible place.
Add to it regularly.
When it's full, either
deliver it or have it
picked up.

7. **The linen closet.** This closet tends to collect stuff that's old, worn and no longer useful. Weed out worn towels and turn them into cloths for washing the car. Fold all the sheets and pillowcases that are part of a set into a pillowcase. The next time you need to change a bed, you'll have all you need easily within your reach. Install a hook on the inside of the closet door to keep freshly ironed tablecloths hung from hangers wrinkle-free. Hang a clear plastic pocket shoe bag on the back of the linen closet door for razors, hair accessories, rolled-up washcloths and other bathroom supplies.

8. **The bathroom.** Use color-coded plastic baskets to keep toiletries neat and separate. Label one for each family member's individual bathroom items. A magnetic strip attached to the back or side of your medicine cabinet is great for holding small scissors, tweezers and nail clippers. Bath toys can be stored in dishpans under the vanity. Or, you can hang a mesh bag from the shower nozzle to conveniently drip-dry toys in the tub.

9. **The laundry area.** Attach a magnetic caddy to the side of the washing machine for items found in pockets and buttons that come off in the wash. Prethread some needles and keep them handy in a pincushion for instant repairs.

10. **The garage.** If there's not enough room to protect your car from the elements, it's time to declutter the garage. Suspend bicycles, ladders, rakes, brooms and other yard equipment from hooks attached to the wall. If the ceiling has open rafters stash infrequently used items such as skis and lumber up there. Corral soccer and basketballs into a garbage can. Medium-size tools, such as screwdrivers and gardening equipment, can be hung on peg board. An old spice rack is just the right size for holding baby-food jars filled with nails and screws. That, too, can be hung from the peg board.

Smart Storage Strategies

Congratulations! You've officially lightened your load. Doesn't it feel wonderful? Now comes the easy part: storing and organizing the rest. You

YOU'RE THE HOME ORGANIZER

can work through the following plan one step at a time over the course of several days, weeks or months. Or, if you're really motivated and still have some of your weekend left, get down to work now. You'll never waste time looking for lost items again.

1. **Conduct a storage survey.** You'll likely need an uninterrupted half hour for this exercise. With a notebook and pen in hand, walk slowly around your house. Jot down all the storage spaces you see. Be sure to check for unusual spots you may have overlooked (behind a china cabinet or under the guest room bed, for instance). This is particularly effective if you've recently moved, are redecorating or are rearranging furniture.

   In a separate column, make note of items that don't have a proper storage space, or aren't located near the place they are used. Have a family member repeat the exercise; sometimes another pair of eyes can turn up spots you missed.

   Once the survey is finished, you can begin matching up items with storage places. If building storage units or hanging peg board will provide the space you need, then get those tasks accomplished with help from your family.

2. **Get the tools you need to get the job done right.** My husband believes (and reminds me every year when he's making up his Christmas wish list) that using the proper tools is the key to completing projects efficiently. The same principle applies to getting—and staying—organized. There are many products in every price range that can help you maximize your storage space. If you're doing a major storage and organization overhaul, I suggest you purchase a wide variety of storage bins and organizing items. Be sure to save your receipts so you can return the ones you don't use.

   One mom I know uses empty, shoe-size boxes to store her family photographs. Whenever she picks up film, she writes a description of the photos (for example, "Summer 2001") on the envelope they're returned in, then lines them up chronologically inside the box. Once the box is filled, she labels the outside with the starting

Go home, and take care of what you have. Provide places for all your things.
—Mother Ann, Shaker Founder

69

*My Favorite
Storage and
Organizing Tools*

■ **Hooks and pegs of
every shape and size**

■ **Wire baskets (single
and double-decker)**

■ **Step shelves**

■ **Three-tier corner
shelves**

■ **Lazy Susans**

■ **Baking sheet
organizers**

■ **Broom and mop
holders**

■ **Over-the-door
organizers**

■ **Under-shelf organizers**

■ **Clear plastic drawer
organizers**

■ **See-through plastic
tubs and crates**

■ **Self-sealing plastic
bags**

■ **Peg boards**

and ending dates of her photos. Her Shoebox Album is stacked on bookshelves in her home office.

Many women tell me empty diaper wipe containers are a mom's best friend. They're brightly colored, kid friendly and can be stacked neatly in a bedroom or play area. Use them to store everything from hair accessories to jewelry to small toy parts.

But don't be afraid to think outside the box. Baskets of different sizes and colors can be an attractive storage option for odd-size items. Another Family Manager I know uses her athletic son's trophy cups to hold kitchenware on her countertop. It's a great look.

3. **Store like items together.** Think in categories. Gather all items used for the same kind of project and put them in one spot convenient to the user. For example, when you put away seasonal items, such as skis or winter wear, keep all related items together. Use this list to help you think about how best to group your belongings:

- Art and craft supplies
- Auto-care items
- Baby clothes (outgrown, to-be-grown-into, sentimental)
- Books (general reading, reference, special interest, children's)
- Boots and rain gear
- Business documents
- Camera equipment and film
- Camping items
- CDs and cassette tapes
- Children's school papers and art
- China, crystal and candles
- Cleaning supplies
- Cosmetics
- Documents (marriage and birth certificates, social security cards, passports)
- Extra food stuffs (canned goods, pasta, rice)
- Extra paper products (towels, napkins, lunch bags)
- Family memorabilia
- Financial records
- First-aid necessities
- Flashlights and batteries
- Games
- Gardening equipment
- Greeting cards/stationery
- Hobby supplies
- Holiday decorations

- Household tools
- Kitchen items
- Kitchen items that are seldom used
- Linens
- Luggage and travel kits
- Magazines
- Maternity clothes
- Medications
- Office supplies
- Pet supplies
- Picnic supplies
- Road kit #1 (toys, maps, wet wipes, snack packages, bottled water)
- Road kit #2 for extreme winter climates (extra clothing and blankets, hand-warmers, shovel, ice scraper, kitty litter for helping with traction on snowy road shoulders)
- Party supplies
- Photos, albums and negatives
- Seasonal clothing
- Sewing supplies
- Silver (flatware, serving pieces)
- Sports equipment
- Tax returns and cancelled checks
- Toys
- Trophies
- Vacuum accessories
- Vases and flower-arranging supplies
- Videotapes and DVDs
- Warranties and care/operation directions for toys and appliances

4. **Store items as close as possible to the place they are used most often.** Instead of thinking, "Where can I store this?" ask yourself, "Where do I use this?" Strive for one-motion storage. For example, the coffeemaker needs to be close to the sink, and the coffee and the coffee filters should be within arm's reach. Other things might seem to have no clearly defined category or place, but don't simply store these stumpers in the first handy space. Think about how you're going to use the object. If you do floor exercises in front of the TV in the family room, then store your mat nearby.

5. **Allocate your most accessible space to the things you use most often.** Shelves between eye and waist level are prime storage areas in the kitchen. Don't store the deep fryer you use to fry fish on the Fourth of July there. And don't put your crepe pan, which you use infrequently, in front of your sauce pans, which you use daily.

71

Take Note

Photo equipment should be stored in an interior closet at room temperature. Extreme temperature change can cause condensation that will damage equipment.

6. **Make finding as easy as storing.** Use see-through containers whenever possible. When you can't, take a minute to label the containers. If you're going to stack containers on top of each other, be sure and label both the side and the top of the box using a fat felt-tipped marker. (If labeling boxes sounds like a chore to you, just think about how much of a chore it will be to find that one item in the seven boxes you stacked on the top shelf in a closet.)

7. **Give every possession a home.** Whenever you acquire something new, be it a pasta maker or a pair of ice skates, decide where it's going to be stored as soon as you bring it into the house. For bigger items, it's a good idea to figure that out before you even think of bringing it home. Will that priced-right antique armoire actually fit up the stairs into your daughter's bedroom? Initially, you may think buying a set of twenty-four marked-down wine glasses for your big spring party is a terrific idea, but where will they be stored after the party? And how frequently will you use them? Always look into the cost of rentals. Often it's the cheapest way to go, plus you get the added benefit of not having to store them once the guests go home.

8. **Create work centers around your house.** With work centers you collect everything you need to perform a task in one place. This eliminates search time and makes you more efficient. Here are some ideas:

• **A Kids' Arts and Crafts Center.** Devote a shelf in their play area to stack construction paper, sketch pads, glue, glitter, scissors, markers, crayons, pipe cleaners and pompoms. No space for a shelf? Pack it all together in a storage bin that they can easily access.

• **A Family Fun and Games Center.** This can be a place for board games, cards, dominos, puzzles and building sets like Lincoln Logs and Tinker Toys. Tip: if you have lots of games and their boxes are falling apart, try removing the contents of each box and storing them in self-sealing plastic bags along with the game's directions.

Corral plastic bags in a basket or shoebox. Game boards can be folded and stacked together nearby.

• **A Gift-Wrapping Center.** Designate a large drawer, plastic crate or part of a cabinet to store everything you need for wrapping (wrapping paper, tape, scissors, ribbon and so on). I know a family who set up a card table in their basement for this purpose. Another family purchased plastic storage boxes that easily slip under a bed. Keep a few generic gifts for adults and children there, too. Stock with blank cards (I love the small gift-size cards because they're cute and cost so much less than regular cards) and cards for birthdays, anniversaries, holidays, graduations, engagements, weddings, babies, confirmations, Bar/Bat Mitzvahs, deaths and retirements.

• **A Sewing Center.** This should have a shelf or basket for family members to put clothes in need of mending. Keep quick-fix mending supplies—needles and thread, a pincushion and tape measure, iron-on patches, fusible bonding and fabric glue—on hand there, too.

• **A Fix-It Center.** This should shelves on which to put broken items that need to be fixed. Keep various types of glue, tape and small tools on hand.

• **A Bill-Paying Center.** This should be stocked with pens, stamps, envelopes, return-address labels, a calculator and a basket to collect bills.

• **A Mail Center.** Use this to organize your mail every day. Keep a trash can close by so you can toss junk mail as you sort. Buy cardboard magazine storage boxes at an office-supply store. Write each family member's name on a box and label one for bills and another for magazines and catalogs. Depending on the space available in your home, your Control Central (see Chapter 1) might also be the place for mail sorting and bill paying.

• **Kitchen Work Center.** This should be arranged according to the tasks you perform there (chopping, baking, lunch making and so on). Try to revolve each center around a major appliance, some stor-

Take Note

When looking for a place to store an item, think, "Where will I use this?" not, "Where can I put this?"

age space and a work surface. Store equipment and food near the center where they'll be used—for example, baking goods and utensils near the mixer and dishes near the dishwasher.

• **A Pet Care Center.** I have two shelves in my house where we keep the dogs' brushes, leashes, bandannas, chew toys, a Frisbee, old towels for bathing them and a plastic bin to hold their shampoo, medicines and other supplies.

• **A Laundry Center.** Detergent, bleach, stain remover, presoak, fabric softener, soap for hand-washables, starch, a zipper mesh bag for delicates, hangers, an ironing board and an iron should all be kept in one place, too.

One Room at a Time . . .

ATTACK YOUR ATTIC

Organizing and maximizing the space in your attic may seem like drudgery, but it will pay off for years to come. Imagine being able to find, within a few minutes, any item in the attic! Follow these easy steps to stress-free storage.

1. **Declutter.** Lots of stuff that ends up in the attic is there because we don't know what else to do with it. Do yourself a favor and clear it out. Toting an empty box labeled Put Elsewhere will get you off to a great start. Take anything that can be fixed or used by someone else to a community organization, drop-off or donation center. As for the rest, take a deep breath and toss it, especially the following:

• Old magazines and newspapers (except those in good condition, since your local library may happily take them).

• Receipts and cancelled checks older than seven years. (Note: Keep only those pertaining to home improvements. Some, like roof repairs, may have long guarantee periods that won't be honored without the paperwork.)

- Outdated office supplies and equipment.
- Mangled holiday decorations and faded wrapping supplies.
- Empty boxes and bags.
- Outdated furniture that needs to be fixed.
- Dishes, cookware and kitchen items you never use.
- High school and/or college essays and notes.
- Moth-eaten clothes.
- Broken toys and sports gear.
- Rusty tools or equipment.
- Broken or torn luggage.

2. **Categorize the remaining items into departments.** Your departments might include seasonal decorations, baby furniture, memorabilia, luggage, a place for next year's garage-sale stuff, technical equipment and/or the boxes the equipment came in.

3. **Reserve attic space for items you access only a few times per year.** Store these items using these space-saving tactics:

- Label all boxes and bins on the top and side for easy identification. Keep an inventory of items stored so you'll know where to find them.
- Use a large plastic bin with a lid for each child to save artwork and other items they will treasure when they're older. Label each in bold letters for easy identification.
- Stash luggage here with smaller suitcases stored inside larger ones.
- Avoid using paper or plastic bags for storage. Instead watch for sales on sturdy, see-through plastic bins that can be stacked and moved easily.
- Purchase inexpensive industrial metal shelving to keep boxes and bins off the floor and safe from bugs, mice and dirt.
- Set up a clothing rack for hanging off-season clothes.
- Attach a pair of old belts to the rafters in your attic to hold things like skis or a rolled-up rug.
- Baby items that aren't currently being used can be neatly stored together in the old crib or playpen.

4. **Don't put certain items in the attic.** These items belong in storage that has a more even temperature and humidity level than an attic:

- **Wood furniture.** Changes in humidity and temperature can cause wood to split and crack.
- **Fur and leather.** Heat, fluctuating temperatures and pests can damage these items.
- **Books.** Mildew and rodents can harm. Changes in moisture can damage old, leather-bound books.
- **Heirloom clothing or formal dresses.** These need a climate-controlled area, and should be professionally cleaned and packed.
- **Camera equipment.** Cameras, lenses and other equipment should be stored in a cool, dry place.
- **Photographs and negatives.** Store these in main areas of your home, away from light and heat. Intense heat or high humidity can cause damage.
- **Stuffed toys.** Squirrels, chipmunks and mice love to chew on these.
- **Rubber and plastic items.** Unless well insulated, attics tend to have extreme temperatures that can damage these items.
- **Important original documents.** Birth certificates and your marriage license don't belong in the attic. Instead, keep them in a bank safe-deposit box. Keep copies in a file at home.
- **Wool rugs.** Moths love to eat through these.

5. **If you use your attic as a clothes closet, follow these recommendations.** Before storing nonheirloom clothing in the attic:

- Wash or dry-clean, because insects and pests are attracted to dirt left on clothes and fabrics. Remove starch, as silverfish like it.
- Hang clothes in canvas garment bags or cardboard clothing boxes with hanging rods from moving companies. You can also install a rod in the attic, hang clothing, then protect with a clean sheet.
- Don't store clothing in dry-cleaner bags or in garment bags made of synthetic fabrics that don't breathe. Moisture trapped inside can cause mildew. Some plastic bags cause clothes to yellow.

Take Note

If you store furniture in your attic, cover it with a sheet to protect it from dust, or plastic tarps if you think your roof might leak.

- Store folded clothing in an acid-free cardboard box (available at home centers, photograph supply stores and archival supply companies) or boxes lined with a clean cotton sheet. Place small cedar blocks in boxes to ward off pests. (Also see page 00, "How to Create a Cedar Closet.")

6. **Practice attic etiquette.**

- Check your roof for leaks. On a rainy day, use a strong-beamed flashlight to locate the spot where water is dripping. Mark the spot with chalk or spray paint. On a sunny day, turn off all lights and look over the entire roof for a pinhole beam of sunlight. Mark it.
- Venting an attic helps cool your house. According to the Department of Energy, ventilated attics may be up to 30 degrees F cooler than nonventilated ones. Before tackling this project, consult a professional.
- Keep a flashlight in the attic to help you see into dark corners and in case the power goes out when you're up there.
- If your attic has a pull-string light, insulate the string against the heat of the bulb by wrapping the string with duct tape several times. Otherwise, if the light is left on long enough, the string could burn.

BANISH CLUTTERED BATHROOMS

A disorganized, messy bathroom is the perfect place for humidity, moisture and bacteria to meet and create a resort for germs—not what you want in a room where people go to get clean. Besides, having an organized bathroom means there's less to clean.

- If you're short on linen storage space, roll towels and display their colors in a wicker basket on the floor of the bathroom.
- Keep bathroom drawers neat with a plastic silverware tray.
- Use plastic totes to store each family member's bathroom items in a cabinet. Install childproof latches on low cabinet doors.
- Mount a magazine rack to the wall to hold magazines and other reading material.

- An over-the-door shoebag on the back of the bathroom or linen closet door can store hair rollers, brushes, washcloths and so on.
- Keep the peace (and save your sanity) by color coding your towels and washcloths. Assign a color to each family member to reduce sibling squabbles and help uncover the mystery of who "forgot" to hang his towel. If you prefer monograms, they serve the same purpose.
- Store bath toys either in dishpans under the vanity, or put them in a mesh bag that hangs from the shower nozzle so they can drip dry in the tub.
- Install hooks on the back of the door for hanging bathrobes and damp towels.
- Make sure you have hooks or towel racks that kids can reach.
- Mount vinyl-coated wire racks on the inside of cabinet doors to hold bathroom items.
- Consider buying a wall-mounted hair dryer for easy access and storage.
- Store prescription medicines and over-the-counter remedies on higher shelves, in clearly labeled containers, out of the reach of small children. I store mine in small plastic crates according to category: topical and skin medications; cold and flu medications; stomach and intestinal medications; and pain relievers. You can also mount a spice rack on the inside of the linen closet door to hold medicine bottles.
- Install a disposable paper cup dispenser. They're neat and provide better hygiene than a drinking cup all family members share. Just be sure to put a small trash basket nearby.

GET-SMART GARAGES

If the square footage in your garage has shrunk, it's probably time to clear the clutter and organize your stuff. Check your local weather report for a sunny day or two. Start early in the morning by taking everything out of your garage. If you have the time, paint the walls a light color. If your floor is badly soiled, saturate grease and oil spots with paint thinner.

Then cover the soiled areas with cat litter or sawdust. Keep the garage door open and give the litter time to absorb the oil. Sweep it away, then wash the floor and let it dry. Finally, put things back in a manner that makes sense to you.

- If you want your garage floor to be easier to clean in the future, consider painting the floor. Several products specifically for this purpose are on the market at home improvement stores.
- Group like items together—for example, sporting equipment, tools, gardening tools.
- Put utility shelves on one wall for storing things like gardening supplies, insecticides, paint and auto-maintenance supplies. (Be sure to put poisonous products on a high shelf.) Assign lower shelves to a family member for their work boots and sports equipment.
- Hang inexpensive kitchen cabinets on the walls for storage. Put peg board on walls for hanging storage.
- "Brand" your tools by painting your initial on them in a bright color. This way, if a neighbor borrows something, your brand will be a reminder to them to get it back to you.
- Install a rack to hold saws, shovels, rakes and extension cords.
- Install large hooks to store garden hoses inside during winter months.
- Use clear, labeled storage containers so you don't have to dump the contents each time you need something. Jelly or baby-food jars can hold different kinds of screws, nails, washers and so on. There are many kinds of hardware-organizing products at the home improvement store.
- Use silverware sorters to hold supplies such as twine, scissors and garbage bag twist ties.
- Store paintbrushes in coffee cans, brush end up, or hang them from a peg board.
- Clip loose sheets of sandpaper to a clipboard and hang it from a wall hook.
- Store single-edged razor blades in a block of Styrofoam. Keep up high out of kids' reach.

Bright Idea

Designate a special fix-it shelf or area in your garage for broken things that need to be fixed.

- Think "up high." Hang bicycles and other sports equipment from the garage ceiling. If you have rafters, put boards across them to make a mini storage loft over part of the garage. (This is a particularly good place to store things you need only seasonally, such outdoor holiday decorations, snow shovels or lawn furniture.)
- String an old hammock along a wall to hold sports equipment and lightweight items.
- Use large plastic trash cans with lids for potting soils, compost materials, fertilizers and so on. Keep them sealed, away from children's toys and equipment, and water. Don't store fertilizer and gasoline close to each other.
- If you have a gas water heater or furnace in your garage, don't store your lawnmower and gas-powered tools nearby. Drain the gasoline for winter storage.
- Keep a trash can on the driver's side of the garage so car debris can be easily tossed.
- Paint parking spaces on your garage floor for tricycles, skateboards, wagons and scooters. (Let your kids take turns being Garage Police and collect fines when equipment is not parked correctly.)
- Use an empty old metal filing cabinet for additional storage space.
- Set up a worktable (you can use sawhorses and an old door) or have a fold-down table handy for repair work and other tasks.
- Install an inexpensive shop light above your primary work surface.
- Keep pet food in a closed container.
- Hang a tennis ball from the ceiling, positioning it so that it rests against your windshield when you've pulled into your garage to the appropriate spot.
- When your car begins to leak oil or fluids, place a flat piece of cardboard under your car until you can have repairs made.

THE EFFICIENT KITCHEN

The kitchen is the hub of the home. A lot of traffic—parents, kids, grandparents, neighbors, guests, and caretakers—flows through this little

Garage Safety Inspection Checklist

☐ Is the circuit breaker box well marked?

☐ Are electrical outlets covered?

☐ Are cabinets containing toxic chemicals locked?

☐ Is the fire extinguisher easily accessible?

☐ Are windows and doors secured against break-ins?

☐ Are there signs of rodent activity?

☐ Are lawn mowers and other cutting machines in good repair with necessary guards?

☐ Are products that have safety packaging properly closed?

☐ Is gasoline stored in approved, clearly labeled containers?

☐ Is scrap wood, sawdust or other waste lying around on the garage floor?

☐ Are solvents and paints in sealed and labeled metal containers and stored away from heat sources, such as your furnace or water heater?

☐ Do any electrical power tools have frayed cords or bad plugs?

☐ Are electrical power tools unplugged and stored when not in use?

---

room, so organization is essential. If your kitchen is really out of control, you'll need to take some time to rethink and reorganize—this will save you time in the long run. Enlist your family to help. If they help you get it in order, they'll be more likely to help keep it that way. Ten questions to consider before you begin include:

1. If you have small children, do you have a lower cabinet dedicated to plastic dishes for them? Do you have safety catches so they can't get into dangerous things? Are there items that need to be stored out of children's reach?

2. Are things you use every day stored where you can get at them? How high can you comfortably reach? Do you have a safe kitchen ladder to extend your reach?

3. Who cooks at your house and how often?

4. Are you right- or left-handed? Particularly short or tall? Do you or other family members have other physical needs or limitations? How might you rearrange your work areas, countertops and storage spaces to accommodate your family's needs? (This could be something as simple as reversing the side of the sink the dish drainer is on.)

5. Do you like to stand or sit when you're working in the kitchen? If you're a sitter in a kitchen designed for a stander, you might consider adding a folding stool. A long-term alternative might be to build a work island at a sitter's level.

6. Do your kids do their homework in the kitchen? Can you devote a drawer or part of a shelf to storing paper, pencils and the other supplies they regularly use? Or use TV trays for temporary work stations?

7. Do you shop in bulk and need a lot of storage space? Or do you buy a lot of fresh foods, in which case you need a lot of refrigerator space?

8. Can you reach cooking utensils without moving from the stove?

9. Are food cabinets well organized so items are as easy to find as possible—like when the pudding has just come to a boil and you need the vanilla?

10. Are table accessories—napkins, dinnerware, place mats, salt and pepper shakers—easily accessible to the dinner table?

If you find the kitchen is in need of a major reorganization, declutter first. Begin with cabinet closest to the sink and work your way methodically around the room. Take everything out of each cupboard. Clean the shelves. Replace only the items that you usually use from that cupboard, leaving the most frequently used at the front. Set the rest aside to be placed in another cupboard during another snippet of time, or place them in a giveaway box. Also consider these kitchen storage tips:

Smart Kitchen Storage
- Keep only the glasses you use regularly in a prime storage space. Store glassware and cups upside down to prevent dust and discourage insects. Line them up in neat rows according to type, or stack them if possible. Let younger kids organize their own lower cabinet for plastic cups and dishes.
- Store extraneous pots and pans, bowls, casseroles and dishes in a high, seldom-used cabinet. Keep only items used at least weekly in prime storage.

- Store pot lids all in one place. Designate a deep drawer to stand them on their sides in order of size, or get a pot-lid organizer, available in houseware stores.

- Install vertical dividers in a lower cabinet close to the oven to store cookie sheets and pizza pans.

- Use only clear-glass or plastic containers for storing food in your refrigerator so you always know what you're saving.

- Hang kitchenware used daily on a wall grid in your favorite color. Store oversize utensils in a crock by the stove.

- Install wire or plastic sliding shelves, or use plastic vegetable bins to store items in the usually dead space under the sink. (Position shelves or bins so that you can get to the shut-off valve easily.) Hang a towel rack on the inside of the cabinet door for wet dishrags and gloves.

- Use lazy Susans on deep shelves or in corner cabinets.

- Hang a foil, wrap and bag organizer inside a cabinet or pantry door.

- Use wall space for wall-mountable dispensers and portable appliances. Some coffeemakers, microwaves and radios can be mounted underneath high cabinets.

- Install slide-out plastic drawers to simplify the retrieval of items at the back of deep cabinets.

- Give away space-taking cookbooks you never use. Cut out favorite recipes and file them in inexpensive photo albums.

- Place a decorative hook on the wall above the kitchen sink so you can hang your watch on it when washing dishes.

- Store canned goods by category and with labels facing forward so you can see what's on hand at a glance.

- Store spices alphabetically or group them by use: baking spices, pasta spices and so on. Avoid lining them up on top of the stove; this interferes with cleaning, and heat can affect the spice's quality. Stair-step spice racks help you see what you have on hand with one glance.

- Attach small containers or racks to the inside of cabinet doors for envelope mixes and other small, hard-to-store items.

- To gain counter space, hang a three-tier wire basket from your kitchen ceiling to hold potatoes, onions, peppers and fruit.

- Store baskets you use only occasionally in the space between your cupboard tops and the ceiling.
- Designate a shelf or roomy basket in the kitchen or near your exit door for errands—for example, shoes to be repaired, film to be developed, books to be returned.
- Screw hooks into the ceilings of your cabinets and hang coffee mugs by their handles.
- Add another shelf inside a tall cabinet to elevate some items and create space underneath for others.

Here are a few more smart moves:

- Bag your own groceries so you can put items together the way they go in your kitchen.
- Most foods store best in cool, dry places in a temperature of 40 to 60 degrees. Do not store food near heating ducts, furnaces, hot-water pipes or other heat sources.
- Rotate food and supplies. Place new items behind old ones. If you buy in bulk, be sure to label all containers. Indicate the contents and date of purchase.
- Discard all bulged or leaking cans.
- If you have partially used containers of the same items, check to see that they have approximately the same expiration dates, and then combine them.
- Save only five grocery bags at a time. They seem to multiply between the counter and refrigerator.
- So dishes won't be exposed to dust and grease, try to store them in cabinets with doors instead of on shelves.
- Keep silverware within arm's length of the dishwasher.
- Save search time by the labeling shelves in your freezer. Mine are labeled Breads and Quick Meals, Vegetables, Desserts and Beverages, and Meat.
- Put a small dish drainer inside a cabinet to tame Tupperware lids. Only buy containers that will nest. Otherwise you're creating more

storage problems. Keep all coffee-brewing supplies near the coffeemaker.

- Keep a measuring cup in the flour and sugar and a measuring spoon in the coffee.
- Use the inside of kitchen cabinet doors to post information such as kitchen measurements and favorite recipes.
- When a new appliance comes with extra packaged parts, write on the package what the parts belong to and store them in a parts box in the garage.
- Designate a drawer for healthy snacks so kids can help themselves when hungry.

CLUTTER-FREE KIDS' ROOMS

Conquering clutter in a child's room is an ongoing process. But don't be discouraged. A few simple organizing techniques can reduce chaos, relieve frustration and turn a Danger Zone into a Children-at-Play Zone.

- When your children get a new game or toy, help them decide where to store it. Involving them in the where-it-goes decision also helps remind them to put it there when they're not using it.
- Have designated toy cleanup times—for example, before lunch, before dinner and a half hour before bed. Make it fun by letting kids take turns ringing a bell announcing cleanup time.
- Make sure children's books are easily accessible. Help them arrange their books by topic or author so they'll have a sense of pride and ownership in a growing library.
- Use a pocket shoe-organizer bag to store not only shoes, but socks, belts, small toys, hair bows and so on.
- Add a to-the-floor dust ruffle to the bottom of a baby crib for hidden floor storage.
- Put a mattress on a platform with built-in drawers, or attach coasters to plastic storage boxes and slide them under beds.
- Keep fragile toys or collectibles on a high shelf so they are on dis-

Bright Idea

Have a rubber stamp made with each child's name. This makes it easy to put their names on their belongings.

play but won't be damaged. (Even if your own kids know certain items are especially meaningful or valuable, their friends don't.)

- Don't keep wrong-size clothes in their closet.
- Keep a small step stool in the closet for kids to reach higher shelves.
- Have a small laundry basket for easy cleanup of dirty clothes.
- Use rolling plastic containers to store toys under the bed or in a closet.
- Buy a chest or use a footlocker to store odd-size toys. These items do double duty when it's time to pack your child's things for camp or college.
- Frame your child's artwork in inexpensive, clear-plastic frames to hang on the walls.
- Lower the bars in your child's closet so he can hang up his own clothes. If your kids share a closet, to prevent bickering, paint each half of the rod a different color or cover it with different-colored plastic shower rod.
- Provide some shelves for your child to display personal treasures.
- Position light switches so your child can reach them easily. Use paint pens to personalize the cover plate with your child's name.
- Make sure furniture is stable and there is no possibility of pulling over tall dressers, shelves, or stacked items.
- Hang a baseball cap rack on the back of a child's bedroom door to keep caps neat and organized.

MORE ROOM IN THE LIVING ROOM

- Have an attractive box on a table to store remote controls.
- If you have small children, keep handy an attractive basket with a lid to hold a few favorite toys in this area.
- Build a high-border shelf around the perimeter of a room to store/display decorative items such as baskets, pretty porcelain dishes, antique dolls or toys, and stuffed animals. But keep in mind, these items get dusty and require regular cleaning
- Buy furniture with built-in storage—for example, trunk-style coffee tables, covered benches with room for hats, mittens and bags underneath, an ottoman that opens with space for games and puzzles.

Take Note

Getting organized is not just about taking care of your stuff. It's about teaching your kids about life. You are doing your kids a favor when you provide helpful organizational supplies and encourage them to take care of their belongings.

- "Behind" storage places are often overlooked. Store your dining-room table leaves behind the china closet or breakfront. A folding game table might fit behind the couch in the family room. A collapsible easel may hang on the wall behind a child's closet door.
- Hang speakers on a wall to free up floor space.
- Convert an old armoire into a cabinet for your TV and electronic equipment.
- Use a felt-tip marker to dot the back of individual pieces from the same puzzle. Use a different color for each puzzle. No more puzzle confusion.

Making Sense of Closets

For closets your mother would be proud of . . .

- Hang work, play and dressy clothes in their respective category, giving prime placement to the kind of clothes you wear most often.
- Group the same types of clothing within each category—for example, shirts with shirts, skirts with skirts and so on.
- Remove all wire hangers and donate them to the dry cleaners. Replace with plastic tubular hangers. They don't misshape clothes or create rust marks, and they space garments nicely.
- Keep empty hangers at the end of a rod so you'll always have one handy.
- Use five-tier space-saver hangers for pants and skirts.
- Hang nicer knits and special-occasion clothes on padded hangers.
- If you have trouble remembering what goes with what, post a list of possible outfits, including accessories, on the inside of your closet door.
- Don't keep wrong-size, -color or -style clothes—or items with permanent stains or irreparable tears—in your closet or in your house. If they're in good condition, give them away. Otherwise, throw them away. (Keep a large paper shopping bag in each closet to collect clothes to be donated.)

Got Serious Closet Issues?

Are your closets filled with clothes the moths have seen more than you have? If so, consider inaugurating an annual **Closet Clearing Day** at your house. Designate a specific day, such as the first Saturday in January or the first Monday in October. Put it on the calendar like you would any other occasion.

87

- Keep clothes to be mended in a designated place.
- Store off-season clothes in another closet or trunk, or put a sheet around them and hang them in the back of your closet.
- Use an over-the-door shoe organizer to store socks, hosiery, shoulder pads, small purses, gloves and so on.
- Store shoes in transparent boxes on a shelf above the clothing rod. Only keep the few pairs you wear regularly on the floor. Roll up magazines and put them in boots to store in an upright position.
- Keep a small step stool in your closet to reach higher shelves.
- Have one clear plastic box or a basket for unmatched socks you still have hope for. Keep another box for hose with runs that you can still wear under pants. (Avoid frustration by keeping them separate from good hose.) Or, snip the tag of the torn stockings in half so you'll easily recognize them.
- Hang a mesh laundry bag for dirty hose and delicate lingerie. Tie it up and toss it into the washer with other clothes.
- Use a tie rack for belts, scarves, leotards, lingerie, ribbons and so on.
- Keep a laundry bag in your closet for clothes to go to the dry cleaners.
- Put a cup hook on an inside closet wall to hold a small pair of scissors to clip loose threads.
- Keep a small wastebasket in your closet for tags, cleaner bags and pocket or purse debris.
- Fill a small box with last-minute fix-up items, including a lint brush or roller, pincushion and a roll of masking tape (for emergency hem repairs when you don't have time to change clothes).
- Move a chest of drawers into your closet to make use of the space beneath your shirts, jackets and skirts that don't hang to the floor.
- Cut (or poke out with your finger) small holes in the paper of a paper-covered wire hanger. Then thread your scarves through the holes. This method keeps them separated and takes up very little closet space.
- Hang a bathroom towel rack on the inside of your linen closet door for tablecloths.
- Sort linens in categories and bed sizes. Label the edge of each shelf in your linen closet to show its contents. If you don't have a linen closet store two sets of bed sheets in the closet of each room with a bed.

- Small rolling carts that fit underneath desks or in closets work nicely for storing and easily accessing art supplies or sewing materials.
- Nest luggage by placing small suitcases or duffle bags inside larger ones. Also, luggage that isn't being used can be an ideal storage place for items such as ski clothes and beach towels.

Making Sense of Drawers

- Try to get family members in the habit of cleaning out one drawer a month. This is a reachable goal if your kids are over the age of seven, and it goes a long way toward keeping clutter under control.
- When cleaning a drawer, remove the contents, then vacuum the inside using a handheld vacuum, or the dusting brush or crevice tool on your vacuum cleaner. (If you only want to suck up the dust and not small items that have fallen to the bottom of the drawer, cover the nozzle of your vacuum hose with a section of panty hose held in place with a rubber band.) Wipe out the drawer with a damp cloth or premoistened disinfectant wipe.
- Line the bottom of drawers with drawer-lining paper or wallpaper scraps so they will be easy to clean. If you spill something in a drawer, wipe it up immediately so it won't congeal.
- Use drawer organizers whenever possible to store like items together and keep drawer contents neat and accessible. You can buy inexpensive plastic or metal drawer organizers almost anywhere. Silverware organizers work well for the kitchen "junk" drawer as well as for organizing silverware. They also work well for costume jewelry and in bathroom drawers for makeup and toiletries.
- If you don't want to buy ready-made organizers, you can use different-size boxes in drawers to corral little things such as curlers, cosmetics and ponytail holders, or bigger things like socks and underwear.
- Don't overstuff drawers. Stack clothing only two or three layers high and arrange so that the most delicate items are at the top of

Bright Idea

Turn an ordinary closet into a cedar closet by installing cedar particle-board on the walls and ceiling. Put weather stripping around the door to keep the scent in.

Bright Idea

Need more bookshelves? Walk through each room in your house and look for wasted space—room corners, spaces between and above windows and door lintels. Don't overlook the top of walls. A single shelf running along the top of the walls in a room makes an attractive place to display books or collectables used infrequently. What about installing a shelf in the bathroom above the toilet? Your local home improvement store will have a section of books describing methods and tools for installing bookshelves.

the stack and the most durable items at the bottom. Leave at least 1 inch between the top edge of the drawer and the top of the contents.

- Place clothes in drawers in ways that make fewer wrinkles. Fold clothes across their width. Creases fall out more quickly than when folded lengthwise. If you store skirts and pants in a drawer, roll them around plastic bags or tissue paper to prevent creasing.

- Don't put overly heavy objects in a drawer. The weight will put extra strain on the bottom of the drawer.

- Use a silicone spray or put soap on drawer runners if a drawer sticks.

- Assign most-used items to the easiest-access drawers in kids' rooms. For example, don't put socks in a high drawer they can't reach if one of their jobs is to put on their own socks and shoes each morning. Label the front of each drawer with details of the contents. (Use pictures for prereaders.) This way they won't have to rummage through drawers to find what they need.

- Don't use drawers as an emergency hiding place for clutter when company comes. It's too easy to forget it's there. Instead put clutter in a laundry basket and stash it in a closet. It will be easy to distribute and put away later.

- Have only one junk drawer. To keep it under control, when you have an extra five minutes—like when you're waiting for water to boil or popcorn to pop—declutter your junk drawer a bit at a time.

- If you keep cooking utensils in a drawer in your kitchen, lay the long, thin objects such as ladles and spatulas so that they all face the same way. This way they won't get jumbled.

Making Sense of Bookshelves

SMART SORTING & STORING

When you start to organize, don't pull out all the books at once. Instead, sort books on shelves and shuffle them around as you go; each section will develop as you work.

- Group your books into categories—by subject matter or by the author's last name—or by types—paperbacks and hardcovers or tall and short books. If you shelve according to subject matter, try alphabetizing the books within the section by title or author. Choose a sorting method that makes the books you use most easy to find.
- Near your desk, put a dozen or so of your favorite books that have had the greatest impact on you. Stand them between bookends or put them in a stack.
- Keep reference books close to your desk.
- Store kids' coloring books or sheet music in magazine storage boxes.
- Small paperbacks can be space-wasters. If your space is limited, store them two deep, or stack two two-by-fours on the backs of your shelves to raise the back row 4 inches and keep the books accessible.
- Create more bookshelf space by donating books you no longer want to a school, a charity or a library. Or try selling them to a used-bookstore.

Bright Idea

If you have a lot of books and haven't dusted in a while, break this huge chore down into smaller chunks. Set a goal to clean two shelves a day until you're finished.

PROTECTING YOUR LIBRARY

- Prevent mildew by rubbing oil of clove on wood bookshelves. Rub it in thoroughly so that it won't stain book covers. If you have bookshelves with doors, open them up to air out the books once in a while.
- Store books in dry places, but not near a radiator or heating vent as heat can crack book bindings.
- Combat humidity by putting small packets of moisture absorber near places that attract moisture.
- Protect your collection by putting bookplates or address labels in your books. Keep a log of where they go when you loan them out.
- If you have a book that is especially meaningful to you, consider having it leather bound.

I have sought for happiness everywhere, but I have found it no where except in a little corner with a little book.
—Thomas à Kempis

KID-FRIENDLY SOLUTIONS

- Encourage reading by installing a bookshelf in each child's room. Make sure it's within easy reach.

- Help children develop a sense of pride and ownership for their collection. Show them how to arrange books by title, topic or author. Buy or make bookplates they can sign and put in their books.
- Use a low bookshelf to store toys or display an older child's personal treasures.
- Secure unstable bookshelves that could topple on a child.
- All you need for a cozy, comfortable reading area—for you or your kids—is a good chair, bright light and a small bookshelf.

MAKE YOUR OWN
- Wood shelves have a natural beauty that wears well. Hardwood is the most elegant and expensive material for bookshelves. Soft wood, such as pine, is cheaper and more casual.
- Medium-density fiberboard is a user-friendly material for bookshelves. It's less expensive and less likely to warp than wood, yet it's still sturdy. You can buy it in a variety of thicknesses; paint or varnish when you're done.
- Melamine-faced board is inexpensive, practical and easy to clean. If shiny, melamine can look cheap; upgrade the look of this shelf by adding a wood trim on the edge.
- Plywood is cheaper than wood, and you can apply an attractive veneer in a variety of wood finishes.
- Galvanized metal shelves are available in kits and can be lightweight to heavy duty. They are difficult to dress up and may corrode over time.
- Plastic shelves are good for kids' books and light toys; they can't hold much weight.

Making Sense of Paper Clutter

Allowing paper to pile up is a little like turning your back on two rabbits. Leave them alone for too long, and they multiply rapidly. To keep paper from proliferating, follow this simple, eight-step excavation plan. Dig in and start digging out!

Reference Books Every Home Should Have

Every home should have a properly stocked library—whether in good, old-fashioned book form or on CD-ROM.

- Dictionary
- Thesaurus
- Book of quotations
- Atlas
- Almanac
- Classic all-purpose cookbook
- Household maintenance and repair handbook
- Encyclopedia
- Family medical encyclopedia
- Etiquette book

1. Put all the papers you need to deal with or file in one place. Get a wastebasket or recycling box, file folders, labels, pens and a stapler.

2. Start with the first paper. Decide if it's valuable and necessary. If not, toss or recycle it. If it's worth keeping, move to step 3.

3. Choose a file heading for it, label the folder and file the paper. You might use some of these headings: Medical Records, Personal Letters, Tax Deductions, Auto Registrations and Vacation Brochures.

4. If there are two or more papers associated with the topic you're dealing with, staple the papers together. Don't use paper clips. They get caught on each other and fall off easily.

5. Pick up the next piece of paper and follow the same procedure, except to file it in the appropriate file if you've already created it. Consolidate as much as you can.

6. When you've finished with all of your papers, sort the files according to the Family Manager departments—Home and Property, Food, Money, Family and Friends, Special Events, Time and Scheduling, Self-Management. (See Chapter 1.) Then, alphabetize the files within the departments. Place files in a file drawer or carton.

7. Stop clutter before it starts. Set up a Mail Center (see page 73) and schedule time each week to deal with paper that's started to accumulate. Treat this time as you would any important appointment.

8. Cull regularly. Each time you refer to a file, thumb through it and discard any papers that no longer are necessary.

MANAGING CATALOGS AND MAGAZINES

- Take the time to clip off address labels from catalogs you don't want. Return them to the company who sent them and ask to be taken off their mailing list. If you get duplicate issues of a catalog you enjoy receiving, send the company the duplicate label and ask it to delete that listing.

- Designate one place to put catalogs—for example, a pretty basket, magazine holder or shelf. Keep them in alphabetical order and cull them every two months.

- Set destroy deadlines for I'll-get-around-to-reading-it magazines. If you haven't gotten around to reading your favorite women's magazine

Additional Books to Have on Hand

- **Children's dictionary**
- **Word usage guides**
- **Special-interest guides or dictionaries, such as foreign language dictionaries**
- **Gardening book**
- **Holy books, such as the Bible or other faith source.**
- **Bible commentary**
- **Concordance**

What the world needs is more love and less paperwork.
—Pearl Bailey

Kids Can Control Paper Clutter, Too!

Here's a workable plan for all those countless works of art your children bring home from school. Purchase clear plastic storage bins; label one per child. Once a drawing or painting has been displayed on the refrigerator or bulletin board for a few days, store it in the appropriate bin. Keep the bins easily accessible in a cupboard or nearby closet. At the end of the school year, have each child pick a few favorites to save in a memorabilia box (I use bigger clear plastic bins—one per child—for this) and store in your attic or basement.

You might also buy your child a filing box or crate. Help him set up files for things like school work, pictures, awards and certificates, personal mail and cards, mementos, stories, articles for future reports and hobby brochures.

In order to seek one's own direction, one must simplify the mechanics of ordinary, everyday life.

—Plato

from two months ago, skim it and cut out articles you really want to read, then throw it away. Old news magazines? Give yourself a couple of weeks, clip stories for kids' reports or future reading, then toss.

- If you've let your magazines get out of control; which is easy to do, schedule a block of time to get them organized. Put it on your calendar.

- Before you start, get some supplies ready that you'll need to do the job efficiently: some boxes (the ones that liquor stores throw away are the perfect size and strength), scissors or a small paper cutter, file folders and labels and some plastic sleeves or magnetic photo pages (the same you use for your recipe compendium [see page 83]). Some of the boxes will be for magazines worthy of donating to a school, nursing home or hospital. The other boxes will hold magazines to be recycled or thrown away.

- Go from room to room and gather all the magazines. If there's an article in a magazine you want to read but haven't gotten around to, cut out the article and put it in a file labeled 'To Read'. If there are recipes you want to save, cut them out for your compendium. Cut out coupons and put them in a file; deal with them another time. (See "Coupons," Chapter 14.)

- When you finish, load the boxes immediately in your car and give yourself a deadline of twenty-four hours to get them where they need to go.

Organized . . . and How to Stay That Way

- Make your family motto, "Put it up, not down." Start the routine of returning everything you get back to where it belongs. (Ten minutes a day looking for misplaced items wastes sixty hours a year.)
- Set some limits on how many toys can be out at one time.
- Start a seven-minute nightly decluttering routine. Sometime after dinner and before bedtime, set the kitchen timer for seven minutes. Put on some peppy music and have family members pick up and put up for seven minutes. Throw away today's paper, plump the sofa pillows, fold the throws and store all toys, games and videos.
- Get family members into the habit of never walking through the house empty handed.
- When necessary play the 'Clutter Be Gone Game'. Give each family member a plastic trash bag. Walk through your house and see how much clutter you can throw away in fifteen minutes. The winner is the person with the most clutter in his bag when time is up.

Cleaning pros estimate that dealing with clutter amounts to 40 percent of the housework in the average home. Believe me, every step you take toward getting clutter under control—eliminating what's not important to you, and organizing what is—is worthwhile. The clutter in your life likely took years to accumulate. Ridding your home of it won't happen overnight, but it will feel good once it's gone. Decluttering is a little like losing weight—it's not easy, but reaching your goal is well worth the sacrifice.

Bright Idea

Reduce the amount of junk mail you receive by registering with the Direct Mail Marketing Association, P.O. Box 9008, Farmingdale, NY 11745-9008. Send a letter requesting that your name be removed from mailing lists. Or visit www.zerojunkmail.com. For $15 a year you can get your name off thousands of mailing lists used by telemarketers, junk mailers, direct marketers and database companies.

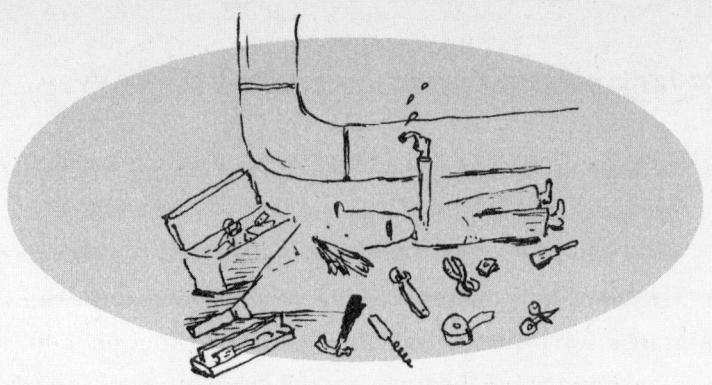

CHAPTER 4

You're the Building Manager

As the building manager, you're in charge of a wide variety of household mainte-nance issues, from fixing broken pipes to ridding your home of bugs. Your job is to care for your home and make it as sturdy as possible. But even if you've never hammered a nail in your life, it's easy to learn how to take charge of this aspect of family management.

The fact is, some basic maintenance—a little money and time spent here and there, on a regular basis—can save big bucks and inconvenience later. Consider these all-too-true scenarios:

Failing to check our washing machine hose left us with a flooded house in the middle of the night; an inch of water covered all of the floors.

We suffered headaches for months because we neglected to regularly examine our heat-ing system. A small crack released the dangerous toxin carbon monoxide into the venting system in our house.

And finally, a good friend has to come up with $10,000 (yes, *$10,000*) to repair a mold and wood-rot problem that came from a leaky dishwasher.

As you can see from these examples, "fixing" it before it becomes "broke" is the way to peace of mind—and pocket.

Home Maintenance

TWENTY-THREE COMMON YET DANGEROUS HOME MAINTENANCE
MISTAKES

1. **Failure to respect electricity.** Make sure you flip the breaker or remove the proper fuse before attempting to repair anything electrical. Don't overload circuits. A frequently blown breaker is a sign of overload or other trouble; flickering lights can indicate a problem and be a potential fire hazard. In either case, call an electrician.

2. **Failure to check heating system yearly.** Carbon monoxide is an odorless gas released when anything burns. Even small amounts can cause headaches and illness, and if allowed to build up, can be a deadly killer. Have your heating system checked yearly by a heating professional before cold weather sets in, and install carbon monoxide monitors in strategic locations in your house; such as in the bedrooms and basement (at least 25 feet away from the furnace). The should not be installed within one foot of the ceiling or at wall intersections where there is little or no air movement.

3. **Failure to check for radon.** Radon is a colorless, odorless substance that is the second-leading cause of lung cancer in the United States. The EPA estimates that one out of fifteen U.S. homes has unhealthy levels of radon. Radon test kits are available at hardware and home maintenance stores for less than $25. If the test indicates that your home has dangerously high radon levels, you should contact local or state EPA authorities for recommendations of what to do. You can also call The National Safety Council's Radon Hotline at 800-SOS-RADON. Generally, curing a radon problem is not a major expense.

4. **Failure to look for and fix water leaks.** Even a small amount of dripping water can do big damage over time to visible things like drywall, cabinets and flooring, but also structural supports such as wall studs and floor joists. Damp areas caused by water leaks promote the growth of mold and mildew. A leaky dishwasher or washing machine connection, drainpipe, faucet cut-off valve, toilet or

The fellow that owns his own home is always just coming out of a hardware store.

—Kin Hubbard

97

shower drain can eventually cost you thousands of repair dollars. Moisture also attracts insect pests.

5. **Waiting too long to paint your house.** When you see small cracks, exposed wood or strips of paint hanging off your house, it's past time to paint. The longer you wait, the more water is penetrating wood surfaces. Not only does water damage the wood over time, but it also exacerbates the cracking and peeling of paint.

6. **Failure to prepare the surface before painting.** For paint to do its job, it has to adhere to the surface and seal out moisture. Scrape and/or sand all loose paint from the surface. If you use a power washer, you still need to scrape and sand some. Repair any damage and prime with a coat of primer or paint. Don't paint over rust buildup or rotten wood. Never prime or paint wet wood.

7. **Putting poor-quality padding underneath carpet.** This can greatly reduce the life of the carpet. And never keep really dirty padding under new carpet. The soil and stains can seep up and spot the new carpet—as well as cause odor.

8. **Overcleaning sinks, tubs and toilet seats.** Too much scrubbing with abrasive cleaners wears off the finish. Use nonabrasive cleaners.

9. **Counting on unreliable warranties.** An extended or aftermarket warranty is only as good as the company behind it. Stick with well-known companies and read the fine print.

10. **Failing to follow manufacturer's maintenance procedures.** Not maintaining almost anything that has a warranty according to manufacturer's instructions will void the warranty. Be careful about trying to repair an appliance yourself. Not only might this be hazardous, but it can void the warranty.

11. **Not putting enough insulation in your attic.** More heat is lost through inadequate roof insulation than through any other part of the home. Lost heat translates into higher heating bills.

12. **Spending too much on plumbing.** If you have a leaky kitchen or bathroom faucet, instead of buying a whole new one (which may be expensive and not match the room and original fixtures), take the leaky valve cartridge to a local plumbing store. Chances are a

$.59 washer will do the job. If not, the plumbing store should be able to replace the whole valve for less than $10.

13. **Failure to keep things clean.** Dirt and dust are often unseen enemies that cause damage and malfunction. For example, dirt in carpet breaks down fibers. Dust that collects on refrigerator coils causes the refrigeration system to overwork, shortening the life of the refrigerator. Dust is the major problem causing CD players to skip.

14. **Failure to change air-conditioning/heating system filters.** Forgetting to clean permanent filters or replace disposable ones monthly not only reduces efficiency, but over time will cause a dirty, unsightly buildup to occur around vents.

15. **Not having the chimney cleaned.** Creosote buildup can occur in all chimneys burning solid fuel, presenting a major fire hazard. There is also the potential of carbon monoxide poisoning. Have your chimney cleaned each spring.

16. **Failure to keep gutters free of debris.** Clogged gutters can cause water to go places you don't want it to go, causing damage to the wood trim and roof of your house.

17. **Not trimming back trees and bushes from your roof.** Overhanging limbs can cause debris buildup and eventually cause damage to the roof.

18. **Failure to prepare for freezing temperatures.** An 8-inch crack in a water pipe can spray 250 gallons of water a day, causing thousands of dollars of damage. Just a little maintenance can prevent this. Remove and store hoses and cover outside faucets and exposed pipes to protect them from extreme temperatures. Open cabinet doors underneath sinks and allow both hot and cold water faucets to drip slightly. Close vents on crawl spaces. In extreme environments, use heat tape or thermal cables on water pipes susceptible to freezing. Seal any leaks that allow cold air to rush in on pipes. If you are going to be out of town, ask a friend to check in regularly and never set your thermostat lower than 55 degrees F.

19. **Not knowing how to shut off the water to your house.** In case of an emergency everyone in the family needs to know how to shut

Take Note

Warning! Never close the fireplace damper while live coals are still burning.

off the water to the house. If a valve near the house isn't easily accessible, keep a water meter key handy in a designated place and know how to use it.

20. **Failure to inspect the dark, out-of-the-way spaces.** Check the attic and crawl spaces twice a year. Take your flashlight and shine it in all of those out-of-the-way areas for water leaks, nesting animals or anything unusual. Small problems unobserved can cause big problems if left unchecked.

21. **Failure to keep things out of direct sunlight.** UV rays cannot only cause damage to your eyes, but to indoor items as well. Carpets and wood floors fade and whites turn yellow in direct sunlight. Consider installing shades in windows with a western exposure.

22. **Failure to replace your washing machine hoses every two years.** Washing machine hoses cause millions of dollars of damage each year. You can replace old hoses with new metal-clad ones, which have a longer life. But don't fail to check them regularly, and shut off the hot and cold water supply when you leave on vacation.

23. **Caulking incorrectly.** Before applying new tub caulk, fill the tub with water and get in. The weight will open the gap around the tub to its widest so you can apply enough caulk in place. Use a damp finger to smooth the caulk in place.

YOUR QUARTERLY HOME MAINTENANCE PLAN

First Quarter: January, February, March

☐ Plan any major remodeling or repair projects. Start getting bids from contractors and schedule work. This is a great time of year for indoor painting or repair projects. Usually less construction work goes on during winter months so contractors are often available.

☐ Check your plumbing system for leaks.

☐ Inspect ceramic tile grout around the tub or shower. Caulk as needed.

☐ Clean mineral deposits from inside the dishwasher by pouring in a gallon of white vinegar and running it through a wash cycle.

☐ Tackle indoor painting jobs.

☐ Repair hairline cracks in walls, which often appear during winter, with spackling paste.

Outsourcing: Should You Hire a Handyman?

In deciding whether to correct a minor repair, tackle a major project yourself, or hire a professional, consider the following:

- What kind of repair is it and do you have the time, tools and knowledge to do it?
- What are the ramifications of doing it wrong? Will it make the problem worse in the long term?
- Do you know a reputable repairman? If not, do you have neighbors or friends who might know one?
- How much will you save if you do the work yourself? Remember that if you start the project then get stuck and need to call in a professional repairman, you will likely have to pay for the full cost of his doing it from start to finish.

☐ Check for wasp nests and remove while they are dormant.

☐ Repair, reglue or replace wallpaper as needed.

☐ Vacuum dust from the coils beneath the refrigerator. (This will increase energy efficiency 6 percent.) Make a note to do this three more times at regular intervals this year.

☐ Replace heating system filters. (Check your manual and note on your calendar how often this should be done. For some, every other month is not too often.) Write the date of replacement on the filter.

☐ Do an attic and basement safety check. Make sure there's no accumulation of trash or dirty rags. Look for evidence of frayed wiring. See that your circuit breaker box is well marked. Make certain that no paint or flammable liquids are stored in the same area as the furnace or hot water heater.

☐ Treat the septic system. (If you have one, make a note on your calendar to do this once a month.)

Second Quarter: April, May, June

☐ Check your attic for roof leaks. On a rainy day, use a flashlight to locate water drips and spots. On a sunny day, stand in your yard and use binoculars to look for broken, or missing shingles or tiles. Hire a roofing contractor to make necessary repairs.

101

- ☐ Clean gutters, downspouts and window wells of leaves and debris.
- ☐ Check the attic and crawl spaces for nesting animals or anything unusual.
- ☐ Watch for carpenter ants and for termites swarming. Call an exterminator if necessary.
- ☐ Hire a chimney sweep to clean soot, remove birds' nests and inspect for cracks.
- ☐ Shut off furnace pilot light for the summer.
- ☐ Change air-conditioner filters now and several other times during the cooling season. If your filter is permanent, clean according to manufacturer's instructions. If you have room units, vacuum the evaporator coils behind the front grille of window units. For central units, have a professional service your system.
- ☐ Check the air-conditioner condenser drain to make sure it is clear.
- ☐ Service and clean lawn mower and garden tools.
- ☐ Remove any new wasp nests on or around your house in the late evening just before dark. Wasps and their kin are less likely to attack.
- ☐ Open foundation vents.
- ☐ Put peel-and-apply weather stripping around windows and doors to reduce air leakage and cut utility bills.
- ☐ Check the grading of your yard and landscaping for settling or erosion. Spread new soil if necessary.
- ☐ Move surplus firewood away from the foundation of the house. Left over the summer, firewood often attracts termites. So store it away from any structures.
- ☐ Trim any branches near a heat pump or air-conditioner condenser so they don't obstruct airflow or tangle the fan.
- ☐ Check air-conditioner condenser drain to make sure it is clear.
- ☐ Make sure windows open smoothly. Give the garage door hardware a squirt of lightweight oil.
- ☐ Check for damage to exterior wood trim. Look for water stains, new cracks, blistering paint, warping and soft places, which can mean dry rot. Repair as needed.
- ☐ Check fences and decks for damage and repair as needed.
- ☐ Test smoke detectors.

☐ Apply lawn fertilizer with pre-emergent to kill weeds before they germinate.

Third Quarter: July, August, September

☐ Replace washing machine hoses.

☐ Have carpets cleaned by a professional or rent a steam cleaner and do it yourself.

☐ Get together with friends or relatives you haven't seen in a while.

☐ Clean out and organize your garage.

☐ Pressure-wash driveways, walkways and the house exterior.

☐ Pressure-wash and reseal your wood deck. This removes dirt and extends the beauty and life of your wood deck.

☐ Trim back any branches or shrubs 2 feet from your roof.

☐ Clean your clothes dryer exhaust vent. Check the flapper door on the outside exhaust vent and remove any lint buildup with a vacuum. If vent is flexible, check for kinks and patch any small holes with duct tape.

☐ Unscrew the aerator from the end of each faucet, wash them carefully and then replace. This will help with low water pressure that often occurs in the late summer.

☐ Caulk all joints and cracks around posts and columns, doors and windows.

☐ Scrape, prime and spot paint any minor blistered, cracked or peeling paint. If you discover a lot of problem areas, consider repainting the entire exterior.

Fourth Quarter: October, November, December

☐ Replace heating system filters; have system professionally serviced and checked for carbon monoxide leaks.

☐ Drain outdoor plumbing; store hoses. Cover outside faucets and exposed pipes to protect them from extreme temperatures.

☐ Rake leaves.

☐ Build a compost pile.

☐ Check fire extinguishers and smoke detectors.

☐ Clean gutters, downspouts and window wells of leaves and debris.

A man builds a fine house; and now he has a master, and a task for life is to furnish, watch, show it, and keep it in repair the rest of his life.
—*Ralph Waldo Emerson*

☐ Add insulation to your attic if necessary.

☐ Check the attic and crawl spaces for water leaks, nesting animals or anything unusual.

☐ Insulate any exposed water pipes inside the house.

☐ Cover any delicate plants before hard freezes.

☐ Take out window air conditioners or cover the outside of units to prevent rusting.

☐ Close or cover foundation vents before the first freeze.

☐ Cover attic turbine vents.

☐ Winterize your lawn mower: clean it, change the oil and drain the gasoline from the tank.

☐ Weather-strip leaky windows and doors or put on storm windows, if needed.

☐ Check the electrical system. Be sure the bathroom, garage and outdoor circuits are grounded and protected by ground-fault breakers.

☐ Wrap plants that need protection before cold weather sets in.

TOOLS OF THE TRADE

Every home should have some fundamental tools readily accessible. Begin with these basics and add to your tool collection as you need more specialized items. It's best to buy name-brand tools that have a lifetime warranty. You don't need to buy a special tool for every job. Consider renting expensive specialized tools from home improvement or rental stores. If you have a do-it-yourself friend who's handy with tools, consider borrowing the tool you need. You might get a helper along with the tool!

BASIC TOOLS EVERY HOME NEEDS

- A 10-inch adjustable crescent wrench
- Pliers (slip-joint and needle-nose)
- 16-ounce claw hammer
- Screwdrivers (both flathead and Phillips head in point sizes 1, 2 and 3)
- Glues (super-type glue and polyurethane glue, such as Gorilla Glue)
- A tape measure (25-foot retractable)
- A level (a 10-inch model is adequate for most home uses)

- A utility knife
- A plunger
- A water meter or water shut-off key
- Assorted sizes of nails and screws

- Duct tape
- Assorted sizes of paint brushes
- An assortment of cup hooks, tacks and picture hangers
- Silicon spray (like WD-40)

OTHER EXTREMELY HELPFUL TOOLS

- A socket wrench set (basic ⅜-inch drive with assorted metric and regular sockets)
- A vise-grip–type wrench
- A cordless electric drill (at least 14.4 volts)
- A set of drill bits (1/16 to ¼ at least)
- A staple gun

- Hot glue gun
- Handheld shop light
- Extension cord (heavy duty, grounded)
- Step ladder (6 foot, or depending on your ceiling height)
- Folding work bench
- Small hand saw

Solving Basement Problems

Dampness in a basement can rot wood, peel paint and promote rust and mildew. If your basement has a damp feel and smells musty, try the following:

- Vent your dryer outside the house.
- Install a window exhaust fan.
- Install storm windows and keep doors closed to keep warmer outside air from entering. (Since the basement air is usually cooler than the air outside, when the warm and cool air meet, humidity and condensation occur.)
- Invest in a dehumidifier.
- Insulate water pipes.

If you have water seeping into your basement, check the following possible sources:

- Cluttered roof gutters causing poor drainage.
- Downspouts may be dumping runoff water toward the foundation of your house.
- Window well drains may be clogged.
- The ground water table may be high.
- Your house may be constructed over a spring.
- The soil may be banked improperly toward the house.

If your basement floods, never touch a wall or anything else, or step into standing water. Have the electric company turn off the power to your house. To have the water removed, call a plumber, an emergency water-removal service or the fire department.

If a basement wall is bowing inward or has cracks that are widening, your house has a structural problem. Call a foundation expert.

BASEMENT TIPS

- Neutralize musty basement odors with activated charcoal or by placing fresh coffee beans in paper bags around the basement.
- Paint the window wells and other basement surfaces white to reflect more outside light.
- Keep a flashlight in a handy place in case of a power failure while you're down there.
- Carpet the top step to trap dust you might track in the house from the basement.
- Place metal utility shelves at the bottom of the basement stairs to hold overflow from the pantry, such as canned goods, extra paper towels and toilet paper.
- Make finding things easy by categorizing like items into "departments"—for example, extra toiletries, seldom-used cooking utensils, lightbulbs.
- Keep boxes off the floor in case of water leakage. If you must store boxes in the basement, place them on top of cement blocks or bricks.
- Store flammable substances, such as oil-based paint and turpentine, well away from the heating system, water heater or other sources of

Bright Idea

Paint the basement floor with a concrete sealer to keep dust to a minimum.

heat. Never store gasoline in a basement. Gasoline fumes travel and can be ignited by a tiny spark.

- Don't store books and papers in the basement unless they are in moisture-proof containers.
- If you need more clothing storage space, consider purchasing a free-standing wardrobe. Be sure to dry clean or wash clothing so stains don't permanently set. Place a fragrant sachet inside the wardrobe to quell musty smells.
- Put a doormat at the foot of the stairs to keep dirt from being tracked to other areas of the house.

Home Building and Remodeling

If building a house is something you dream of doing in the future, start planning now.

- Begin by collecting ideas you like and don't like about other homes. Clip photos from magazines that show architectural styles, appliances, fixtures, and colors that you would like to incorporate into your dream home.
- Determine how many bedrooms and bathrooms you'll need. How big a living room would suit you? Do you need an office/exercise/hobby space? Exceptional storage space? Consider how much upkeep you can handle, inside and out.
- Evaluate your property needs. How much maintenance do you want to do? What about location? What areas are convenient to transportation, shopping, schools or other places of interest to you?
- Attend open houses and home shows. You can examine model houses as well as find potential builders.
- Study all of a model home's construction features: the grade of carpet, cabinets, trim and paint. Ask lots of questions, and make sure you get specific answers. Keep notes of discussions with potential contractors.
- Remember that more expensive does not necessarily mean better quality.

Life is a serious attempt to make something of oneself, and one's surroundings.
—Angus Wilson

107

OUTSOURCING: CHOOSING A CONTRACTOR

Whether you are building a new home or remodeling your existing home, the biggest decision you will make is choosing the contractor. Be aware that professional repair people and home improvement contractors rank high on the complaint list of the Better Business Bureau and the U.S. Counsel of Consumer Affairs. Here are tips to help you make a wise decision.

- Ask friends for recommendations. Be leery of contractors who make unsolicited visits or calls.
- Ask recommended contractors for a list of their recent projects and names and numbers of references. Drive by to see the homes. If homeowners are around, say hello and explain that you're checking the work of a recommended contractor. Ask if they are satisfied with their home. Have they had any problems? Were they corrected quickly? Would they purchase another home from this builder?
- Shop around. Obtain estimates from at least three contractors. Don't let anyone pressure you to make a quick decision, even if he/she offers a discount.
- Ask about everything:

  - How long have you been in business?
  - How long will it take?
  - How much will it cost, and what is included in this figure?
  - How many workers will you use?
  - What grade of materials will you use?
  - Do you have liability insurance? Workmen's compensation?
  - Do you belong to the local builders association (one that is affiliated with the National Association of Home Builders)?
  - What kind of energy features do you install?
  - What kind of warranty do you offer on your projects? (Ask for a written copy.)
  - Who will haul away the trash?
  - Who will correct problems with major appliances, and whom do I call if something goes wrong?

- Deal only with licensed professionals. Contact the licensing board to confirm a contractor's home improvement license. Check with the Better Business Bureau and/or Consumer Protection Agency to see if a particular contractor has had complaints filed against him/her.

- Check the contract carefully. Ask someone experienced in building to go over your contract with you. It should include:

  - A complete definition of the job to be done
  - Grade of materials that will be used, and their cost
  - Cost of labor
  - Subcontractors' names
  - Starting and completion dates
  - Payment schedule/financing details
  - Warranty agreements
  - Cleanup responsibilities

- Protect your funds. Don't pay anything until both parties have signed a written contract. Never use cash, and never pay an advance of more than one-third of the total contract. And make sure you're completely happy with the job before you pay the final balance.

Bright Idea

Protect your computer and other electronic equipment from the dust created during a remodeling project. Cover them well.

Combating Insects and Pests

Pests are one annoyance over which you have some control. To do battle with them safely try these tips.

- Wait till after dark to spray wasp nests with insecticide. Wasps cling to the nest after sunset and will not attack you.
- To catch a wasp in your house, spritz it with a water mister. Water will weigh down its wings, making it easier to kill.
- Buy citronella-scented geraniums from a nursery. Plant several near your patio to help keep bugs away.
- Plants and herbs will help repel insects if you lightly rub the leaves to release the scent and natural repellents.

109

- Sprigs of basil tucked in your fruit bowl will help keep fruit flies away.
- Large sprigs of rosemary are good for moth control. They work better if closet doors are kept closed.
- Place bay leaves on pantry and cupboard shelves to help keep them bug-free. A bay leaf in your flour can help prevent weevils.
- Basil, bay leaves and mint help keep flies to a minimum.
- Control slugs by placing a shallow pan of stale beer at the infested area. Or just sprinkle the slugs with salt. To discourage slugs from slithering under a door, pour a line of salt across the outside of the doorway.
- Discourage ants by washing down any area they might enter with full-strength white vinegar or boric acid. Or mix equal parts red pepper and sugar; sprinkle it where ants travel.
- Any infestation of bugs in the house can be cleaned up by sucking them into the vacuum cleaner, followed by sucking up some powdered bug killer. Let it sit a few hours, then remove the vacuum cleaner bag, and put it outside in the trash.
- A few pieces of mint gum in the pantry may help deter bugs.

BEFORE YOU CALL THE BUG MAN

You may be able to exterminate the bugs yourself. Try these remedies before calling in a professional to rid your home of insects and other pests.

- Cockroaches, crickets and silverfish will consume a bait called Niban, which is made from boric acid.
- Crickets are attracted to duct tape. Place a piece of tape, sticky side up, on the floor near where you hear crickets.
- Bait mousetraps with chewy candy, gumdrops or peanut butter.
- If you know where ants are coming in, sprinkle dried mint, chili powder or laundry borax across their trail. Plant mint near windows and doors.
- To kill cockroaches, leave a mixture of equal parts flour, cocoa powder and laundry borax or a mixture of equal parts baking soda and

confectioners sugar in shallow dishes. (Keep away from children and pets.) Or try boric acid at a 99 percent concentration (one registered for use as a pesticide). Inject it via a "dust bulb" into cracks and crevices. *Don't* apply this ultrastrong, ultra-effective poison in areas children and pets use.

- A telltale sign of carpet beetles is their shed skins, usually found around carpet edges. Though these pests are difficult to eradicate because they get into well-hidden places, try this: sprinkle laundry borax around the carpet edges, and also over the padding before a new carpet is laid down.
- Sprinkle baking soda all over your carpet. Leave on for fifteen minutes, then vacuum thoroughly. This will discourage pests and neutralize odors.

PEST PREVENTION

- Carpeted closets are an ideal environment for moths and carpet beetles, which eat hair, lint, dust and clothing. Regularly vacuum carpeted and uncarpeted closets.
- Rub cedar walls in the closet with a fine sandpaper to restore the scent.
- Regularly check pantries for infestation. Pests such as the Indian meal moth and a variety of worms and beetles, including weevils, like to share your grains, flours and cereals. Protect food by sealing it in plastic bags. In case of infestation, vacuum the shelves, then clean with an all-purpose cleaner.

ATTIC PESTS

Depending on where you live, various animals can cause havoc in your attic. Squirrels love to nest in insulation. Raccoons and rats like attics as well. They cause damage by chewing on electrical wiring, boxes, books, textiles and wood, and by leaving droppings. You can try to eradicate them yourself by scattering mothballs in hard-to-reach recesses or by filling old socks with mothballs or flakes and hanging them near suspected entrances and pathways. Another idea is to soak rags with ammonia and place them in buckets or shallow pans next to entry holes or squirrel nests.

Take Note

If your clothes have holes with jagged edges or white larvae, you've got moths. If you see round holes, you've got carpet beetles. And don't think of crickets as harmless little chirpers; they eat clothing, too.

111

Outsourcing: How to Choose an Exterminator

Ask friends and neighbors for recommendations. If you don't know anyone who's hired a pest control firm recently, check the yellow pages and call three nearby companies. Consider both national firms and smaller local contractors. Make sure the company has a license and is insured. Get quotes from all three companies.

Don't be shy about obtaining references. Call the Better Business Bureau and ask if there have been complaints against the companies. Discuss your problem with the company representative. They may want to inspect your home before making recommendations. Ask what techniques and products they intend to use. Tell them you want to see copies of labels and Material Safety Data Sheets (MSDS).

Research the pesticide products a contractor recommends to control your problem, especially if you have young children, elderly adults or people with asthma or allergies in your household. (Call the National Pesticide Information Center at 800-858-7387, or visit npic@ace.orst.edu.)

Learn what procedures you should follow to reduce your exposure to pesticides (such as vacating the house, emptying the cupboards, removing pets and so on.). The company representative should be able to discuss what you can do to prevent or minimize future pest problems.

Finally, read and understand the contract you sign. Ask the salesperson to clarify anything you don't understand.

The more squeamish should call a professional exterminator to get rid of pests before one dies or has babies in your attic (this happened to us). (See "Outsourcing: How to Choose an Exterminator.")

Once the animals are gone, seal up all entry points with heavy-duty screening. Stuff holes with steel wool.

SAFETY: MAKE SURE PESTICIDES HARM BUGS, NOT YOU

Do:

- Read and follow package directions carefully.
- Mix pesticides in a well-ventilated area.
- Wear rubber gloves.
- Store in original containers that are tightly closed and clearly labeled.
- Store in a locked, well-ventilated area away from heat and direct sunlight.

- Wrap empty containers in thick layers of newspaper before discarding them.
- Remove food, utensils, pets and their dishes before spraying indoors.

Don't:
- Use near children.
- Smoke, eat, drink or chew gum when using pesticides.
- Inhale sprays' dusts or vapors.
- Store near food.
- Dump in places where they could endanger fish or wildlife, or contaminate water.
- Reenter a treated room for a half hour after it has been sprayed.

CHAPTER 5

You're the Interior Decorator

What truly makes a house a home is the love that is shared by the people who live there. Decorating your dwelling is one way of reflecting the uniqueness of your family. For some, choosing paint, fabric and furniture is fun. Others view decorating as an expensive necessity—they buy a sofa because they need a place to sit.

Regardless of where you stand (no pun intended), it's important to do some research and make well-thought-out choices since decorating mistakes can be costly.

Before you spend a dime or pound a nail, think carefully about the purpose of every room and each piece of furniture you currently own. Maybe the house you live in lacks a family room so your living room is where you relax and entertain. Bedrooms aren't just for sleeping. Many provide office space, too. Kitchen tables often double as homework areas for children. Here are six steps to guide you through the planning process.

Do-It-Yourself Decorating Plan

1. **Survey your home and family.** First, ask yourself the following questions to get a better understanding of how your home is used:

- How large is your family? What are the ages of each family member?
- How long will each person live in the house with you?
- How long do you plan to stay in the house?
- How often is each entry door used?
- Where does everyone sleep?
- How many people use each bathroom?
- Where do individuals go when they need to spend time alone?
- Where is food consumed? In the kitchen, dining room, in front of the TV?
- How many clothes, linen and coat closets do you have?
- Is there room for more than just cars in the garage?
- Is there storage space in the basement or attic?

> *Make every room a living room.*
> —*Alexandra Stoddard*

Then, address specific space and furniture needs with the questions below:

- Where does the family gather for leisure activities?
- Do you have/need an all-purpose family room or area to play board games and watch TV?
- How often do you entertain and what is your style—casual buffets or dining room sit-down dinners?
- Is a media center, laundry area, play space or home office required?
- What about a workshop, exercise room or playroom?
- Does your family require storage for books, sports equipment electronic equipment, or collectibles?
- How much electronic equipment—TV, CD player, stereo, speakers, video games, computer—do you have? How often is it used? Where is it stored?
- What kinds of tables would be helpful or enhancing: end tables, coffee tables, night stands, or a table for board games, cards, puzzles or hobbies?

2. **Create an inventory.** Make a list of what you've got now, including furniture, lighting, art and all the accessories. Note what you plan to keep and what you'd like to replace. If you have antiques, create

a separate section for them (see "All About Antiques" page 129). If there are pieces you're unsure about, don't keep them. It's easier to leave a space empty rather than to fill it with furniture you don't really like. Take photographs of the items you're keeping to simplify shopping for coordinating pieces later.

Now for the fun part—making up the dream list of pieces and/or accessories you'd like to add. Be sure to prioritize your dream list to determine which purchases are most important. This process helps ensure that you purchase items in a methodical manner and helps minimize expensive impulse buying.

3. **Start a resource/idea book.** Buy a binder with pockets or a looseleaf notebook with tab dividers and a box of plastic insert sheets. Use it to store product literature, clippings from magazines, paint chips and fabric swatches. Give each room or project its own section in the notebook. Have one page at the beginning for names, phone numbers and comments about recommended professionals, craftspeople, service companies and tips from friends.

Whenever you see a photo of a room or piece of furniture you like, clip it from the magazine and put it in your notebook. After you've collected twenty or so, spread them out and look for similarities. You may see oriental rugs in many of the room photos you like. Or perhaps you've amassed a pile of clippings showing French provincial furniture or buttery yellow walls. Continue adding things you like to your notebook and periodically cull items that no longer interest you. The result is your personal style guide.

4. **Create a room decorating envelope.** Put samples of all your existing materials for each room in large, separate envelopes. Include the drapery and upholstery fabrics, carpet swatches and room measurements. If you can't get a small cutting of your carpet, buy a spool of thread that's close to the color or take a photograph of the rug. Be sure to include the furniture photos from your to-keep list in each corresponding envelope. On the back of each photo record the dimensions of each piece. When it's time to shop, take the envelopes along with you.

5. **Shop widely and wisely.** With the decorating envelopes in hand, visit furniture, decorating and fabric stores, as well as tag sales and

Outsourcing: Should You Hire an Interior Designer?

If you're too busy to shop, are unsure of your "eye" for color or fabric or don't enjoy the process, working with a professional decorator is probably a good move. Designers charge either a flat fee for the project or an hourly rate. Most also take a percentage of the cost of goods you order through them.

Should you decide to hire a designer, ask friends for references and interview several candidates to find the designing style and personal demeanor that makes you feel most comfortable. Don't hire anyone who makes you feel intimidated or pushed into decisions. If the designer loves the colonial look and you want contemporary, he or she's not the right person for you. Try to get a sense of the designer's ability to stay within a budget and specified time frame. Ask to see photographs of their finished work, or better yet, ask if you can view their work in person. A call to the Better Business Bureau is a good way to check on work history.

An interior designer usually begins by spending time in your home to learn about your family's personality and tastes. They'll also finalize your budget, work out a delivery schedule and take lots of measurements. Based on this information, the designer then makes a preliminary selection of fabrics, paint colors, carpet, light fixtures, furniture and furniture placement.

Designers are also trained to make floor plans, suggest renovations, recommend window treatments, oversee contract workers and design custom furniture. They will either bring samples to your home to review or take you directly to showrooms. In fact, many furniture showrooms and home design stores have in-house design staffs that will work with you for a reduced fee if you buy merchandise from the store.

Before you agree to work with someone, discuss the following points:

- Have a budget in mind and describe what you want to accomplish. Determine if that's feasible and realistic for both of you.
- Be clear about the designer's fee. Are you billed by the room, the hour or the project? Some designers also charge for shopping time, which is the time they spend looking for furniture for your home.
- Can the designer help you create a master plan that you can implement yourself over time?
- If your designer works for a department or furniture store, ask if you have to purchase all of the furniture from that store, or if you can shop around.
- Is it possible to incorporate some of your existing furnishings and/or items you purchase on your own?
- Would reupholstering or slipcovering some of your existing furniture be an acceptable alternative to buying all new furniture?
- Don't assume that size matters. Perhaps you're only interested in decorating the first floor of your home. Or, you need help with your living room. Don't rule out a designer's input. Many are delighted to take on smaller projects, especially those that are just getting started in their careers.

local and online auctions and flea markets. Note what you like, and what things cost, so you can plan a budget. If the house you're in now isn't the one you plan to live in forever, only invest in furnishings that can move with you. Look for furniture and fabrics that will work anywhere, go for neutral colors and avoid trendy looks. Another way to ensure that new acquisitions will work in future homes is to decorate using colors you've consistently liked over the years.

6. **Try the $100 test.** Before making a purchase over $100, always ask yourself how long you think you'll keep it. If your answer is less than three or four years, don't buy it. Be patient. As painful as waiting can be, it's always worth it. New products constantly come on the market and your tastes are likely to change. You may find a lamp or accessory that you like even more in the next store or catalog. When you can, shop sales. Furniture is expensive and getting something you love for less is a great feeling.

DIY Decorating: Tips from the Pros

ARRANGING A ROOM

- Before deciding where to place furniture, start with the focal point of your room—the fireplace, a tall piece of furniture, a bookcase wall or windows with a great view—and plan the seating from there.
- If the room you're decorating is small, don't be tempted to use smaller-scaled furniture. It will look cluttered. Instead, use fewer pieces of normal-size furniture.
- Don't crowd a room with too much furniture. Let the space breathe, especially at all the corners.
- In rooms with low ceilings, staining, carpeting or painting the floors a darker color than the walls will make the room feel bigger.
- Add warmth to your kitchen by using as many organic materials as possible—for example, wood, tile, cork, baskets, terra-cotta pots.
- Wallpaper with vertical stripes will make the ceiling of any room appear higher.

SELECTING FURNITURE

- Keep your room from becoming too "leggy" by striking a balance between upholstered pieces and wood pieces.
- The sofa is one of the most important pieces of furniture you can buy. If your room is large, an 84-inch sofa that seats three people is ideal.
- Every chair and sofa requires a corresponding table or flat surface for books, magazines, drinks and food.
- Place a coffee table 18 inches in front of your sofa and allow another 18 inches between the ends of the sofa and other furniture to allow ample walking space.
- Avoid a glass coffee table or one with sharp corners if you have small children, a clumsy spouse or elderly relatives living with you or visiting often.
- End tables don't have to match, but both should be about the same 26- to 30-inch height. A 1-inch difference between the height of two tables is not noticeable.
- Placing a stool in the kitchen will promote conversations there. Use 24-inch high stools for counters and tables and 30-inch high stools for higher bars.
- A skirted table at one end of a sofa or next to a chair is a great place to display photographs and small paintings.

CHOOSING WINDOW TREATMENTS

- Almost all windows look more finished with some sort of shade, curtain or drape.
- Pretty tea towels and sheets can be turned into lovely curtains for a kitchen or bedroom.
- For bedroom windows in sunny rooms, consider a roll-down black-out shade behind the curtains for undisturbed sleep.
- Valances above the curtains, made of the same fabric, create a formal, finished look around the window.
- Swags, pull-backs, tassels and fancy-looking curtain rods are relatively inexpensive ways to dress up windows.
- Curtains made of horizontally lined fabric that falls to the floor makes ceilings appear taller and rooms bigger.

- Extend curtains or drapes approximately 8 inches beyond the window to allow the greatest amount of sunlight to enter the room.
- Balloon shades, which roll up into billowy folds, can be a prettier alternative to a vinyl pull-down shade.
- For a dramatic-looking window, create a bishop's sleeve. Loosely tie back two side panels of lightweight fabric above the window's midpoint to form a poufy drape with a flowing effect.

CHOOSING LIGHTING TYPES AND USES

There are three basic types of lighting: general, task and accent lights. A good lighting plan incorporates all three types and takes into consideration the function and style of each type. Here's a brief course in how to use lighting:

- General lighting replaces sunlight and provides overall illumination to help you see and walk safely through your home. Ceiling or wall-mounted fixtures, chandeliers and recessed and track lights are examples of general lighting.
- Task lighting provides special lighting for reading, working on the computer or paying bills. Task lights should be free of glare and shadows, and be bright enough to prevent eye strain. Pendant lighting, bedside lamps, table lamps and some track lighting are examples.
- Accent lights provide visual interest or dramatic focus and add mood and character to a room. This type of lighting can spotlight plants and art, or highlight the texture of a wall or drapery. Accent lighting requires at least three times as much light on the focal point as general light. Examples are pinspots, floor canisters, under-shelf lighting and torchères (the tall floor lamps that uplight a ceiling).
- In the family room, arrange lighting so each seating area is bright enough for reading.
- You can achieve a warm glow in your dining room or hallway using wall sconces.
- Three-way bulbs and dimmer switches give you easy-to-change lighting options. With one flick, a bright living room can be converted to an inviting place for drinks and conversation.

- Colored lightbulbs can be used to create different types of light. Incandescent bulbs add a warming yellow cast, while cool fluorescent lights lend a slightly gray tone. Halogen bulbs show true colors. Pink lightbulbs provide a softer color than the standard white bulbs.

ADDING MIRRORS AND WALL HANGINGS

- Suspend a mirror between two windows to add light and space to a room. At the end of a hallway, a mirror will give the illusion of continuing space.

- Place a favorite painting or mirror in your entrance hall so you and everyone else can enjoy it coming and going. Be sure to double hang your picture or mirror (use two hooks instead of one), so it will remain stable when the door is slammed.

- Before you hang a mirror, check to see what it will reflect. You don't want to see the inside of bathrooms, the driveway next door or a dark corner of the living room.

- In the bathroom, a counter-to-ceiling mirror will make a bathroom seem bigger.

- Hang pictures at eye level. Sixty inches from the floor to the center of the picture is about right.

DECIDING ON FLOOR COVERINGS

- Use a colorful rug as a welcome mat inside your front door. Make sure the background is a medium color so dirt won't show.

- Buy the most expensive carpet you can afford for high-traffic areas such as stairs, corridors and family rooms. Cheap carpet wears quickly and, after replacing it, eventually costs as much or more than higher-priced options.

- Less expensive carpet is acceptable in bedrooms since there is less wear. With careful care and regular cleaning, carpet and rugs can last at least ten years.

- Large area rugs and oriental carpets immediately warm up a room, but dark background colors make rooms feel smaller.

- Dhurries, the inexpensive cotton rugs from India, add lots of color to hallways and small bedrooms.

- Natural fiber carpets, like sisal, jute and coir, are fine for rooms where you're unlikely to walk barefoot and feel their roughness. If you have young children, avoid sisal rugs. Their natural fibers are itchy on little feet plus they are difficult to clean.

ADDING THE EXTRA TOUCHES

- Add warmth and color to a room instantly with nature. Try fresh flowers in your grandmother's vase, a colorful plant in a terra-cotta pot or a basket of apples or lemons in a pretty bowl.
- Use personal treasures to decorate—for example, frame a restaurant menu to remind you of a memorable meal, hang your grand-mother's plates on the wall or buy an old wooden high chair at a flea market and set a favorite teddy bear in it.
- But use them sparingly. Too many treasures on display almost always looks cluttered. Instead, rotate your things. You'll appreciate them more and it will keep the space open.
- When displaying collections, group objects by color or type. For example, display green plates of different sizes together on a dining room wall, or place a pitcher collection along a shelf in the kitchen. Scale objects from largest to smallest, from back to front.

Your Painting Plan

HOW MUCH PAINT DO YOU NEED?

One gallon of paint normally covers about 400 square feet. To calculate the number of gallons you need, multiply the total wall length by the ceiling height. For example, if you have a 12 × 12 room (48 feet of walls) with an 8-foot ceiling, you have 48 feet times 8 feet or 384 square feet of wall space to paint. So, you'd buy one gallon. Assuming there are doors and windows in the room and you are able to achieve your desired results in one coat, you will have a little left over for touch up later. It's always good to have at least a pint left over for touch up.

Much of the character of every-man may be read in his house.
—John Ruskin

SELECTING A COLOR

Most paint stores and large building supply stores have sophisticated paint-matching systems. If you want to match an existing color, take a piece of trim, cabinet door or something with the color you want to match. If you have some of the paint you want to match left in a can, you can paint a small amount on a piece of white cardboard, let it dry and take that in to match.

If you are selecting a new color, be sure to take several paint samples in the general color range you desire home with you from the paint store. The lighting in your home can make a major difference in how a color looks to you. Hold the paint chip on the surface you will paint and observe it there. Then make your choice.

Even though some paint brands claim to cover in one coat, you will invariably need additional coats of paint if you are making major shade or color changes, for example, light to dark or dark to light. If in doubt, ask for advice in the paint store.

Buying expensive paint does not guarantee a better-quality or longer-lasting paint. Most interior paint lasts about five years but that can be an eternity if you don't like the color. Of course, it's just paint and can be changed fairly easily and inexpensively. But some extra time and coordination up front makes sure you get the look you want.

Here are some further tips on selecting a paint color:

- Start your color selection by looking at the amount of natural light in the room. A sunny southern or western exposure often needs neutral, softening hues to balance the strong, bright light. Conversely, the cool light of a north or east facing room usually requires warmer tones to brighten the natural light.
- Room location also determines how color appears. Blue on a wall in a room with southern exposure can feel relaxing. But that same color on a wall with a northern exposure could feel depressing, because of the duller natural light.
- Color looks quite different under daytime and nighttime conditions. A hue that looks vibrant in sunlight, for instance, may wash out in artificial indoor light at night.

- Usually warm hues, like red, yellow and orange, are best in spaces where there is activity, and cool colors, such as blue, purple and green, are good for restful places.
- Light cool colors, like pale blue, make a room look larger. Maroon and other dark colors make larger spaces seem smaller and more intimate.
- White paint reflects light and gives a clean, fresh look to the dreariest of rooms.

TESTING A COLOR

If you purchase paint using small color chips on a paint fan or card, always buy the color that is one shade lighter. That's because light colors are brighter and stronger when painted on a wall and dark colors look deeper and darker.

To gauge the intensity of a color look at the inside of the paint can. The shadows inside the can will give a similar appearance to what it will look like in a room.

Purchase small quantities of two or three shades and paint patches of each in different locations of the room, like a spot with direct sun and then one in a dark corner. Look at the patches over a few days before deciding if the color is right or wrong.

PAINTING TIPS FROM THE PROS

- Begin by moving furniture away from the walls and tarping the floor and furniture. Protect windows and windowsills with newspaper. Cover floors and furniture with inexpensive plastic tarps available at your paint store.
- Remove all hardware and switch plates rather than try to paint around them, and replace when paint is completely dry.
- Don't take a shortcut and fail to prepare your walls before you begin. Repair nail holes with spackling paste, using a putty knife to fill the hole and scrape away excess. Then rub the area with a rag to wipe away excess before it's dry. Fill all cracks with acrylic caulk. Use as little as possible, then smooth and remove excess with your finger.

- If you are using multiple gallons of paint for a room, mix them all together in a 5-gallon bucket (available from your paint store). Even though the shade is calibrated, one can of paint will vary slightly from another. By mixing them together, you eliminate shade changes that will give you less than the look you want.

- Paint the ceiling first and then the walls. Next paint the trim: crown molding, window, and window frames and doors and door frames. Paint baseboards last.

- Using a 3- or 4-inch brush, begin by painting at least a 3- to 4-inch border of paint (called "cutting in") around your ceiling or wall and around all woodwork. Then use a roller to complete your work.

- Consider using a 5-gallon bucket and paint grid when rolling, rather than a roller pan. Ask about it at your paint store.

- When using a brush, paint from a smaller paint bucket rather than from the paint can. Just pour up what you think you'll need for the next hour—up to about 2 inches—and reseal the paint can.

- Always thoroughly reseal the lid on a can of paint after you use it. It will keep it from drying out, but also keep you from accidentally spilling a can of paint later.

- Even though great advances have been made in water-based enamel paints, nothing beats the look and durability of oil-based enamel paint for trim.

- When repainting, never paint latex enamel over enamel. It will not adhere properly and could peel prematurely.

- Good brushes produce superior results, especially for trim work. However, cleanup can be a real pain and they are too expensive to use and throw away. To avoid having to clean up oil-based paints every day, you can wrap the brush in aluminum foil or use a plastic bag to seal up the brush and put it in the freezer until you are ready to paint again (within the next few days).

- Dip the tip of the brush into the paint only about an inch and drag off any excess on the edge of your paint bucket.

- When you take a break, leave the brush in the paint to keep it from drying out.

The homeliest tasks get beautiful if loving hands do them.
—Louisa May Alcott

■ When it's time to clean up, clean your brushes thoroughly. If you are using oil-based paint, be sure you are in a well-ventilated area away from any flames, and hang out rags to dry rather than throw them in a container (fire hazard). Brush bristles with a wire brush, smooth and set aside to dry. Dry and store brushes laying flat so bristles will not be bent and damaged.

PAINTING TECHNIQUE

■ Painting the ceiling and walls the same color pulls the ceiling closer to the floor. Heighten a room by using a different, lighter color on the ceiling.

■ A home feels coordinated when all the trim—base, crown molding, window and door frames—is painted the same color. This principle also applies to ceilings, although the trim and ceiling colors do not have to match.

■ Using similar shades in adjoining rooms makes the transition between two rooms visually pleasing.

■ Be adventurous and try faux finishes (to create a marbleized look), rag rolling and even splattering. If you don't like it, just paint over it.

SPECIFIC ROOM ISSUES

■ In a family room, paint is usually better than wallpaper. You can hang paintings, photographs and quilts without a distracting background.

■ To lighten a dark, wood-paneled family room, consider painting it a light color. Or ask your paint store how to apply a light wash over the wood.

■ For entry halls, or other rooms with few windows, consider a pale yellow paint, which brings the outdoor sunny cheerfulness into the space.

■ The front door is the first and last thing your family and friends see going in and out. The paint should be high-gloss white on the interior to match the trim. The exterior can be a different color.

■ When painting the exterior of your house, two little mistakes can ruin the job: not scraping away loose or flaking paint before repainting, and painting outside when the temperature is above 50 degrees F.

A Little Decorating Goes a Long Way: Ten Tiny Improvements That Make a Big Difference

1. Install new hardware on your entry door for a solid first impression. Consider a brass kick plate knocker, handle or knob.
2. Replace old bath and kitchen knobs, as well as switch plates, electrical outlets, central heat and floor air grates throughout the house. Then color-coordinate new ones for a clean look.
3. Crown molding will give a room a more finished look.
4. Install a dimmer on your overhead entry-hall light for a warmer look.
5. Declutter countertops for a spacious appearance. Store small appliances that aren't used every day.
6. To easily and inexpensively coordinate a kitchen, recover the seats of your kitchen table chairs or make thin seat pillows that tie to the backs of the chairs. Then buy or sew napkins from coordinating fabric.
7. A variety of tropical trees and plants add life to any room. Fresh flowers in guest bedrooms and baths are a welcoming touch.
8. When framing artwork, buy the best frames you can afford. Use wood around paintings and limit chrome and metal to framed posters only.
9. Coordinate picture frames that are grouped together. Using all-silver, gold or leather frames on a tabletop makes photos stand out.
10. Always have something red in the living room and family room to draw your eye into the space.

Selecting Wallpaper for Your Room

Wallpaper can make an inexpensive yet striking change in a room. When choosing your wallpaper, remember:

- Beginners should use pretrimmed, prepasted wallpaper without a design to have to match up.
- Match your pattern to your room size: large ones for large rooms and so on.
- Make a room seem taller by using a paper with vertical stripes.

127

- Make a room look deeper by choosing a paper with large, geometric designs on a light background.
- A wallpaper border placed under ceiling molding makes the ceiling seem lower.
- Make a room more elegant by wallpapering above chair-rail molding.
- In your most-used rooms, skip bold prints that will wear on you quickly.
- Make your wallpaper last longer by coating it with clear polyurethane.
- A wallpaper with a faux finish will attract eyes away from wall flaws.
- Wallpapering the ceiling makes a room seem smaller.
- If you like a certain expensive wallpaper, buy just a roll. You can create panels from it and paper against a solid background.

Getting Ready for Summer

A few simple, affordable touches can lighten and brighten your home. Try these ideas to give your house summer spirit.

FRESHEN UP
- Arrange old bottles and shells on your mantel to remind you of the sea.
- Wash large seashells you collected on vacation and use them to create a centerpiece for your dining room table.
- Bring some of the fresh outdoors into your home with fragrant flowers such as miniature irises, wax flowers, hyacinths, roses, gardenias, hybrid lilacs, lilacs and white jasmines.
- Keep a dish of pretty seashells on your kitchen table or counter.
- Put citrus-scented soaps in a small basket by your bathroom sink.
- Hang wind chimes fashioned from seashells or driftwood outside your back door.
- Set seasonal fresh fruit out in a colorful bowl.
- Put plants against a mirror panel to exaggerate foliage.
- Place seasonal potted plants on either side of the entrance.

Never buy what you do not want, because it is cheap; it will be dear to you.
—*Thomas Jefferson*

All About Antiques

Having your antiques appraised is the best way to determine if particular objects are worth preserving carefully, or if the only value is the enjoyment they give you. The value of antiques and collectibles varies dramatically, depending upon the rarity of the item, its overall condition and the current market for the item.

When appraising antiques, find trustworthy experts who specialize in specific types of collectables, like furniture, toys, comic books and so on. For an accurate estimate, consider having two or three specialists look at an item. Or, hire an independent appraiser who is professionally trained to do the research required. It costs more, but may be worth the expense if you've got lots of different types of antiques.

Once you've determined an item's value, you can then decide how to repair or restore it. If it's valuable, find a reputable restorer. Often local antique stores, flea markets or even high-end furniture stores can make recommendations. For simple repairs or just a fresh coat of paint, do it yourself. Before you polish, clean or restore an old item, make sure the methods and materials you use will protect and highlight the finish of that item. Again, asking a professional and doing some research beforehand can help you avoid mistakes.

For very old or very fragile pieces, be mindful of your home's climate. Temperature and humidity fluctuations can wreak havoc on furniture. Use air conditioners and humidifiers to help you regulate indoor conditions. Avoid subjecting paintings, drawings and books to ultraviolet light or direct sunshine. On bright days, shut blinds or use shades and curtains. Never store valuables near radiators or heat vents.

Important family photographs and paper documents should be protected with acid-free paper and stored in a light-proof container. Make copies for day-to-day use. Documents such as birth and marriage certificates should be stored in a bank's safe deposit box.

- Frame vacation photos from summers past. Display on bookshelves and tables to bring back fun memories.
- Place varying-size candlesticks on the mantel; alternate different colors of candles—for example, bright green, yellow or pink.

COVER UP
- Cover old counter stools with bright fabric.
- Consider a tie-on slipcover to give a sofa a new lease on life.

129

- Rejuvenate an old lampshade with pastel ribbon or beading.
- Drape a pastel patchwork quilt over a table and add a green plant in a white pot.
- Put a colorful vinyl tablecloth on your kitchen table. (The kids will be eating more meals at home.)
- Give a chair or two a new cover. Casually tied loose covers that fit over standard-size chairs are now widely available through mail-order companies or from large department stores. You won't be so worried about the furniture when the kids come in from play.
- Put out a new welcome mat.
- Place a colorful rug inside your front door. Make sure the background is a medium color so dirt won't show.

LIGHTEN UP

- Revive an old tabletop by spattering it with blue and white paint.
- Give an old wicker chair a fresh coat of white paint and a new floral cushion.
- Give bookshelves an open air by removing not-so-favorites and placing books with darker jackets vertically. Lean light-colored books against the back wall to show off attractive covers. Feature a favorite summertime novel by standing it upright.
- Use casual accessories—for example, straw and wire baskets or birdhouses—to create a lighthearted atmosphere.
- Treat yourself to a new, brightly colored tea towel and hang it on your oven door.
- Roll up large rugs and leave floors bare, or use scatter rugs here and there.
- Take down draperies or heavy curtains, have them cleaned, then store. Replace them with white sheer panels for the summer.
- Replace dark, heavy bedspreads with old-fashioned white cotton ones.
- Brighten up any room with a few decorative throw pillows.

CLEAN UP

- Physically lighten up a room. Put away heavy throws, knickknacks and other unnecessary clutter.

- Air out comforters, blankets and pillows on a sunny day.
- Sweep winter debris from the picnic table and patio.
- Store a collection of pretty pitchers on top of your refrigerator for easy retrieval when making lemonade or iced tea.
- Buy some new place mats and cloth napkins. Keep your table set to make summer suppers easy and inviting.

Before You Start

Decorating mistakes can be expensive so take your time before bringing anything home permanently. One of the best pieces of advice I ever received was not to spend a lot of money on furniture when my children were young. No matter how hard you work at keeping food in the kitchen and messy craft projects outside or in the basement, kids will be kids.

Of course, I'm not suggesting that ugly or poor-quality furniture is the way to go. However, the time for being practical is now. In a few years—when the peanut butter and jelly period is behind you—you can have the living room of your dreams. Until then, save your money. Besides, your taste will likely change by the time your youngest finally goes off to kindergarten!

Style Glossary

Few homes are clearly definable as one style. Most of us have furniture and accessories from a variety of different styles that we've collected over the years. When you're shopping for furniture in catalogues, furniture stores or flea markets, it's helpful to understand some style terms so you can articulate your needs and feel knowledgeable about your purchases. And it's fun to see how new items reflect older styles of furniture.

Art Nouveau: A curvilinear style that developed across Europe during the late 1800s that often uses iridescent colors and designs of landscapes, animals and insects.

Art Deco: Dating from the 1920s and 1930s, this sleek geometric style began in France and features rounded corners, and clean, sleek lines.

Asian: A broad category of style incorporating Japanese, Chinese and Southeast Asian influences.

Beidermier: Furniture, which started in Germany in the late 1890s, that is made of blonde-colored wood, accentuated with deep green or black elements.

British Colonial: Often ornately carved and made of teak or mahogany finish, this look is most often seen in heavy desks, chairs and beds.

Colonial: From the American colonial period, a rough-hewn and plain style, often including furnishings with spindly legs.

Contemporary: An all-encompassing term for furniture designs of the past twenty years.

Eclectic: This style is a mish-mosh of a number of different styles that work together for a unique, indefinable look.

English Country: A warm, classic look, incorporating floral chintz fabric, fringed lamp shades and dark, comfortable furniture.

French Country: Designed around the warm yellow and terra-cotta color palette of Provence, this style features lots of pine and oak rustic furniture.

Georgian: A style of elegant furnishings form 1714 to 1820, including Sheraton and Chippendale, often with claw and ball feet and cabriole legs.

Industrial: An office look reinterpreted for home furnishings, usually using stainless steel, chrome and black rubber.

Mission: Also known as arts and crafts, this heavy, boxy style uses broad slabs of wood connected with raised joints. It was popular from the 1880s until the mid-1920s.

Modern: A broad term that includes furniture from the 1940s, 1950s and 1960s and features a functional, clean look.

Neo-classical: A revival that occurred in the early 1800s of furniture that looked like ancient Greek and Roman furniture with curved arms, slightly flared legs and ornate carvings.

Primitive: This folksy, rustic look includes chunky, rough-hewn furniture and accessories like quilts and camp blankets.

Scandinavian: Made of light-colored woods with a mid-1900s look, this style is warm and straightforward. Also known as Danish Modern.

Shaker: An extremely simple, functional look, like refined colonial furniture, that was started by the American Shaker communes.

Southwest: A look that exemplifies Santa Fe, New Mexico, using silver, turquoise, sunset reds and burnt oranges with rough, heavy Spanish-like furniture.

Traditional: The classic, familiar look is any mix of English Country, Georgian or Colonial styles.

Victorian: Named for the long-ruling British monarch, this style includes deeply carved, dark mahogany furniture and heavy accessories.

Don't forget that the purpose of decorating your home is for your family's use and enjoyment, seven days a week, and not to impress the occasional guest. Whether you're a do-it-yourselfer or are a danger to your home with a paintbrush and ladder, it doesn't matter. The end goal is the same: a warm and welcoming home.

CHAPTER 6

You're the Gardener

I'll admit that my thumb is not the greenest one out there. Creating a beautiful lawn and lush gardens has always been a challenge for me—I've had to kill a lot of things in order to figure out what works. Here, I'll share some of what I've learned so you won't have the same experience. And an opening word of advice: don't become too emotionally attached to plants. If something gets frostbitten, devoured by pests, trampled by the dog or wilts to a stub, you can always start over.

Outdoor Gardening

THE BIG LANDSCAPE PICTURE

Begin by determining what you want in your landscape. Ask yourself lots of questions. Do you want all lawn? Or the no-lawn, natural prairie look? Lots of flower gardens? Or just a rock garden? A vegetable patch? A fruit-bearing tree or shade trees? A patio covered with plants and hanging baskets?

Then look deep within yourself and honestly ask just how much time and money you're willing to put behind your ideal plan. If you can afford weekly gardening help to mow, prune, deadhead and rake, then labor-intensive landscapes are completely possible. But if you're relying upon yourself and your family for all of these outdoor chores, then carefully consider your decisions. Luckily, there are lots of easy-to-implement plans with easy-growing plants for lawns, flower and vegetable gardens, and containers to choose from.

PLANNING YOUR PERFECT LAWN: NINE THINGS TO CONSIDER

1. **Study the site.** The climate, soil conditions and the amount of daily direct sunlight largely determine what type of grass seed will grow best. Look at your neighbors' lawns and ask what's worked for them, and trust the advice of the people at the garden center. Buy the best seed you can, as it contains more seeds and less nongrass particles. You don't want to repeat the planting process more often than necessary. If your yard is planted already, but entirely covered with weeds, it's simply easier to replant instead of weeding.

2. **Planting grass.** You'll probably want to plant a mix of different cultivars, or types of grass. In cooler climates, wait until the temperature is above 60 degrees F before planting. Prepare the soil by raking it into pea-size balls. If the soil is dry or sandy, add enough topsoil to create 6 inches of planting soil. Using a scattering machine spread the seed and a fertilizer, specifically designed for planting, on the same day. Then water daily for the next three weeks or so. With new seed, only water about a half-inch a day, as the roots are growing just under the soil and deep watering isn't required. Wait until the grass is 2 inches tall before cutting, and make sure the mower's blade is sharp, so it won't pull out seedlings.

3. **Planting on hills.** Hilly areas require some ground cover to prevent erosion. If you choose grass, follow the same planting instructions as above and then cover the new seed lightly. The straw prevents the seeds from blowing away, but too much straw prevents sunlight and water from reaching the seeds. Sod is an easier but more expensive option for hilly areas. When planting sod, place it horizontally across the hill and make sure it receives at least 1 inch of water weekly.

4. **Watering grass.** During the growing season for established lawn areas, grass requires a minimum of 1 inch of water a week. Measure

Kids Can . . .

Elementary school kids can . . .

- **Water the lawn**
- **Water plants**
- **Rake leaves**
- **Pull weeds**
- **Plant flowers**
- **Shovel snow**

Teenagers can do the above, plus . . .

- **Mow the lawn**
- **Trim plants and shrubs**

135

Bright Idea

Recycle your old leaky garden hose by using it as a sprinkler. Poke additional holes consistently throughout the length of the hose and use it to water your garden or lawn.

your sprinkler's hourly output by placing at least three small cans within the range of the sprinkler. After an hour, pour the water from the cans into one container, measure the amount and divide by the number of cans. That's the hourly rate. Then plan accordingly. Less frequent and deeper watering creates stronger root structures. Also watering after a light rain ensures deeper water saturation, as the top is already wet and water easily flows down into the soil. If possible, water in the early morning and avoid evening watering that may promote fungus growth. However, if the lawn looks dry, then water anytime.

5. **Making the cut.** Taller grass means less sunlight for ground-hugging weeds to grow. That's good. So set the mower's blade at 2.5 to 3 inches during the peak growing season. For your last cut of the season, set the blade to a 2-inch setting. Only cut off one-third of the overall height of the blade. If the grass has grown too long, don't drop the blade height, which could burn the grass. Instead, cut at the preferred height and then do another cut a few days later. Use an edger to clip around trees, flowering vines and other plants. If someone besides you uses the edger, point out all tender or new plantings before any damage is done.

6. **Clippings and mulch.** With dry clippings, leave them and let them compost down into the grass, as they're an important source of potassium and nitrogen for growing grass. Avoid cutting wet grass, as the clippings will just clump on top of the grass.

7. **Fertilizer facts.** In addition to the nutrients the grass receives from the clippings, a complete lawn fertilizer is usually necessary. In northern climates, experts recommend applying fertilizer in the spring and fall. In warmer areas, just a spring application should do. But there is some debate. So turn again to the neighbor with the best lawn and ask them.

8. **Weeds.** A healthy lawn with long blades of grass is the best defense against invaders like dandelions, crabgrass and chickweed. The presence of weeds usually means the lawn is watered irregularly, fertilized erratically or grows in poor-quality soil. Spend a bit of time examining what types of weeds are growing in your lawn and learn

to identify the seed pods they produce. Then, cut the lawn before the seed pods open and pick up all the seed-infested clippings, instead of leaving them in the grass to germinate. This is time-consuming, but it works.

9. **Aerating and thatching.** If your lawn is the neighborhood playfield, or if the soil is heavy, consider aerating the grass once a year. Rent a machine that opens the soil, allowing air and water to penetrate root systems. A dethatching machine rids the yard of dead grass stems and roots that build up on top of the soil. The type of grass seed you've planted determines if and how often this process is necessary.

CREATING A FLOWER GARDEN

1. **Create an outdoor style guide.** Buy a looseleaf notebook with tab dividers and fill it with items you like. Pull pages from magazines, newspapers and plant catalogues. Take lots of photos and file them here too. Local garden tours, community gardens and the gardens of historical properties are wonderful sources of what grows in your area. Interview gardeners of properties you enjoy. Most are quite proud of their work and willing to share advice (and cuttings, if you're nice). After a few months of collecting, see what you've got. Do any color combinations or types of plants keep appearing? Do you see lots of one specific style, like Japanese or English cottage gardens? Use these as a starting point. If nothing jumps out from your guide, then ask a gardener friend or a friendly nursery employee to take a look and see what they see.

2. **Evaluate your garden area.** Once you've determined where you want your garden, take a close analysis of the area. How much sun does it receive every day? Determine if it's full sun, partial sun, partial shade or full shade. When it rains, where does the water flow? You'll need to remedy any areas that collect water. Finally, do a step most people skip. Have your soil tested by the local agricultural extension office. The information they provide is invaluable for determining what kinds of plants will grow in your soil. Plus, it details which nutrients are present and which are missing—important to know when choosing fertilizers.

Bright Idea

Keep the care tag of any new plant or shrub in a recipe-card holder so you can refer back to the tag for pruning, watering and fertilizing instructions.

137

3. **Create a garden plan**. Trust me, there is no shorter path to insanity than arriving at the garden store without a clue as to what you're looking for. It's guaranteed that you'll buy the wrong quantity, settle for a color that doesn't work or purchase items solely based on how they look as opposed to how they'll work in your garden. Start with some basic design tenants: build in height from shorter plants in front to taller plants in back. Use a mix of colors, textures and foliages. Choose plants with varying bloom times, so there is always some color in the garden. Once you've made some decisions, then go shopping.

4. **Color made simple.** There are a few tricks to combining color in the garden, and getting a color wheel from an art store will decode much of the mystery. Try to mix contrasting colors (those across from each other on the color wheel, like blue and orange) with harmonious colors (those next to each other on the color wheel, like blue and green). Because it's a combination of all colors, white is not on the color wheel, but it's a great color for separating parts of the garden, or for making a single other color, like red, pop out. Don't be afraid of hot color combinations like red/yellow/orange. Used sparingly, these colors draw your eye right into the garden. A good rule of the green thumb set is that fewer colors are always preferable to more.

5. **Prepare the soil**. For most soils, you'll need to add some peat moss, compost and a 10-10-10 fertilizer. If you're an organic gardener, then substitute an organic fertilizer like aged manure. With a spade, dig down about a foot deep and turn the soil with a pitchfork. Then work in the peat moss and other additives. Make sure the mix is even across the garden. If your soil is especially sandy or clay-filled, then change your add-ins accordingly. Be realistic in what you can and can't change in your soil. Completely re-creating a Richmond garden in Tucson is unlikely, but some overlap is possible.

6. **Selecting the plants.** When buying plants from a garden center or nursery, select healthy-looking ones and avoid any that look dry or tired, even if they are on sale. Don't worry if roots are growing out of the bottom; these are trimmed before planting. If a plant looks easily divisible, then split it in half. Always buy three to four kinds

of the same plant, perhaps in more than one color, for an in-ground garden. If you buy fewer than that, the plant won't visually register in the landscape. A garden with lots of different plants looks smaller and requires much more upkeep than a garden with different kinds of the same plant.

7. **Perennials versus annuals.** Perennials are plants that rebloom year after year. Every two to three years, you can divide perennials and plant the offshoots in other parts of the garden, which makes them economical in the long run. The downside is how long they take to grow and the fact that the bloom time is often just a few weeks. The rest of the year perennials are dormant or just foliage plants. Conversely, annuals, while only living one year, grow rapidly, bloom constantly and provide color all season long. Experienced gardeners recommend using a mix of both. Plan your beds with long-term perennials and use annuals to fill in any empty spaces.

8. **Perennials that produce.** Plant these perennials in the sun: globe thistle, helianthus, liatris, aster, candytuft, clematis, daylily, gold-enrod, rudbeckia, stachys, sedum, peony, lupine, lunaria, phlox, monarda, gaillardia, chrysanthemum, coreopsis and delphinium. In shady areas try bleeding heart, creeping phlox, Jacob's ladder, lady's-mantle, periwinkle, astilbe, columbine, foamflower, forget-me-not, hepatica, hosta, galax, Solomon's seal, polmonaria and primrose.

9. **Tender perennials.** Tropical or sub-tropical plants grown in much colder climates are called tender perennials. In their native areas, these are perennials; but in most of the country these plants will die at the first frost. But don't let that dissuade you; most can move indoors for the winter. This classification includes the fragrant angel's trumpet, deep blue agapanthus, sweet potato vine and lan-tana. All are colorful additions to the garden.

10. **Biennials for another option.** These types of plants bloom in the second year after planting, showing only some foliage the first year, then seed and die. Some favorites include foxglove, dianthus, sweet William, silver sage, milk thistle and money plant. In warm cli-mates, impatiens are actually biennials.

⑥ *Everything I have earned has gone into these gar-dens. I do not deny that I am proud of them.*

—Claude Monet

139

11. **Annuals for guaranteed color.** For ground cover, use candytuft, creeping zinnia, periwinkle, portulaca, toadflax, ageratum, Johnny jump-up or sweet alyssum. For cuttings, use zinnia, sunflower, snapdragon, aster, calendula, cosmos, salvia, rose mallow, cleome, or stock. For climbing plants, use hyacinth bean, moonflower, black-eyed Susan vine, cardinal climber, cup-and-saucer vine, moonflower, morning glory, trailing nasturtium, scarlet runner bean or cathedral bell.

12. **Planting the plants.** Once the soil is ready, place each plant on top of the soil and step back to see how the arrangement looks. Tread carefully to avoid crushing anything. Now's the chance to move things easily. Remember to plant in clumps instead of rows to avoid that soldiers-in-a-line look. If you're planting with plants in a plastic container, knock the plant out of the container. Spread open the root ball by cutting into it with pruners. Drop the plant into a hole slightly larger than the root ball. Tap soil around the plant until it's firm, and water thoroughly. If some part of the garden doesn't look right when you're finished, then pull the offenders out, move them someplace else or give them to a friend. Planting in the spring or fall is preferable to the height of summer, when new plants need the most attention.

13. **Water wisely.** Purchase an inexpensive water gauge and keep it near the back door, so you can easily see how much water has fallen in any given week. Or place a small can marked with inch increments inside the flowerbed. A well-watered flowerbed requires 1 to 2 inches of water a week. When watering with a hose, attach a water wand, which dissipates the water flow to simulate a gentle summer rain. Try and water first thing in the morning, so plants get a full day to absorb the water. Avoid watering in the evening as water on foliage overnight often encourages diseases. You can create your own soaker hose by picking up an old hose at a garage sale and poking holes along the length of it.

14. **Fertilizer 101.** Fertilizer labels list the percentages included of nitrogen (N), which produces a plant's leaf growth, and phosphorus (P) and potassium (K), both of which invigorate plant growth.

The numbers are always listed in this order—NPK—and a zero indicates that the nutrient is not present in that fertilizer. Ask at your garden supply store about which fertilizer is correct for your specific needs. Also consider a pellet fertilizer, which is applied only once each growing season. Handle all fertilizers carefully, keeping them away from pets and children.

15. **Bugs.** Bugs love a good flower garden, because you've made such a pleasing place for them. However, before reaching for the spray can, determine what kind of bugs you've got. Butterflies, moths and bees, for example, are instrumental in pollinating flowers and eating destructive bugs. An inexpensive guide can help you decipher an aphid from a whitefly. Then plan your attack accordingly. Toads are good garden company as their diet is bugs, bugs, bugs. You can attract toads to your garden by placing one or two 6-inch-high terra-cotta pots sideways on the soil. The shelter keeps them dry and warm all summer long.

16. **Weeds.** Even for the finest of gardens, weeding is a necessary chore. For fully established beds, there is little room between plants for weeds to start. But for up-and-coming gardens, weeds will invariably sprout up. Digging them out with a weeding tool works perfectly well; just make sure you remove the entire root system or you'll soon see it again. It's an easier and less daunting task to do a bit of weeding every week instead of facing several weeks of weeds.

17. **Deadheading and pruning.** Encourage your plants to produce as many flowers as possible all summer long by deadheading spent blooms. Just pinch them off. For annuals, this discourages seeds and encourages more blossoms. While some perennials rebloom with some deadheading, the process mainly serves to keep them neat and tidy looking. Walking through a garden of dead flower heads is too depressing. Also, many perennials benefit from a pruning halfway through the summer.

18. **Putting the garden to bed.** If your ground freezes in winter, you'll need to do some work in early winter to protect your plants during the cold season. For a cleaned-up look, trim all the dead stems to

an inch or two. However, this isn't required for good plant care. But do pull up all dead annuals, so you'll save some time in the spring. When the ground is frozen (meaning temperatures have been below freezing all day for seven to ten days) spread a 2-inch covering of an organic compost over the garden. This will enrich the soil over the winter and is an important step for first-year gardens. To secure the mulch, cover with pine branches from your Christmas tree. If you need more greens, see if your community has a centralized drop-off point for discarded trees, or ask your neighbors for theirs.

19. **Record wins and losses.** Celebrate your gardening victories and avoid repeating any mistakes by keeping a garden journal. Save all those tags that come with the plants and at the end of the season, flip through them and see what worked and what didn't. This will simplify some of next year's planning. Also, photograph your garden at different times during the growing season so you can determine which color combinations you like and how your plants look together.

GROWING A VEGETABLE GARDEN

1. **Start small.** Don't be too ambitious with your vegetable garden, or you'll be zucchini and tomato crazy by summer's end. Keep your first garden to no more than 80 square feet and then, as you determine your needs, you can expand accordingly. Where rabbits, pets or other animals are an issue, fence the area and cover the fence with climbing vegetables like peas and beans. Raised beds take some effort to construct, but beautifully define an area and are a one-time expense for years of use.

2. **Select a garden spot.** Most vegetable are sun lovers, so choose a location that receives at least four to six hours of full sun per day. However, most leafy vegetables do well in partial sun. Since you'll be watering often, an area near a water source is ideal. You won't want to carry buckets of water across the yard if there's a better alternative.

3. **Choose your selection.** It's important to grow similar crops with similar maturation times together. Early growers like spinach, early

If you would be happy for a week, take a wife; if you would be happy for a month, kill a pig; but if you would be happy all your life, plant a garden.

—*Chinese proverb*

lettuce and English peas can be replaced with warm-weather plants such as cucumbers for the heat of the summer and then fall crops of late lettuce, arugula and chicory for tasty autumn salads.

4. **Starting indoors.** You can easily start seed indoors, on windowsills that receive six hours of direct sun or under a growlight. Use potting soil or inexpensive seed starter cubes, then move the seeds outdoors as soon as the stems are 6 inches high and the threat of a late freeze has safely passed. For a very early-blooming plant, a "hardening off" step is often necessary for two weeks before planting. Place the pant outdoors in a protected area for several hours a day on mild spring days to acclimate it to colder outdoor temperatures.

5. **Planting outdoors.** One old gardening friend always plants her gardens when the oak leaves start to bud. Sow seeds in rows and identify your plants. If the plants grow too close, then thin them out. It's better to have fewer but stronger plants. And remember to rotate your crops each year, returning to the original area only after three years. This ensures the soil isn't continually depleted of the same nutrients.

6. **Supplement your soil.** Like flower gardens, vegetable patches need fertilizers and additives to enrich the soil. However, since you'll be eating these vegetables, use only organic materials like leaf mold, aged manure and household compost for improving drainage and enriching the soil.

7. **Stick to a watering schedule.** Like other areas of your yard, the vegetable garden requires at least 1 inch of water a week. Water in the morning to minimize rot and discourage funguses. If you're on vacation or away on business for many days, consider installing an irrigation system. Just be sure it works properly before you leave town.

8. **Mulch for success.** Mulch helps vegetable gardens retain moisture, maintain even temperatures and ward off weeds. Avoid peat moss as it just absorbs water. Better kinds of organic mulches are shredded leaves, wood chips or even dried grass clippings. As these materials decompose, they create soil-enriching hummus. Be careful to place organic mulches away from the base of each plant. This keeps the plants safer from fungus, disease and bugs that are

143

naturally attracted to organic mulches. Similarly, only let tomatoes and other fruits touch mulch as they grow and ripen. They'll rot by touching the soil. Staking helps minimize this.

9. **Weeds.** Mulching helps eliminate weeds, as does planting quick-growing, large-leafed vegetables. If weeding isn't your favorite chore, try corn, tomatoes, beans, cucumbers and squash in your garden. A quick walk through the garden every day to see how the vegetables are progressing and to pull any weeds that grew overnight minimizes any lengthy weeding sessions.

10. **Bugs and disease.** Try hand-removing bugs and obviously diseased parts of plants as soon as you spot them. If there is a real infestation, then make sure you've correctly identified what type of insect or disease is causing the problem. No one herbicide will remedy every problem, although insecticidal soaps and sticky insect traps are helpful. If slugs are feasting on your vegetables, then spread pans of beer, eggshells or sand around the plant's base. That'll fix them.

11. **Continually harvest.** As the vegetables ripen, keep gathering the fruits of your labor and share it with your friends. More picking pushes the plant to grow and produce more, which will keep everyone in fresh vegetables all summer long.

STARTING A CONTAINER GARDEN

1. **Choosing a container.** You can plant in just about any container, including pots, buckets, wheelbarrows, casks and even old shoes. Just make sure there are drainage holes in the bottom. Add a layer of broken bits of pots or a few small stones over the drainage holes to keep the soil from running out, then add your plant of choice. If drainage holes are impossible to make, layer the bottom of the container with a deep layer of crushed rock.

2. **Sizing the container.** Usually the bigger the plant grows during the summer, the bigger the container you'll need. Most flowers, herbs and small vegetables perform perfectly in about 8 or 9 inches of soil. Bigger plants, like tomatoes and large tropical plants, require 15 inches of soil and very wide-mouthed containers. For all con-

tainers, raise them off the surface by setting wooden blocks, flat rocks or bits of broken brick underneath.

3. **What to plant.** Perennials like yarrow, lupine, chrysanthemums and columbine do well in containers. Vines such as passion flower and moonflower, and trailing plants like licorice, petunias and fragrant alyssum, all thrive in pots. Good choices among annuals are coleus, geraniums, zinnias, pansies, salvia, snapdragons and nasturtiums. Summer vegetables such as tomatoes, bell peppers, cucumbers, summer squash, leaf lettuce and eggplant all do well in containers that receive six hours of sun daily. Even berry plants such as blackberries, raspberries and strawberries thrive in containers. And most herbs are ideal container plants.

4. **Guidelines for looking good.** If you're planting containers with a variety of different flowers and foliage plants, try to combine those with varying heights and textures, all in coordinated color schemes. Don't forget to include trailing plants that will visually soften the edges of the container. Set a board across the top of the container and set the chosen plants on top to see how the group looks before planting. Make sure all the plants in the container have similar sunlight requirements—for example, shade lovers versus sun lovers. When in doubt about adding more plants to a container, do it. A full, lush look is the desired result, and cramped plants will grow just fine.

5. **When to plant.** Planting time depends upon your hardiness zone and when the danger of any damaging frost has completely passed. This could be anytime from early April to late May. And it's always better to plant too late than too early.

6. **Move indoor containers outdoors.** In the summer, you can move your houseplants outside. But do so carefully. They're used to the diffused light of your house and will require several days in a semi-shady outdoor spot before moving into a sunny spot. If leaves show any sign of burning, then remove to a shadier spot. Before taking them back inside for the winter, place them in the same semi-shady spot to wean them off the strong outdoor sun.

7. **Soil of choice.** Use potting soil from containers instead of soil from your garden, as it's more porous and free of insects. If you don't

Take Note

Water plants and flowers in the morning or evening. Watering them in the heat of the day may scorch the leaves and flowers.

145

want to worry about fertilizing, then purchase potting soil with fertilizer already added in. You may have to repot if the plant grows quickly. Roots emerging out the drainage hole are a sure sign to repot.

8. **Vigilant watering.** Because containers are small, they dry out quickly. For pots in full sun or windy areas, like hanging baskets, daily watering is required. To test if the pot is dry stick your finger about a half-inch into the soil. If it's dry then water until water flows from the bottom. Anytime soil has pulled away from the side of a pot, then water immediately. In containers without drainage holes, closely monitor the soil moisture level. Root rot will occur if the plant is over-watered.

GROWING HERBS

Herbs are a wonderful addition to any gardening plans. They're easily adaptable for containers, look great in perennial borders and fragrantly spruce up a vegetable garden. Best of all, herbs are easy to grow and useful in cooking, making teas and as ingredients home remedies.

1. **Annual herbs.** Many herbs are annuals, including basil, dill, fennel, marjoram, parsley and rosemary. Plant some together in a container, like a strawberry pot, near the kitchen, so they're easily accessible for cooking. An inch of water per week is ideal. Don't over water herbs or they get leggy and loose their intense flavor.

2. **Perennial herbs.** Chives, catnip, lavender, lemon balm, mint, sage, tarragon and thyme are usually perennials herbs, depending upon your growing zone. Plant them in the perennial bed or among the vegetables. When these herbs grow back the following spring, cut back the woody stems to encourage new, tender leaves.

3. **Seeds or plants.** Most annual herbs are easily started from seed, but if you're impatient consider buying the seedlings. Either way, the cost of starting the herbs is quickly recouped during the next few months. Imagine how much money you're saving not buying big bunches of herbs, only using a few springs or leaves and then tossing out the rest.

4. **Watch the mint.** Mint is invasive and difficult to remove once its roots are set. To minimize this, plant mint in a container and sink the container into the ground, which should control it for two years. At that time, remove, trim off half the roots and replant.

5. **Fragrant choices.** Many herbs are prized for their scent. These include chamomile, lavender, lemon balm, lemon verbena, rosemary, sage and spearmint. Use the leaves in teas and as linen drawer fresheners.

6. **Shady options.** While most herbs require full sun, chives, mint and parsley all grow easily in partial shade areas. You can even plant a border of herbs along a shrub line if you like the particular look of the foliage.

7. **Picking for cooking.** Try to pick herbs in the morning after the dew has dried and leave them to air on a paper towel in the kitchen until you're ready to use them. But if you're rushed and need the herbs immediately, skip the previous step.

8. **Drying and preserving.** When dried, herbs last about two years in a dark glass jar, tightly sealed. There are several methods for drying herbs. For all methods, rinse and towel dry any dirty plants before starting. You can spread the leaves in a single layer on a tray and leave in a dark, dry room for several weeks. Or tie the stems together and place in a paper bag, with a few inches of the stem protruding, and place in a warm, dry location for two weeks. Microwaving herbs is easy. Just place herbs between two pieces of paper towel on a nonreactive rack and use half power for no more than three minutes, until they feel brittle. If additional time is needed, do so in twenty-second intervals, then check again.

9. **Pick often for more.** Herbs easily and quickly grow new leaves. So pick lots of leaves and enjoy herbs all season long. Be sure and pinch back flowering herbs, like basil, to encourage more foliage growth.

10. **Extend the season.** In late summer, bring rose geranium, lemon verbena and basil inside and place in a bright window. Or try planting root cuttings from the outdoor plant inside and enjoy herbs all fall and winter.

BULB BASICS

Planting bulbs are an easy way to grow flowers that brighten your landscape. And quick cuttings from your yard, arranged in vases, are a wonderful way to bring instant color and beauty inside your home.

1. **Choose your season.** A wide selection of spring flowering bulbs grows in most regions of the country. These include allium, anemone, crocus, fritillaria, hyacinth, iris, muscari, narcissus or daffodils and tulips. For later color in summer, consider any of these summer flowering bulbs: begonia, calla lilies, canna, dahlia and gladiola.

2. **Where to plant.** You can easily intersperse bulbs in your existing perennial beds, scatter them across the lawn for a blanket of color in spring or create entire beds just filled with bulbs. Most bulbs require at least eight hours of sun a day. However, daffodils, crocus and some hyacinth thrive in partly sunny locations.

3. **When to plant.** For spring bloomers, plant bulbs in the fall when the soil temperature has cooled to about 60 degrees F and well before the ground freezes. If you ordered bulbs and you can't plant them immediately, then store them on a tray filled with peat moss in a dry place. Summer blooming bulbs are planted at the same time you plant your annuals.

4. **How to plant.** A good gardening rule is to plant bulbs at a depth equal to three times the diameter of the bulb—for example, a two-inch bulb should be planted 6 inches deep. When planting, the squat, rooty end faces down and the pointy end stands upright. If the top and bottom are indiscernible, then plant sideways. Bulbs perform best in well-drained soil. Consider adding some sand if your soil is especially dense or compact. Dig the hole with a specially designed bulb digging tool or a trowel and add a bit of bulb fertilizer and a thin layer of soil on top. Don't let the bulb touch the fertilizer, as it will burn. Cover the bulb with the soil, and water thoroughly to eliminate any air pockets.

5. **Naturalizing bulbs.** This terms means the bulbs bloom year after year, like perennial flowers. Daffodils are excellent naturalizers and

Take Note

Gently scrape away the dry roots on the bottom of bulbs. They will root faster and be less likely to rot.

quickly spread. After six or seven years, dig up the bulbs and divide them. This prevents overcrowding and encourages new growth. To create a field of daffodils across part of your lawn, scatter a handful of bulbs. Plant them where they fall and let them grow in over several years. Crocus, scila and muscari also naturalize easily and quickly.

6. **Avoiding the bulb-eaters.** Squirrels are notorious tulip bulb nibblers, causing irreparable damage to your carefully laid plans. Either coat each bulb with a deterring agent, like Bulb Guard, or skip tulips and plant fritillaria, daffodils and snowdrops. Squirrels will pass these bulbs right by.

7. **Cutting the foliage.** After spring blooms fade, the bulbs need at least four weeks of photosynthesis in order to create next year's blooms. Although it turns an unattractive yellow, leave the foliage alone so it can feed the bulb. Either let the grass grow long to cover it up or tie the leaves loosely together for a tidier look.

8. **Taking up bulbs.** Tender bulbs like tulips and hyacinth will reperform the following year if removed from the soil by early summer and replanted in the fall. Summer bloomers like dahlias and tuberous begonias are taken out of the soil before the first frost and kept indoors over the winter. After the first light frost, lift out cannas and gladioli bulbs. Keep all bulbs lightly covered with moistened peat moss in a cool, dry location. Usually a heated garage or basement is ideal. Make sure the bulbs don't dry out, as they'll die.

PLANTING TREES

Trees serve a variety of functions: creating privacy and windscreens, offering a habitat for small animals and birds, reducing noise and air pollution and eliminating soil erosion. If planted to shade a house, trees reduce annual energy consumption by 30 percent during the summer months, quickly recouping their cost.

1. **Choosing a location.** Before choosing a tree, pick a site for the tree, steering clear of any obstacles above or below ground. Avoid septic systems, pipelines, underground power lines, overhead power lines,

149

driveways and walkways. Plant at least 5 feet away from a sidewalk and 10 feet back from intersections. Also, pick a sunny spot that's undisputedly on your property to avoid any future conflicts with your neighbors.

2. **Choosing the type of tree.** Pick a tree based on your specific criteria. Do you want shade from an oak? A colorful maple for the autumn landscape? An apple or citrus tree for fruit? Do you want a fast-growing willow or pine, or a slow-growing ornamental, like a weeping cherry? Whatever you decide, make sure the tree is hardy for your region, and can survive the soil and moisture conditions of your yard. Also, always err on the side of a smaller tree, especially in a smaller yard or interior garden. Big trees make small spaces look smaller.

3. **Selecting a tree.** Trees are usually sold one of three ways: wrapped in ball and burlap, inside a bucket container or bareroot. If your tree is balled, make sure the tree is not loose from the ball. If it's in a container, remove the container and only buy the tree if the roots are smaller than the diameter of a pen. Otherwise, it's been in the container too long. Bareroot trees are the easiest to plant, but need planting as soon as possible. When you're ready to plant, cut off any damaged roots and rehydrate the remaining roots in a bucket of water for an hour. If the tree is dormant, make sure it's alive before purchasing it. Scratch a bit of stem off a branch and see if the undergrowth is moist and green. Also, ask if your nursery or plant store offers a guarantee on the tree's longevity in case any problems arise.

4. **Soil drainage test.** Even if a chosen spot looks perfect for your new tree, perform a drainage test to make sure water will absorb into the soil. Dig a hole 1 foot wide and 1 foot deep and fill it with water. If, after six hours, any water remains in the hole, plant the tree elsewhere.

5. **Planting the tree.** In most areas, the best planting time is early spring. The proper-size hole for a tree is two to three times wider than the root ball and slightly shallower than the depth of the roots. Spread the roots out across the planting area, making sure that no

roots are curling under each other. Also, make sure no loose soil is below the roots, as it causes air pockets to develop. Don't use any soil additives. Instead, force the tree to immediately adjust to your property's natural soil. Place the tree squarely in the hole and back-fill with half the soil. Then water completely. Once the water settles into the ground, add the remainder of the soil. Keep 2 inches of the crown, where the roots join the stem, visible. Fertilize with a gentle, slow-release product designed for newly planted trees.

6. **Watering the tree.** Lack of water or insufficient watering methods is the number one reason trees die. Careful monitoring, especially through the first summer; is crucial to developing strong roots. Trees require at least 1 to 2 inches of water weekly during the first year. This is best done with a slowly-trickling hose, or a soaker hose placed upside down around the perimeter of the planting area. Deep watering encourages stronger root growth, so less frequent but longer waterings are ideal.

7. **Staking.** Only consider staking a tree if its trunk is truly crooked. A slight bend is natural. If a tree does requires staking to correct a serious leaning problem, then only stake it for one year. Use old cotton rags to cover any rope that touches the tree. Secure the tree with two opposite-facing stakes and allow room for the tree to move. Pound the stakes 18 inches into the ground.

8. **Pruning.** Removing dead branches is the only reason for pruning in the first year. In subsequent years good pruning controls growth, encourages flowers and removes dead wood. When to prune depends upon the type of tree. For flowering trees, only prune after the flowers have bloomed. Shape leafy trees in the fall after the leaves are down, but do so judiciously, as mistakes take a long time to grow back. Conifers, like most evergreens, are best pruned in the spring.

WORKING WITH HEDGES, SHRUBS AND BUSHES

A hedge is a row of any type of plant—trees, shrubs, bushes or roses—grown closely together to create a unified look, irrespective of height. Hedges are perfect for lining walks, screening out unattractive foundations and views and providing protection from winter winds if planted on the north end of your property. A mixing and matching of any combination of plants within the same hedge is perfectly acceptable.

Basically, shrubs and bushes are interchangeable terms for any plant growing taller than a groundcover and shorter than a tree. Lilacs, viburnum and mock orange are example of taller bushes with fragrant flowers. Azalea, rhododendron and mountain laurel are types of shorter flowering bushes. Similarly, low evergreens, like dwarf juniper and spreading English yew, are often called bushes. Taller evergreen bushes like privet, Japanese holly, American boxwood and wintergreen barberry create beautiful hedges.

1. **Planting a hedge.** For a row of dense hedges, planting two rows of plant closely together is the easiest way. Carefully draw the straight line of the first hedgerow and then draw another straight line 18 inches behind it. Space plants 3 feet apart, alternating between the front and back rows. Plant and water like new trees, except follow the pruning schedule below. With quick-growing plants, the hedge will take shape in just a few years.

2. **Pruning a hedge.** When a hedge is first planted, remove one-third of the plant to encourage dense, bushy growth. The following year remove another third, following the pruning timetable described in the tree section. In the third year of growth, only prune the branches to shape the emerging hedge. Keep the top slightly narrower than the base, which allows light to reach the base. The "A" shape also provides stability during wind and snowstorms.

PLANTING ROSES

A rose is a rose, everywhere. Roses are among the most versatile and diverse of plants. Climbers artfully cover trellises and arbors. Miniature roses make perfect container plants. Hybrid teas provide fragrant cuttings all summer, while floribunda and shrub roses easily grow into dense hedges. Some rose are easily cared for while others will require hours of pampering, so choose your rose based upon your schedule and its needs.

1. **Planting landscape roses.** Roses thrive in at least six hours of sun a day, preferably all in the morning, although some new roses are tolerant of partial shade. Their soil must be rich, so pile on the compost and bone meal. If you're planting roses from containers, carefully remove the entire container, or cut just one side of the container before planting and then pull the rest out of the hole after planting. Dig a hole 6 inches wider and 6 inches deeper than the container. For roses shipped bareroot, trim off any dead roots and then trim all the roots to 10 inches. Plant these roses in a hole that is 18 inches in diameter and 14 inches deep. Most roses are grafted, meaning that the upper portions are melded together with a different type of hardy rootstock. The union, where the two portions meet, is clearly visible. When planting, keep the union 1 inch below the soil line. Water thoroughly after planting and pile 4 inches of mulch around the base of the rose. Since roses are always thirsty, ensure they receive at least 2 inches of water a week.

2. **Fertilizing and overwintering.** Most types of rose require three applications of a 5-10-5 rose fertilizer annually, before the buds appear in the spring, after the first round of flowers and lastly in mid-August. In colder climates, no later than Thanksgiving, cover the rose's base with 12 inches of mulch to protect the plant from extreme fluctuations of winter temperatures. Remove the mulch in early spring.

3. **Pruning and pests.** The pruning of roses is an art form, requiring a good eye and good instruction. Invest in a well-illustrated, simple-to-follow booklet about pruning to understand the nuances. It's not complicated, just time-consuming. Roses are a dietary staple for a variety of insects and susceptible to numerous diseases. Again, a guide to identifying and treating rose ailments in your region is well worth the cost.

4. **Planting container roses.** Choose wooden or terra-cotta containers for roses, as these allow for better air and water circulation. Miniature or shrub roses are ideal for sunny patios and decks, providing compact mounds of flowers for several months. Planters that are

about 12 inches wide and 12 inches deep are the right size. Larger roses, like hybrid teas and floribundas, also work in containers, just make sure the diameter and depth are at least 16 inches. Water the containers at least twice a week and fertilize weekly. In hot climates, place the roses away from light-colored exterior walls that reflect sunlight and might burn them. Container roses need overwintering if the temperature routinely dips below freezing. Keep them in an unheated protected area, perhaps a garage, away from light, and ensure the soil stays just slightly moist. Return outside once the final frost has passed.

GARDENING: TIPS FROM THE PROS

Any gardener worth her trowel has some tips about what's worked for them. Below are an array that I've collected from gardening friends. Hopefully some will work for you.

- You can do most gardening work with just a good spade, a hoe, a trowel and a wheelbarrow. Do use gloves all the time or invest in a good fingernail brush. (Before you garden, dig your fingernails into a bar of soap for easier cleaning later.)
- Know how to determine what kind of light is in your yard. Full sun means an area that gets unfiltered sunlight for six to eight hours per day. Partial sun means an area that receives light sunlight all day, or about four hours of direct sunshine per day. Partial shade refers to areas that receive two hours or less of sunlight a day. Filtered sun or broken shade means areas that get sunlight through branches, but no direct sun.
- In moderate climates, liriope plants are excellent for defining flower beds. Five liriope plants will become twenty-five or thirty in just two years.
- Daylilies multiply easily and need very little care.
- Depending on the variety, iris can cost several dollars for a single plant, but in about two years you'll have at least twice as many and it will continue to multiply.
- Daisies are a wonderful bargain. In two seasons, an inexpensive 3-

inch plant will grow to fill a square foot of your flower garden with beautiful blooms.

- For hedges, choose red-tipped Photinia or Ilex. Small plants are inexpensive and grow tall and full in just a few years.
- Consider planting fruit trees instead of ordinary shade trees. Many varieties of apple trees will grow in a small space without much care and provide shade, beauty and bushels of apples for up to thirty years.
- Spread ashes from the fireplace around rose bushes in early spring as an alternate to fertilizer.
- Swap with neighbors. Many people would be happy to share plant divisions with you in exchange for cuttings and seedlings you may have.
- Buy perennials on sale. Many garden centers try to get rid of their entire growing stock at the end of the season.
- Consider wildflowers for large, open areas. Contact the National Wildflower Research Center, one of Lady Bird Johnson's favorite causes, in Austin, Texas, for more information.
- Investigate native plants for your area. These are guaranteed good growers, often requiring little work for lots of results.
- If you have space outdoors, consider making a compost area and recycling nonmeat kitchen scraps and yard clippings. Turn it with a spade and water occasionally and in several months, you'll have rich, organic mulch for the garden. Just don't use it in containers, where potting soil is best.
- Buy in bulk whenever possible. Seed, mulch and even bulbs can be cheaper when purchased in large quantities.
- Shop garage sales and church bazaars for tools like clippers, pruners, spreaders and lawn mowers.
- Remember, they're just plants.

Bright Idea

Shop the same end-of-season sale for gardening equipment. High-quality rakes, shovels, hoes and other gardening tools can often be picked up for less than you would pay for inferior ones early in the season. Good tools will last a lifetime and can make gardening an even more pleasant experience.

Lawn and Garden Safety Tips

When working outside:

- Put on goggles when mowing the lawn.
- Wear long pants and sleeves to prevent against insect stings.
- Use sunscreen on all unprotected areas.
- Wear garden gloves.
- Use a plastic-covered pillow or wear old hockey or skating knee pads for weeding and planting comfort.

If you use chemical products in your yard:

- Work on a windless day.
- Wear goggles and a nose-and-mouth mask while spraying or spreading fertilizers or pesticides.
- Read labels and follow instructions carefully.
- Keep children and pets away while you're working with any chemical.

If you find poison ivy:

- Clean any tools that touch the ivy, as the oil will stay on the tools.
- Wear a long-sleeved shirt, work pants, gloves, socks and sneakers.
- Work on a windless day.
- Never burn poison ivy, as the smoke can carry the particles.
- Remove and wash your clothes, including your sneakers. Take a shower and use plenty of soap.

Indoor Gardening

IT'S EASY BEING GREEN: KNOW 'EM AND GROW 'EM

In addition to brightening indoor rooms with some outdoor greenery, houseplants provide several functions. They absorb chemicals like paint, tobacco smoke and cleaning agents from the air, as well as noise from outdoor sources. Plus plants soak in carbon dioxide from indoor air and excrete oxygen, making our homes healthier breathing spaces. Many require just a little care and maintenance to stay in top condition and several do well in low light conditions.

CHOOSING HOUSEPLANTS

When picking out plants in garden centers and nurseries, take the time to choose healthy-looking plants, meaning those with erect leaves, no browning leaf edges and a full shape. Inspect the underside of the leaves carefully making sure there are no insects destroying the plant. Most plants usually come with brief care instructions, including light and water requirements that you should follow carefully. Almost all houseplants should avoid direct sunlight indoors but can be moved outdoors in warmer weather. Keep them in a shady outdoor spot for a few days, so they can adjust to the brighter light.

1. **Light requirements.** Plants that flower, as well as some foliage plants, do well in bright but not direct sunlight and include:

   - African violets
   - Aloe vera
   - Ficus
   - Jade plant
   - Mother-in-law plant
   - Pathos
   - Rubber plant
   - Spider plant
   - Christmas cactus

   Plants for low light conditions include many foliage plants:

   - Algerian ivy
   - Asparagus and Boston ferns
   - Chinese evergreen
   - Dracena
   - Peace lilly
   - Philodendron
   - Weeping fig

   When regular waterings are a problem, opt for these arid loving plants:

   - All cacti
   - Bromeliads
   - Kalonchoe
   - Mother-in-law plant

157

Bright Idea

For a bargain, call plant rental companies to see if they will sell plants they are no longer using.

Take Note

You can cool the water drained from cooking spaghetti or potatoes and use it to water plants, rather than buying fertilizer. Plants like the starch.

2. **Watering.** As with outdoor plants and lawns, less frequent but more thorough waterings are best. For all plants the best way to determine when to water is to stick a finger into the soil. If it feels dry, then water slowly until the water runs out the bottom of the container. When a plant is especially dry and the soil has pulled away from the edge of the pot, then put the pot in a shallow pan of water for twenty minutes, allowing it to absorb water more slowly. The humidity of most houses is too low for ideal growing conditions. Increase the humidity by putting a tray of pebbles under each plant and keep the stones partly covered with water. Also weekly light mistings will raise the humidity.

3. **Fertilizing.** Overfertilized plants turn brown around the edges, a result of burned roots. Underfertilized plants look pale and pallid. To take the guesswork out of fertilizing, add one-quarter the strength of regular liquid fertilizer to your watering can every time you water. Flowering trees like oranges, lemons and limes do better with fertilizer sticks inserted into the soil annually. Flowering plants, like African violets, should only be fertilized when they are in bloom and never during their dormant period.

4. **Diseases and pests.** Houseplants are often susceptible to diseases and pests like aphids, scale, whiteflies and spider mites. Treatment depends upon identifying a problem in its early stages. Every month check the underside of leaves and remove any dead foliage from the plant. If you notice any insects on just a few leaves then removing the infected leaves will usually resolve the problem. For a complete infestation, use either an insecticidal soap or add 2 tablespoons of liquid detergent to 1 gallon of water and carefully wash both sides of every leaf. With either type of soap, use warm water to rinse the soap from the leaves. To kill any eggs or bugs missed by the initial treatment, repeat the washing at least two times, with a week between each application.

5. **Potting and repotting.** When roots begin growing from the bottom of a pot, it's time to replant. If you'd rather use the same pot, just remove the plant, trim back the root ball by one-third and repot it.

Poisonous Houseplants

Many plants cause skin and soft tissue irritations when their leaves are ripped or eaten. Luckily, few plants have any fatal side effects. Chewed leaves and stems are especially a problem in houses with small children and animals. If you suspect your child or pet has eaten any of the following toxic plants, then contact your pediatrician, veterinarian or local poison control to determine what immediate care is required.

- Aloe vera
- Amaryllis
- Chrysanthemums
- Crown of thorns
- Cyclamen
- English ivy
- Heart leaf philodendrun
- Hydrangea
- Poinsetta
- Swiss cheese plant

If you can't identify some of the plants in your yard, enlist a fellow gardener, landscaper or nursery employee to help. Get rid of dangerous plants and poison oak, ivy and sumac. Also remind your children that many seeds, berries and nuts are *not* for eating. Make sure kids' play areas are free of toxic plants. If a neighbor's or friend's yard contains some, ask that they remove or fence them. Lastly, remember that the water houseplants sit in can be as poisonous as the plants themselves.

If you want the plant to grow larger, choose a clay or plastic pot that is only an inch larger in diameter, as replanting in a bigger pot creates a shallow root system that hampers growth. Cover the hole in the bottom with a small stone or a piece of a broken pot and spread out the roots of the plants. Then cover with soil, leaving at least 1 inch of the inside rim exposed. Water the plant thoroughly before and after potting. When plants become too leggy or bushy, trim back the branches and reshape the plant into a symmetrical sphere. Cuttings can be left in a shallow glass of water until new roots sprout and then potted as a new starter plant.

Bright Idea

Use a shoehorn as a small trowel when transplanting small plants.

There is material enough in a single flower for the ornament of a score of cathedrals.
—John Ruskin

MAKING YOUR OWN FLOWER ARRANGEMENTS

Flowers are a colorful addition to any interior, whether they come from your backyard, a fancy florist or the flower section of your local supermarket. With the help of global greenhouses and overnight airfreight services, the most exotic of flora are now available everywhere year round. Following some simple steps keeps flowers looking fresh for as long as possible.

1. **Cutting and storing.** If you're cutting flowers from your own garden, do so early in the morning when the stems are full of water they've absorbed overnight. Cutting in the evening is also acceptable, but try avoiding the hot midday when flowers are dehydrated. Choose stems that are full of slightly opening blooms, cut them with sharp scissors at a 45-degree angle and drop them into a pail of cool water for several hours, unless you need them immediately. While you don't want to decimate the garden, don't hesitate to cut enough flowers for full-looking arrangements.

   At the florist or supermarket, also look for about-to-open stems and flowers with no yellowing or wilted leaves. When you get home, leave the flowers in water, covering three-quarters of their stems, until you're ready to arrange them. If you want to use several different types of flowers in an arrangement, hold them together in the store to make sure the color combination is pleasing. At the florist, where someone else is selecting the flowers for you, tell them which colors you prefer and your price range. Should the florist cut the arrangement before giving them to you, don't cut them again when you get home. But do refresh them with a good misting.

   If you're not using the flowers immediately, or if you bought a bouquet on the way home to take to an office colleague the next morning, store them in water overnight in a dimly lit, cool room before arranging. Make sure the container is far away from drafts—including fans and air conditioners—and direct sunlight.

   When you're ready to arrange the stems, fill your sink with several inches of water. Remove the stems one at a time from the pail, and holding the stem under water, cut at a 45-degree angle another

1 to 2 inches off the bottom. For long-stem roses especially, this step is an important one, because it prevents air bubbles from blocking the stem while allowing more water up the stem. Then use a paring knife and scrape off 2 inches of the stem's green outer layer, exposing an even greater area for water absorption. Next, remove all leaves below the water line so they won't rot in the water. I know this sounds like more work than you ever imagined. But, really, these are quick steps that you'll easily master, and the beautiful, long-lasting results are worth the effort.

2. **Containers and water additives.** Choosing a container for the arrangement is as easy as opening your cupboard. Pitchers, goblets, serving bowls and everyday glasses are just as appropriate as vases and urns. If you're using a colored container, make sure the colors coordinate with the arrangement. For all containers, follow the one-third or two-third rule. Either cut the stems one-third or two-thirds taller than the container for good visual proportions.

Fill your container of choice with room-temperature water. To feed the flowers and keep the water free of contaminants, add either 2 teaspoons each of white vinegar and bleach, a shot of clear liquor like vodka or gin or one packet of Floralife. Remember to change the water every other day in cool locations and every day in hot, humid locations.

3. **Useful tools for flowers.**

• For arrangements in short containers or with a small number of stems, a frog helps create order from chaos. A frog is a metal, glass or ceramic disk or square with holes or spikes, placed in the bottom of the container, that secures stems upright.

• Create your own frog by wrapping several plastic hair curlers with a rubber band. Only use this in nontransparent vases, so no one sees your ingenuity.

• Two inches of clear marbles in the bottom of vase provide a good alternative to frogs, especially in glass and crystal containers where the base of an arrangement is visible.

• An oasis is a brick-shaped foam block that provides a stable base for building more complicated arrangements. Trim the oasis with a

Bright Idea

The next time an out-of-town friend or family member sends you a plant or floral arrangement, enclose a Polaroid picture of the gift with your thank-you note. That way the sender can see exactly what he or she sent to you.

Bright Idea

Refrigerate your cut flowers while you're out for the day to lengthen their indoor life.

Bright Idea

Be ready to make a fresh flower arrangement for any occasion. Keep a collection of vases, pruning shears, blocks of oasis, arranging frogs and dried baby's breath.

paring knife to fit into the container, and then submerge the oasis in water for a minute or so until it stops bubbling. Place the water-logged oasis in the container and insert the flowers into the foam. Stick greens around the base to cover up the foam. Rewet the oasis with a half-inch of water every day, or when it feels dry.

• Top-heavy flowers like Gerber daisies need some assistance to stand tall. Push a 2-inch piece of a clear drinking straw up the stem to the base of the petals to hold the flower upright.

• Keep a hammer handy in springtime. Branches of flowering trees, such as apple, crabapple and lilac, look spectacular in a tall vase. Hammer the bottom 2 inches of the cut stem to increase water absorption.

FLOWER ARRANGING: TIPS FROM THE PROS

- Usually flower arrangements are built as flat (the flowers are all about the same height) or cone-shaped (gradually building from shorter flowers on the outside to the tallest flowers in the middle). Either shape is suitable for dining table centerpieces, just limit the height to 6 inches or less so guests can comfortably talk over the flowers.

- When creating an arrangement with fewer than ten stems, use an odd number instead of an even number of stems for a cleaner look.

- To hold long stems secure in a wide-mouthed vase, create a cross-hatched design across the rim of the vase with clear cellophane tape and insert the stems. The same technique also holds floppy flowers, like peonies, in place in a low container. Just trim the stems to just touch the bottom of the container.

- Tulips will grow a few inches once arranged, so trim the stems back to an acceptable length. Dropping a penny into their water prevents a tulip from opening too quickly.

- Minimize wilting by recutting the stems underwater after a few days and then rearrange.

- Cut flowers last longer when kept out of direct sunlight.

- If the blooms, especially roses, begin wilting, then float the flowers in a sink full of tepid water for a few hours. There is no guarantee, but this is worth a try.

ONE LAST BLOOMING THING

If you're overwhelmed by flower care, don't enjoy flower arranging or need a quick, colorful gift, buy one or more flowering plants. African violets, gloxinias, poinsettias and begonias all provide long-lasting flowers with minimal care. Mix and match in baskets, pitchers or other containers for instant arrangements. Also bulb plants such as paperwhites, tulips, hyacinth and amaryllis are another attractive option.

CHAPTER 7

You're the Safety Officer

"Be prepared." It's the scout motto, and it's also the Family Manager's motto. The unexpected happens to all of us. We can't prevent sudden home emergencies, but good preparation and a little know-how can keep a bad situation from becoming worse.

Coping with Disasters

Natural disasters—hurricanes, floods, wildfires, tornadoes, earthquakes—strike suddenly. Taking the necessary steps can make a life-or-death difference. Make sure your family will be ready if disaster strikes, particularly if you live in an area where one or more of the above can occur.

- Twice a year, designate the day you adjust your clocks for daylight savings time as Home Safety Day. Use this day to change the batteries in your smoke detectors and see that fire extinguishers and flashlights are in working order.
- Make an inventory of all your possessions and keep a copy in a safe place away from your home. Take several photos of any valuable items. (See page 178.)

- Make sure everyone old enough knows how to turn off the water, gas and electricity at main switches.
- Keep the following emergency phone numbers handy so you can easily call when you have a crisis:

  Emergency services (fire, police and ambulance)
  Nearest hospital
  Physician, dentist and pharmacist
  Poison control center
  Emergency numbers for gas, electric and water companies
  Neighbors
  Immediate family
  Taxi
  Veterinarian

EMERGENCY PREPARATION PLAN

- Call your local American Red Cross chapter or Emergency Management Office and ask which disasters they suggest you be prepared for in your area. Do they have any free booklets they can send you? Ask how you would be warned of an emergency, and learn your community's evacuation routes. Ask about special assistance for elderly or disabled persons.
- Discuss with your spouse and children how you would respond to various disasters—fire, severe weather and other emergencies.
- Identify the safest places in your house in case of a tornado or earthquake.
- Instruct family members to turn on the radio for emergency instruction.
- Outline escape routes from each room of your home.
- Pick two meeting places: a place near your home in case of a fire and a place outside your neighborhood in case you cannot return home after a disaster.
- Designate one out-of-state and one local friend or relative for family members to call if separated by disaster.
- Practice emergency evacuation drills with all household members.

- Learn first aid and CPR.
- Keep family records in a water- and fire-proof container.
- Post emergency telephone numbers near telephones.
- Teach children how and when to call 911.

DISASTER SUPPLIES KIT

FEMA (Federal Emergency Management Agency) and the American Red Cross suggest that each home create a Disaster Supplies Kit. Store supplies in an easy-to-carry container such as a backpack or duffel bag. Include:

- ☐ A portable, battery-powered radio or television and extra batteries
- ☐ A flashlight and extra batteries
- ☐ Matches in a waterproof container
- ☐ A first aid kit and prescription medications
- ☐ Credit cards and cash
- ☐ Personal identification
- ☐ An extra set of car keys
- ☐ Extra eyeglasses
- ☐ A signal flare
- ☐ A map of your area and phone numbers neighbors and family members
- ☐ Blankets or sleeping bags
- ☐ Special items for infants elderly or disabled family members

EVACUATION SUPPLIES KIT

In case of an emergency in which you need to evacuate your home, you'll want this kit on hand in addition to the Disaster Supplies Kit. Put these items in an easy-to-carry container, such as a large, covered trash container or cargo container for the roof of your vehicle. Label it clearly. Include:

- ☐ 3 gallons of water per person
- ☐ A three-day supply of nonperishable food
- ☐ Kitchen accessories: a manual can opener, mess kits or paper cups, plates and plastic/disposable utensils; a utility knife; water purifica-

tion tablets or household bleach; sugar, salt and pepper; aluminum foil; plastic resealable bags

☐ A change of clothing for each family member, rain gear and sturdy shoes

☐ An A-B-C-type fire extinguisher, emergency preparedness manual, tent and compass

☐ Sanitation and hygiene items

☐ Entertainment, such as games and books

☐ Tools and other accessories: paper and pencil; needles and thread; pliers, shut-off wrench and shovels; tape

FOURTEEN COMMON HOME EMERGENCIES AND HOW TO HANDLE THEM

1. **Grease fire**. Never throw water on a grease fire. If the fire is small enough, turn off the burner and smother the flames with a lid or damp towel. Contrary to popular belief, you shouldn't use baking soda to douse flames as it can cause the fire to flare. Keep a fire extinguisher (chemical or foam, not water-based) stored in the kitchen where it easily can be grabbed—not in the cabinet space above a burning stove. (Check extinguishers regularly according to manufacturer's instructions to make sure nozzles aren't clogged and pressure is sufficient.) When using a fire extinguisher, stand 6 feet from the flames when spraying. (Also see "Fire Safety.")

2. **Electrical fire**. Unplug the appliance and use a fire extinguisher (chemical/foam, not water-based) to douse flames, or smother the appliance in a heavy blanket or rug. Never throw water on a burning appliance.

3. **Overflowing toilet**. Turn the stop valve clockwise underneath the toilet to shut off water. Bail out half of the water with a cup and bucket. Use a plunger to open a clogged toilet. (Put petroleum jelly on the lip of the plunger, which helps stabilize its position on the drain hole, then place the plunger securely over the bowl's drain hole and pump the plunger up and down.) If plunging doesn't work, try a toilet auger (also called a snake) to

loosen the blockage. Most rental companies rent augers by the hour.

4. **Burst pipe**. Shut off the water supply either at the stop valve (underneath the sink) or at the main shutoff valve, which is usually located in the basement, crawl space or utility room near the water meter. *(Find out where it is before an emergency arises.)* Call a plumber. Turn off the water heater to prevent overheating and cracking. If possible, bind the pipe with a rag or waterproof tape. Keep a bucket under it. Close the doors to the room where the pipe has burst and stuff towels under the door to keep water from running out. If ceiling plaster is bulging, move furniture and carpets away, and place a bucket under the area. Pierce the bulge to let the accumulated water out. This will limit the damage to one area.

5. **Frozen water pipe**. When you turn on a faucet in subfreezing weather, only to get trickling water or none at all, ice has built up inside the pipes. Keep the faucet turned on. (If it's closed, pressure from the thawing water can cause the pipe to expand and burst.) Next, wrap electrical heat tape (sold in hardware stores) around the suspected ice blockage until it thaws and the water is flowing freely once again. You can also apply heat to the frozen pipe with a hair dryer. Never leave a heat appliance unattended or in a closed area. If you suspect a hard freeze could have caused a frozen pipe to crack, turn off the water supply and follow instructions for a burst pipe (see no. 4 above) as the pipe thaws.

6. **Flooded basement**. Never step into standing water in a basement. Even if you can see that there's no danger of electrical shock from cords plugged into outlets, you may forget about a hidden electrical outlet that's now under water. First, have the power company turn off the gas and electricity to your house. Bail out water with buckets or soak it up with a mop or a wet-dry vacuum. For deeper water, rent a submergable electric pump from a rental company, or call a plumber. Place fans in opposite sides of the room to dry it out.

7. **Washing machine hose burst**. Turn off the water faucet connected to the hose behind the washing machine. (Be cautious about any electrical appliances that are standing in water.) Move

Take Note

If the electricity goes out frozen food will last about 48 hours provided you don't open the freezer.

any furniture or rugs that could be damaged, then mop up the water or remove with a wet-dry vacuum. If water has seeped into rooms with carpet, pull the carpet and pad back and dry with a fan. Replace washing machine hose.

8. **Water heater leak**. Shut off water-supply valve to hot water heater. If it doesn't have one, or you can't locate it, turn off the main water supply to your house. Switch off the gas or electricity supply to the water heater, and call a plumber.

9. **Gas leaks**. Extinguish all fires, cigarettes and other open flames and open as many windows as possible. If you smell a strong gas odor, get everyone out of the house immediately. Call the emergency service number of your utility company from a neighbor's house. Cut off the supply of gas to the house by turning off the valve beside the gas meter. If the odor is faint, check pilot lights to see if one has gone out. If so, wait for the gas smell to diminish and relight. If you can't find the source of the odor, call for an emergency service.

10. **No electricity**. Check to see if all the lights in your neighborhood are off. If only your house is without power, turn the main switch at the top of your breaker box off and then back on. (The breaker box, sometimes called a service panel, is usually in the basement or utility room.) If the panel has round glass fuses, pull the handle attached to the main fuse completely out of the panel. You may need to replace old fuses with new ones. Never touch the panel if the floor around it is damp or your hands are wet.

   Shut off and unplug all appliances and electronics; they might draw a rush of electrical current when power is restored and could cause damage to fuses and circuitry. Switch on appliances and lights one at a time.

11. **Loss of heat**. For gas heat, check to see if pilot light is burning. If it's not burning, relight, following manufacturer's directions. For electric heat, check for a blown fuse or tripped circuit breaker. Call a repair person if necessary. To keep in warmth, shut exterior doors and close all curtains and shades, except those that allow direct sunlight in.

Take Note

Never use a candle for light when checking pilot lights. The flame could ignite fumes.

169

12. **Jammed garbage disposal.** Push the reset button on the bottom of the unit. If it still won't work, turn off the power to the unit. Then use a wooden spoon or broom handle to move the blades back and forth to dislodge the object. Never put your hand inside the unit.

13. **No phone line.** Check with neighbors to see if their phones are also out of service. If they're not, and if your home was built after 1982, there may be a diagnostic jack in a box near the location where the phone line comes into your home. Plug a phone into this jack; if you get a dial tone, the problem is inside the house. Check your accessories—cordless phone, answering machine, modem—to see if they are functioning properly. If the phone works without an accessory on the line, the problem probably is in the accessory.

14. **Sink clog.** Bale out water into a bucket. Boil a large pot of water and pour it down the drain. If this fails, position a plunger over the drain and push it down forcefully three times. Repeat if necessary. If the blockage is in the U-bend pipe, place a bucket underneath the bend and unscrew the U-bend. Carefully poke a piece of wire up the pipe until you free it. If this doesn't work, try using a plumber's snake.

Childproofing Your Home

Every year, 4.5 million children are injured in their homes—2 million seriously enough to require medical attention. Supervising your child and taking simple steps to ensure a safer home are the best ways to prevent household accidents.

KITCHEN SAFETY

- Teach your toddler to stay away from the stove at all times. Mark off a zone that he knows is not safe to enter.
- If stove knobs are within a child's reach, use protective covers to prevent turning.
- When cooking, turn pot handles toward the back of the stove and use the back burners whenever possible.

Keep Your Drain Clean and Clear

- **Pour boiling water down the drain on a weekly basis.**

- **Clear your sink drain once a month. Pour ½ cup of baking soda down the drain followed by a cup of vinegar. Let it sit for a few minutes and then run the hot water. This will also help keep the sink from smelling.**

- **Place a strainer over the drain to stop big bits of food from descending into the pipes.**

- **Never, ever pour coffee grounds or grease down the drain.**

- Place a pot or pan over a hot burner until it's cooled down.
- Keep highchairs, chairs and step stools away from counters and the stove.
- Store cookies and treats your child might reach for far away from the stove area.
- Keep your child out of the kitchen when you are frying.
- Install cabinet locks on low cabinets and drawers that contain sharp knives and potentially toxic cleaning products.
- Place kitchen appliances away from the edges of counters. Make sure electrical appliance cords aren't dangling from countertops.
- If possible, stow trash and recyclables in a locked cabinet or closet.
- Keep plastic bags, plastic wrap and foil out of reach. Tie plastic bags in knots before storing or recycling them.
- Use place mats instead of a tablecloth so your child cannot pull the entire contents of the table down on top of himself.
- Set your water heater to 120 degrees F or cooler to prevent scalding from the kitchen faucet.
- Load silverware into the dishwasher with the handles facing up.
- Remove small magnets—potential choking hazards—from your fridge.
- Never hold a hot beverage while carrying your child, no matter how careful you plan to be. Make sure baby-sitters and grandparents know this rule as well.
- Clean up broken glass slivers with a damp, disposable cloth, then vacuum. Mop thoroughly before letting your child back into the kitchen.
- Keep a working fire extinguisher handy.

BATHROOM SAFETY

- Make sure electrical appliances, such as blowdryers, are unplugged, away from water, and out of a child's reach.
- Store hazardous items, such as razors, scissors, and medicines, out of a child's reach, preferably in a locked cabinet.
- Keep the toilet seat down and the door to the bathroom closed or gated. Or, buy hinged toilet lid locks that clamp to the lip of the bowl.

171

- Set your water heater to 120 degrees F or cooler to prevent scalding from the bathroom sink and tub.
- Place a nonskid mat or decals in the bathtub and a nonskid rug on the bathroom floor.
- Toss a small hand towel over the top of a bathroom door when your child is using the restroom so it won't close completely. This way, little ones are less likely to lock themselves in.

LIVING AREAS AND BEDROOM SAFETY

- Secure unstable furniture such as bookshelves, entertainment centers or dressers that could topple if a child pulls on them.
- Install cushioned corners on sharp corners of tables and other furniture with pointed edges.
- Move your TV, DVD/VCR and stereo out of reach.
- Run electrical cords along baseboards, securing them to the floor when possible. Bind up any extra cord. Check regularly to make sure they're not frayed or overloaded.
- Install short cords on phones or secure the cords up high out of reach. Better still, use cordless phones. You eliminate the choking hazard and make yourself mobile, which means you never have to leave young kids unattended to answer the phone.
- Shorten long cords for blinds or draperies. Wrap them around wall brackets, wind them up and tie the cords with a short string, or buy a cord wrap.
- Set up safety gates at the bottom and top of staircases to protect small children.
- Position your child's crib or bed away from windows, drapery and electrical cords. Put night-lights at least 3 feet away from bedding and draperies to prevent fires.
- Keep pocket change and jewelry off the top of your dresser and out of reach.
- Light hallways and staircases to prevent falls.
- If you have older children whose toys have a lot of small pieces, buy organizing boxes with lids that close tightly.
- Use plastic outlet covers to prevent electrical shocks.

- Install a screen or locked glass enclosure on your fireplace. Remove irons and tools. Install screens around radiators, wood-burning stoves and kerosene heaters.
- Cover fireplace hearths with protective cushioning.
- Install smoke detectors on the ceiling outside sleeping or napping areas. Test the alarm monthly and replace batteries twice a year.
- Keep a list of emergency numbers—fire, police, pediatrician, poison control—by the phone.

SAFETY INDOORS

Conduct a room-by-room inventory of potential dangers. If you have younger children, get down on all fours and view each room from their eye level. Make sure all potentially harmful items—cleaning products, perfumes, shoe polish, hair products, makeup, vitamins, mouthwash, medicine, alcoholic beverages, cigarettes, matches and lighters—are out of a child's reach.

- Keep potted houseplants in inaccessible locations; some are poisonous.
- Put childproof covers on all electrical sockets.
- Secure radiator covers and floor vents so a child cannot pull them off.
- Affix decals at a child's eye level to glass doors or windows that extend down to the floor.
- Put slip-proof guards on uncarpeted stairs.
- Use nonslip carpet tape or sticky matting under area rugs to hold them in place.
- Use safety gates on rooms without doors to keep kids from wandering into dangerous areas.
- Install gates at the top and bottom of stairs. Don't use a tension-mounted gate at the top of the stairs. If a child leans on it, it could become dislodged.
- Put covers on doorknobs to rooms you don't want a child to enter. Or install hook-and-eye latches to keep doors closed.
- Make sure you can unlock any door inside your home from the outside in case a child gets locked in a room.
- Consider installing plastic guards along the hinge side of frequently used interior doors to prevent pinched fingers.

Take Note

Never leave a child unattended in a room with a lit candle.

- To prevent choking, remove plastic end caps on doorstops or replace the stops with a one-piece design.
- Attach bells on exit doors to warn you if a child opens one.
- Install latches to prevent windows from opening far enough for a child to slip through.
- Don't place furniture in a way that a child could climb to a window or ledge.

SAFETY OUTDOORS

- Make sure any raised porch or deck has a railing and that the railing isn't wide enough for a child to climb through. If it is, cover the railing with Plexiglas, strong mesh or lattice. Do the same for fences surrounding your property.
- Keep patio furniture away from the railings, so a child cannot climb on them and fall over.
- Check wooden decks regularly for splinters.
- Install a latch on the door leading to your balcony or yard.
- Regularly check swings and other play equipment for rust, loose screws, splintering wood or sharp edges.
- Make sure children's play equipment is securely anchored before use. Test it yourself to detect potentially unsafe structures.
- Put covers on swing chains to avoid caught fingers and torn clothes.
- Put wood chips, sand or mulch under your swing set or play area. The deeper the fill goes, the safer your child will be in case of a fall. Make sure the fill extends out far enough so that if your child is propelled from a swing, he will still land on a softer surface.
- Never take a child for a ride on a garden tractor or riding mower.
- Do not mow the lawn with a child nearby. The blade often kicks up sharp objects.
- Return gardening equipment to a locked shed or an inaccessible part of the garage immediately after its use.
- If your yard is not fenced off from the street, establish a safety zone along the front yard in which your child knows to stay. Buy orange safety cones and teach your child not to go past them.

Take Note

Install a hook-and-eye on the outside of the gate to your yard so you can reach it, but your child can't.

- Keep the play area clean of pet droppings. Keep cats out of the sandbox by covering it when not in use.
- Coil and return the garden hose to its hanger when it is not in use.
- String clotheslines out of your child's reach.
- Make sure wooden fences have rounded, well-sanded posts. See that a chainlink fence has no barbs sticking up.
- Teach your child to stay away from the barbecue grill.
- Get rid of highly poisonous or toxic plants growing in your back or front yard. Call your local Poison Control Center for a list of plants in your area.
- After a rainy period, remove any mushrooms or toadstools since they could be poisonous.
- Store ladders out of reach, or secure them to the wall horizontally, so they will not tempt your child to climb them.
- Keep your car locked to prevent your child from climbing inside, activating the garage door opener or knocking the car out of gear.

Crime Prevention

According to Bureau of Justice Statistics, there were more than 2.7 million household burglaries in the year 2001—not a statistic to take lightly. Your home is a precious commodity. Take the time to safeguard its contents.

THIRTY-ONE WAYS TO CRIMEPROOF YOUR HOME

1. Replace hollow entryway doors with solid ones made of fiberglass, wood or steel.
2. Install dead-bolt locks, either the single-cylinder type, which turns with a key on the outside and a lever on the inside, or the double-cylinder type, which requires keys on both sides. The double-cylinder locks are best if a door contains glass. A burglar may break the glass, but he won't be able to turn the dead bolt without a key.
3. Lock all doors and windows every night and whenever you leave your home. Most burglaries occur during workday hours.
4. Make sure your door's hinges are on the inside. Pins in hinges on the outside are easy for a thief to remove with a screwdriver.

175

5. Install a security system that includes sensors on all doors, motion sensors in the master bedroom and living room, and a loud siren.

6. Advertise your alarm by displaying security system decals on doors and windows.

7. If you don't have a security system, try battery-operated units with motion detectors and alarms. These can hang from doorknobs or sit on tables.

8. Make sure your doors have peepholes, and use them before opening your home to a stranger.

9. If a stranger knocks and asks to speak with you, ask him to show ID before you open the door.

10. Don't hide a key in the usual places—for example, under the doormat, on top of the door frame, in the mailbox, in a flower pot. Give a copy to a nearby neighbor or relative instead.

11. Case your own house for burglary: what unprotected entry points do you see?

12. Better yet, call in the experts. Many police departments provide free security inspections for area residents.

13. Mark your possessions. Engrave valuable items with your Social Security or driver's license number, or get a personal Operation ID number. Operation ID is a nationally sponsored program that makes personal property identifiable in the event of a burglary. Your local police department should know where you can sign up for this service.

14. Get together with a few neighbors and create a Neighborhood Watch program. Don't overlook residents in apartments and condos. They need security, too.

15. Keep trees and shrubs trimmed so your yard is easily visible to neighbors and hard to hide in for thieves. Be on the lookout for easy access to the second floor from tall trees close to windows.

16. Plant bushes with thorns under your windows.

17. If someone asks to use your telephone, make the call for him or her rather than letting a stranger into your home.

18. Make sure your doors and main floor and basement windows are lit well. Consider using motion detector lights or lights that come on automatically when it's dark.

19. Make sure windows have locks.

20. Lock your garage door and keep it that way.

21. Don't leave major appliance or electronic boxes on the curb after a purchase. These alert thieves to your latest buys. Break down the boxes and tie them so the wording doesn't show on the outside. If possible, dispose of them at a nearby dump.

22. Keep an eye on appliance repairmen and cleaning people when they are in your home.

23. If you have sliding glass doors, install bolt locks on them.

24. Don't put your home address on luggage; use a business address.

25. Call the police if you notice any suspicious cars or persons in your neighborhood.

26. Lock up ladders and tools burglars may use to break into your home.

27. Display a "Beware of Dog" sign whether you have a dog or not.

28. Leave curtains open a little; a closed-up house signals it's empty.

29. Teach your kids not to tell strangers their parents aren't home; they should say you're busy instead.

30. Close curtains at night.

31. Don't put your address on your key chain.

DON'T LEAVE HOME WITHOUT . . .

Take the following precautions before leaving town:

- Have the post office hold your mail when you're away; don't let a bulging mailbox signal your absence.
- Ditto for the daily news. Stop delivery of newspapers when you're away, or ask someone to pick them up for you.
- A neighbor or friend might also be willing to pick up any packages that are delivered when you're away.
- Hire a teenager to mow the lawn or shovel the snow if necessary.
- Before you leave on vacation, put your TV, lights and/or stereo on

Take Note

If you come home and notice that your house has been broken into and burglarized, leave immediately. Call the police on a cell phone or from a neighbor's house. Once the police arrive, you can go into the house and begin to take inventory of what is missing. Call your insurance company when you have a complete list of what has been stolen.

177

timers. Set them to go on and off at different times, just as they would if you were home.

■ Leave a car in your driveway when you're away. Let a friend use the car, or move it occasionally, to make it look like you're home.

FILMING A HOUSEHOLD INVENTORY

To determine the replacement value of your home, insurance agents recommend creating a videotape inventory of your possessions—room by room—so any claim for theft, fire or flooding is readily backed up with visual documentation. Include all items you own—for example, furniture, electronics, jewelry, clothing. When in doubt, film it.

■ Open all your closets, cupboards and drawers, and don't be shy about pointing out special features or the value of certain items. Include all those possessions in the basement, attic, storeroom or laundry area. Take focused close-ups of smaller items for better identification. Also, film the outside of your home; include the landscaping, decks, tool sheds and outdoor furniture.

■ Keep receipts or other written proof of the value of items in your home, in addition to the videotape. Use the checklist below for the written descriptions, including all the relevant information about the item.

■ Consider having expensive items—jewelry, furs, collections, silverware—appraised so you'll have written proof of their value.

■ Record serial numbers of theft-prone items whenever possible. Engrave your driver's license number on items that don't have serial numbers for an increased chance of recovery.

■ Never consider a home inventory complete. Every time you buy something, film it, file the receipt and add it to the inventory.

■ Store copies of this invaluable inventory in a safe-deposit box, with an insurance agent or at the home of a close friend.

HOUSEHOLD INVENTORY CHECKLIST

Use a household inventory checklist as a master guide to what you should record.

LIVING AREA

What I Own	Age	What It's Worth	Description/Identification Information
Carpeting, Rugs			
Couch			
Chairs			
Tables			
Cabinets/Contents			
Books/Shelves			
Window Treatments			
Lamps			
Television/VCR			
DVD Player			
Home Stereo Equipment			
Computer			
Artwork			
Collectables			
Other			

KITCHEN AND UTILITY ROOM

What I Own	Age	What It's Worth	Description/Identification Information
Table and Chairs			
Refrigerator			
Stove			
China/Silverware			
Pots and Pans			
Small Appliances			
Microwave Oven			
Dishwasher			
Deep Freezer and Contents			
Washer/Dryer			
Vacuum Cleaner			
Sewing Machine			
Other			

BEDROOMS

What I Own	Age	What It's Worth	Description/Identification Information
Carpeting, Rugs			
Beds/Mattresses			
Linens			
Chests			
Tables			
Chairs			
Desk and Contents			
Window Treatments			
Radios/Stereos/TVs			
Lamps			
Chairs			
Mirrors/Décor			
Personal Items			
Other			

STORAGE CLOSETS AND GARAGE

What I Own	Age	What It's Worth	Description/Identification Information
Extra Furniture			
Luggage			
Photo Equipment			
Sports Equipment			
Hobby Materials			
Power Tools			
Hand Tools			
Camping Gear			
Fishing Tackle			
Guns			
Lawn Mower			
Garden Tools			
Lawn Furniture			
Bicycles			
Other			

HOME OFFICE

What I Own	Age	What It's Worth	Description/Identification Information
Computer Equipment			
Printer/Copier			
Fax			
Communications Equipment			
Furniture			
Office Supplies			
Other Equipment			
Filing Cabinet/Contents			
Other			

Fire Safety

According to the National Safety Council more than 500,000 residential fires occur annually in the United States. Cooking is the number-one cause of home fires. Most fatal home fires occur between 10 P.M. and 6 A.M. The major killer is smoke inhalation, not flames. Here are some wise ways to avoid fire danger at your house.

- Clean your dryer's lint filter after every use and remove accumulated lint from around the drum. Always turn the dryer off when you leave home.
- Replace outlets and light switches that feel warm to the touch.
- Don't use more than one extension cord per outlet, and never run extension cords under rugs or carpet.
- Store flammable chemicals, including machines with gas tanks, in outbuildings or garage, and never inside the house.
- Dispose of oil- or solvent-soaked rags safely to avoid spontaneous combustion. Never wad them while they are wet; hang or spread them to dry thoroughly, allowing combustible elements to dissipate, then dispose of them. Consult local waste-management authorities for requirements for disposal of toxic materials. Don't dry or dispose of them near material that can ignite. Never use gasoline as a cleaning agent.
- Do not leave stovetop burners unattended. When preparing slow-cook foods, set a timer for 20- to 30-minute intervals to remind you to check the stove. Always turn off burners when you leave the house, even for a short time.
- Wear short or close-fitting sleeves when cooking. Loose clothing can catch fire.
- Keep the oven door shut and turn off the heat to smother an oven or broiler fire.
- Establish escape routes so that everyone in your home knows how to leave quickly in an emergency. Assign a meeting place outside the home. Practice using the routes.

- Install fire escape ladders in second-floor bedrooms; check existing ladders regularly for safety. Practice using the ladders, dropping to the ground and going to the assigned meeting place.

- Have an A-B-C fire extinguisher on each level of your house, plus in the kitchen and garage. Keep them fully charged and teach family members how to use them.

- Only use candles in sturdy holders that won't tip over. Don't assume candles in glass holders are safe; the glass might break. Keep candles away from items that can catch fire, like clothing, paper, books and curtains.

- Always use safety screens in front of fireplaces.

- Maintain your fireplace and furnace chimneys, flues and vents. Schedule annual professional inspections, cleaning and repair.

- If you use live Christmas trees, assign someone to check and water it daily. Position a tree at least 3 feet away from a heat source. Always unplug lights before leaving home or going to bed.

Smoke Alarms

- Install at least one alarm on each level of your home, using battery-operated or battery-backup alarms that detect both smoke and heat even when the power goes out. Ideally, place one in each bedroom and hallway.

- Mount alarms on the ceiling, away from corners and ductwork.

- Test alarms every six months by holding a blown-out, smoking candle near the alarm.

- Do *not* mount smoke alarms or fire detectors anywhere that smoke is routine—for example, in the kitchen, bathroom, utility room, workshop or garage. It might set off the system unnecessarily.

CHAPTER 8

You're the Chauffeur

According to the Nationwide Personal Transportation Survey, a mom drives an average of 32.14 miles a day. When my children were young, there were many afternoons when I clocked more than 100 miles driving them to various activities on opposite ends of town. Some days my hands felt permanently affixed to the steering wheel!

As the head chauffeur at your house, you'll want to do everything you can to make the many miles you drive as merry as possible. This starts with taking care of your car. Experts say it's possible to actually double the life of your car by sticking to a regular maintenance plan. In this chapter, you'll learn how to save time, stay safe on the road and keep your car running trouble-free so you can get your family where they need to be.

The Ten Car Care Commandments

1. Change your oil and filter every three months or 3,000 miles. (When you change the oil, make sure the radiator and coolant tanks are full, too.)

2. Regularly check tire pressure when tires are cool—for example, in the morning or before a long trip. Check your car's owner manual for the correct pressure.

3. Don't overload your car. This has the same effect as driving on underinflated tires. Both cause excess wear and may lead to a flat. ("Peeling out" also hurts tires, potentially erasing hundreds of miles from their tread life.)

4. Have your tires balanced and rotated about every six months or 6,000 miles.

5. Have engine hoses and belts checked and adjusted periodically. Replace them as needed.

6. If a belt squeaks when starting your car, get it adjusted as soon as possible. A broken belt can lead to further damage and a lot of inconvenience.

7. Have your coolant (antifreeze) checked before summer heat and winter cold.

8. Tune up your car according to the recommendations in your car's owner manual.

9. Never drive when your car is overheated.

10. Find a reliable mechanic you can trust. Having the same technician get to know you and your car can prevent a lot of expensive problems.

Automobile Warning Signs You Shouldn't Ignore

Be alert to the onset of any of the following and report them to a mechanic as soon as possible:

- Difficulty starting
- Unusual vibrations
- Brake-pedal softness or hardness; brake noise
- Unfamiliar engine noise
- Engine roughness and loss of power
- Stalling at traffic lights
- Steering-wheel pulls to the left or right while driving
- Uneven tire wear
- A ride that is noticeably less comfortable

Good Clean Habits

- Keep moist towelettes in the car to clean up spills and remove gunk from sticky fingers.

- At the end of the day, remove everything from the car that was added during each trip.

- Stow a plastic grocery bag in the door of your car to collect trash as it is generated. At the end of each day, empty the trash bag in a garbage can you keep in the garage near your car.

- Get in the habit of picking up trash and emptying the ashtray every time you fill your car with gasoline.

- Wash your car out of direct sunlight so the soap won't dry too quickly and spot the finish.

187

- Clutch chatter or slipping
- Exhaust-system roar; rust holes in the muffler
- Horn failure
- A gauge that shows an abnormal reading
- Fluid leakage on the pavement beneath a parked car
- The smell of gasoline or the visibility of thin, watery spots (be very careful; gas leaks are the leading cause of car fires)

Car Cash Savers

- You may not need to buy higher-octane gas. Use the lowest-octane gas that does not cause your engine to knock when you accelerate.
- Fill up before the light comes on. Make it a habit to fill up when the tank is half empty. It is safer and allows you to stop when you are passing a station with the best price. Buy gas in the morning. Because the warmth of the sun expands the gas in a station's fuel tank, you'll get as much as 5 percent more fuel for your money by purchasing it early.
- Avoid the urge to top off your fuel tank. Gas can expand in your tank and overflow.
- Keep it light. Don't drag around extra weight in your trunk, and if you have a detachable roof rack, remove it if you're not using it. Your car will use fuel more efficiently.
- Keep your tires filled properly. As much as 2 percent of your fuel can be wasted if your tires are not fully inflated.
- Avoid long periods of idling. Restarting actually uses less fuel than idling for more than a minute.
- Change your air filter regularly. Gas mileage sinks when the filter is dirty.
- Save as much as 17 percent of your fuel by driving 55 mph instead of 65.

Outsourcing: How to Find a Good Mechanic

Ask friends or neighbors for recommendations of a good car-repair facility. Don't rely on coupons to find a good mechanic. Just because a place is offering a discount doesn't mean it will best serve your needs.

- When choosing a shop, look for a neat, well-organized facility with cars in the parking lot equal in value to your own. There should be a courteous, helpful staff as well. Look for any evidence of training. Some shops will post certificates on the walls. Don't be afraid to ask the shop for names of a few customers—and call them for references.

- Before you take your car to a mechanic, read your warranty. Find out what's covered and for how long. Some parts are covered past the average three-year or 36,000-mile warranty.

- Clean your car before you take it in. When you show you care about your own vehicle, there's a good chance the mechanics will care more about it, too.

- Don't try to fake advanced knowledge of engine repair. But do know the basics. The best way to start is to read the owner's manual.

- Once you choose a repair shop, start off with a minor job. If you're pleased, then trust them with more complicated repairs later.

- If you are not pleased with the service you received at a shop, don't just rush to another one. Instead, discuss the problem with the manager or owner, and give the business a chance to solve the problem. Reputable shops value customer feedback.

Tips from the Pros: Help Your Car Keep Its Cool

According to experts, when the mercury rises, a car's interior temperature can easily hit the 200-degree-F mark. Here's how to beat the heat:

- Apply a solution with ultraviolet-ray protection to your vinyl dashboard and doors (available at auto supply stores). These surfaces are vulnerable to sun damage; this step may save maintenance costs later.

- Turn off the air conditioner when you're stuck in traffic. If your car idles for a prolonged period, and your engine temperature gauge

189

Take Note

It's usually more expensive to buy tires at a service station or car dealership. Specialty tire outlets usually have better prices for popular name brands.

continues to rise, turn on the heater. It will act as a little radiator that will increase the circulation of the engine's coolant.

- Pay close attention to the condition of your battery. Note that warm weather decreases its life span.

Don't Drive Me Crazy!

THIRTY-ONE TIPS FOR DE-STRESSING DRIVE TIME

1. Whether it's a trip to the grocery store or the mall, create a list before you leave home. Write down the items you need and the stores you plan to visit.

2. Do your business with stores, banks, cleaners and gas stations that are close together so you can make a faster trip with fewer stops.

3. Think of ways you can cut back on repeated errands. Unless it's an emergency, don't take only one item to the dry cleaners. Wait until you have two or more. Accumulate several reasons to visit the pharmacy or discount store.

4. Avoid doing things at times when everyone else tends to do them. Don't go to the bank at lunchtime, on Fridays or the day before a holiday. Go out to lunch a half hour before or after the general population. Go to movies on a weeknight or early on weekends.

5. Consolidate errands. On your way to mail a package, drop off videos or film to be processed. When you're at the post office, stock up on stamps.

6. Call before you make a trip to see if a store has a certain item, if a plane is leaving or arriving on time, if a friend is home before you drop by and if your doctor, dentist or beautician is running on time.

7. Avoid zigzagging around town. Plan an efficient route for running your errands in the least amount of time.

8. Keep an envelope in your car for receipts or stubs needed for picking up items such as dry-cleaning, photos or shoes being repaired.

9. Squeeze in errands at odd times. Pick up toiletries on your lunch hour. If an evening meeting or dinner party for which you've booked a sitter ends early, get your grocery shopping done too.

10. Reduce car chaos with car-organizing products such as CD or tape holders, trash containers, over-the-seat organizers and a Tempo Car Case for your visor.

11. Consider your children's schedule. Avoid running errands or shopping when they are hungry or overly tired.

12. Always have your kids go to the bathroom before you leave home.

13. Always plan time for rush-hour traffic, busy salespeople and the inability to find what you want.

14. Give yourself some extra time. Set your wristwatch, house and car clocks five to ten minutes fast. If you still chronically run late, try adding an extra 20 percent time margin to your scheduled activities.

15. Have a plastic basket in the backseat of the car to keep small packages together so you can transport them easily into the house.

16. Store a cooler in the trunk of your car. You can stop for groceries without having to go straight home.

17. Keep a wastebasket in your garage so car debris can be easily dumped. Make a rule that every time anyone gets out of the car, he or she takes all trash along.

18. Explain to your children the errands planned and establish what your expectations are—for example, "We need to stop at the fabric store and the office-supply store. Please stay with me and remember not to touch." Praise your child for cooperative behavior.

19. Turn errand time into a fun game. Count the number of buses, police cars or traffic lights you pass. Listen to audiobooks or sing-along music.

20. Keep a canvas tote bag in your car. Make a rule that whenever kids take off their shoes or socks, which they always seem to do, they put them in the bag. When you reach your destination you won't have to scramble for the missing shoe or sock that slipped between the crack in the backseat.

21. Keep your doors locked at all times while driving. Carry an extra key to your car in your purse.

22. Keep a stackable plastic shoe box for each child in your car. When eating, kids can set these in their laps to hold their food. It helps them balance their meal, and, if something should overturn, the

191

Take Note

Never leave a child or pet in a parked car, even for a minute. The end result could be fatal.

mess will be contained in the shoe box. Keep towel wipes or a roll of paper towels in your car for kids to use as a bib. Then, after eating, use it to wipe out the containers.

23. Arrange with another mom for once-a-week, kid-free errand time. Each mom gets a couple of hours to tackle tasks while the other mom watches all the kids.

24. Keep several self-closing plastic bags of various sizes in your car. They come in handy for wet bathing suits, dirty diapers, souvenir rocks and the like.

25. Always keep a small amount of nonperishable food, such as dried fruit or crackers, juice boxes and bottled water, in your car in case you're out longer than you anticipate.

26. Use a cosmetic bag to create a small emergency medical kit for your car. Keep a sampling of pain relievers, Band-Aids, antibacterial ointment and antacids.

27. Have plenty of change for tolls, parking meters and vending machines. Keep important phone numbers and insurance and personal information in your car in case of emergency.

28. Make the most of time spent waiting in the car:

   • Organize your glove compartment.
   • Dust your dashboard and console and wipe off rearview and side-view mirrors.
   • Gather coins that have fallen between the seats.
   • Read magazine articles you cut out beforehand, put in a self-sealing bag and store in the door-well of your car.
   • For kids, a cake pan with a sliding or snapping metal lid doubles as a storage box and lap desk in the car. Let kids pack it with small toys and art supplies.

29. Prevent squabbling in the car by planning ahead. Change seating arrangements on the first and fifteenth of every month so the kids won't argue over who sits where.

30. Keep a pair of sunglasses in the car for each child. Bright sunshine can cause headaches and short emotional fuses.

31. Plan to make your last errand the bakery or place where your child can buy a small treat. Be sure to have towel wipes on hand for quick cleanup.

Driving Emergencies

HOW TO BE READY FOR A DRIVING EMERGENCY

- Carry your cell phone with you whenever you're in the car.
- Join an organization that provides roadside assistance and keep the membership card and phone number in your glove compartment.
- Move your car as far away from traffic as possible. Turn on your emergency flasher lights.
- To signal for help, tie a white cloth to your antenna or hang it out a window.
- If you have to stop on the side of a highway, exit the car from the passenger side.
- Never leave children alone in the car while you go searching for help.
- Regardless of the kind of emergency, your first concern is for your own safety and that of your passengers.

WINTER WEATHER DRIVING

- Plan extra time for a trip in winter. A trip that might take thirty minutes in May could take forty-five minutes or an hour in the winter.
- Keep these items in your car: a blanket, a small shovel to dig out snow, sand to help get traction if needed, a flashlight, a first-aid kit, jumper cables, an ice scraper/brush and a lock de-icer.
- Before going on a road trip, check the antifreeze. See that wipers are in good shape to handle snow and ice. (Always remove them from frozen glass before turning them on.)
- Be ready for changing conditions. Make sure you have good all-season tires that can handle different types of weather. Check with your auto mechanic or a professional at a tire store to discuss your options.

Bright Idea

Keep a duffle bag in your car packed with items you might need in a pinch, such as a towel, rain poncho, change of clothes for a child, rope for tying down large purchases and a small bag of toiletries (toothbrush and toothpaste, feminine products and so on).

193

Hope for the best, prepare for the worst.
—*Anonymous*

- Know how to react to trouble. If you have antilock brakes don't pump them. Instead, press them down as hard as you can. If you start to skid, turn the steering wheel in the direction you want the front of the car to go; that will keep the vehicle from skidding out of control. Then prepare to counter steer two or three times.

- Leave space between cars. Follow the three-second rule. After the vehicle in front of you passes a stationary object, you should be able to count for three seconds before your vehicle passes the same object. Add one more second for each hazardous driving condition you encounter.

WHAT TO DO IF YOU ARE INVOLVED IN A CAR ACCIDENT

According to the National Safety Council, one in every eight drivers will be involved in a motor vehicle crash this year. It's important to know what to do and which questions to ask. Since most people are reasonably upset after an accident, the National Safety Council offers this list of eleven easy steps to remember. You might also keep this information in your glove compartment in case of a fender-bender.

1. Stop your vehicle if it is clear, safe and legal.
2. Move the vehicle out of the traveled roadway, if it is clear, safe and legal. (In some states it is against the law to move the vehicle from the place where the crash occurred. Know the ordinance in your area.)
3. Turn off the ignition of your car.
4. Make a first-aid check of all persons involved in the crash.
5. Call the police and, if necessary, emergency medical services.
6. Mark the scene of the crash with reflective triangles.
7. Gather the names of all persons in the motor vehicles and people who witnessed the crash.
8. Make a quick diagram of where the vehicle occupants were seated and indicate the vehicle's direction of travel and lane. Also note the date, time and weather conditions.

9. Ask to see the other driver's license and write down the number.

10. Exchange insurance company information. Do not discuss "fault" or make statements about the crash to anyone but the police.

11. Get a copy of the police report of the crash from the local precinct.

As the family chauffeur, you've got a lot to think about. But most important, you're in charge of carrying precious cargo. The time, effort and resources it takes to do your job well are of inestimable value. The next time you're rushing to pick up your daughter from soccer practice or fighting traffic to get your son to a birthday party on time, keep in mind that you're doing important stuff—so slow down and enjoy the trip!

Roadside Emergency Supplies

Remember the Family Manager motto, Be prepared. Keep the following items in your car:

- First-aid kit
- Aerosol tire inflator
- Roadside reflector triangles or flares (two or three)
- Flashlight (with extra batteries or auto-charger kit; check batteries every few months)
- Bottled water for drinking
- A gallon of water for the engine
- Rain poncho and umbrella
- Wet wipes
- Small fire extinguisher
- Nonperishable food (packs of dried fruit or protein bars, for instance)

PART II

Taking Charge of Meals and Entertaining

In our home, food has always involved a bit of humor; when I cook, antacids are always the first course at our dinner table. Julia Child I'm not. But kidding aside, overseeing the food and nutritional needs of a family—whether we consider cooking among our stronger or weaker points—is an enormous task. It requires thinking about, shopping for and preparing three meals per day, not to mention snacks, special-occasion dinners and impromptu get-togethers. It involves how we buy food and cook it, who does it and on what schedule. Then there are considerations about where we eat, with whom and what goes on at meal-times.

I've learned through trial and error that if you effectively manage food, your entire day runs more smoothly.

To eat is human; to digest, divine.
—*Charles Townsend Copeland*

You eliminate time-robbing, last-minute trips to the store and you save money by cutting back on fast-food outlets when you need food in a hurry. The transition from afternoon to evening is less stressful because there's a thought-through plan for dinner and you have the food and ingredients on hand. When old friends drop in, you don't panic, you simply shift into guest mode, pull out the hors d'oeuvres (kept hidden from your kids for times such as this) and enjoy the unexpected company.

Developing a good strategy for handling meals and entertaining is a worthwhile endeavor. It will get you in and out of the kitchen faster, which is good news for those of us who hate spending time in front of the stove, and ever for those of us who don't. Fortunately, it's not necessary to be a gourmet cook to adequately feed and nourish your family. No CEO worth his or her salt ever claimed to do all things equally well. For me, *teamwork* has solved many of my kitchen challenges. I felt indescribably free when I decided it doesn't make me less of a woman, mother or Family Manager to allow someone else—often my husband, who is infinitely more talented and comfortable in the kitchen than I am—to cook sometimes. And I hope the girls who marry our boys appreciate the fact that they know their way around a kitchen!

So whether you regularly "kick it up a notch" a la Emeril Lagasse, or open jars and boil pasta like me, this chapter has hundreds of ideas to remove the madness from your mealtimes. These tips are entirely trustworthy because everything I know I learned from an expert, longtime friend, author and cook extraordinaire Judie Byrd. She's taught thousands of women, from gourmet cooks to the culinary challenged like me, quick and easy ways to get great food on the table. Judie makes this potentially overwhelming task definitely doable.

Come and tackle this more-than-manageable department. Bon appetit!

CHAPTER 9

You're the Menu Planner

Keep in mind that you manage no less than 1,095 meals per year for your family—and this doesn't include snacks and parties! Since coming up with that many different menus will tax the brain of even the most creative person, it's a good idea to have at least a simple plan.

Dealing with the What's-for-Dinner? Issue

1. **Get the whole family involved in menu planning.** Schedule a brainstorming meeting. Remind everybody of the basic ground rules of brainstorming before you start.

- There are no stupid or wrong ideas. Every food mentioned goes on the list.
- No commenting on another person's suggestions. No "groans" when meatloaf is mentioned, for example.
- As with any other meeting, only one person talks at a time.

Get some paper and a pencil to take notes, then have everybody call out his or her favorite foods, what they'd like to eat that you haven't fixed for a while and maybe something you've never served but a child had at a friend's house. You can organize the brainstorming list as you go by meal—breakfast, lunch, dinner—or by category—fruit, vegetable and so on. Or you can simply list everything and organize the foods into reasonable menus later.

2. **Write a family menu of various meal choices.** Every Sunday night, let each family member "order" the meal for one night that week. Post the resulting weekly menu on the refrigerator door. The first parent home knows what to start for dinner. If you have a motivated teenager in the house, try to enlist his or her help on dinnertime prep as well. This works especially well if your teen likes what's on the menu for that particular night.

3. **Develop a repertoire of five meals you can prepare in less than thirty minutes.** Always keep the ingredients on hand. For example, keep a jar of prepared spaghetti sauce in the pantry and one pound of Italian sausage in the freezer for a quick dinner. Sauté 1-inch slices of sausage, add the jar of sauce and simmer for ten minutes. Tastes like homemade! Serve over pasta. Have on hand a couple of kinds of cheese, like Cheddar or Monterey Jack, plus flour tortillas and elbow macaroni. Then you can make two other fast meals: cheese quesadillas (garnish with chopped lettuce, diced tomato, bottled salsa and sour cream) and quickie macaroni and cheese. Boil the noodles while you grate cheese, then drain the noodles, sprinkle cheese over the top and microwave briefly.

4. **Try an alternating cooking arrangement.** Your husband cooks on Mondays and Wednesdays; you cook on Tuesdays and Thursdays; eat out or order pizza on Fridays; and be flexible about Saturdays and Sundays. If you have teenagers, they can take part in the schedule as well.

5. **Have "Planned-Overs."** Whenever possible, double or triple a recipe and freeze the leftovers for a quick meal on a busy night. Do this regularly and you'll find you spend a lot less time cooking. Leftovers from one night's roast chicken can be turned into chicken potpie, tacos, stir fry, salad or sandwiches on another night. Make enough pasta one night that you'll have extras for another evening. Serve with tomato sauce one night, then toss with

sautéed garlic, juice of one lemon and a can of undrained chopped clams for another night.

6. **Create three weeks' worth of dinner menus.** Unless you have a lot of extra time to kill, keep them simple. After three weeks, recycle your hard work by reusing the weekly menus again and again. You don't have to have roast chicken every third Thursday. Have it on Monday in the fourth week instead. This basic meal plan can carry you throughout a year, making allowances and changes for seasons—what fresh fruits and vegetables are available and what foods your family especially likes to eat at various times of the year—without anybody ever even figuring out you're eating the same basic foods in a rotating schedule. It also simplifies grocery shopping!

7. **If you're not a great cook, develop recipes you're comfortable with** Prepare one week of different breakfast menus; and two weeks of different lunch menus; three weeks of different dinner menus; and two or three simple company menus. You'll never find yourself without ideas again.

8. **Consider inviting two or three women to a menu-planning party.** Choose women who struggle for ideas the way you do, or who like to "talk food" and always seem to have lots of ideas. Depending on you and your friends, this could be a more "visionary" meeting, talking about how you each plan menus and look at food. You'd all come away with strategies to apply. Or it could be a more nitty-gritty meeting in which you share menu plans and recipes, and talk about specific problems, like nine year olds and vegetables or teenagers and junk food.

9. **Don't feel like you have to reinvent the wheel every week.** Some of the best family traditions revolve around food. Start your own! Maybe Dad grills hamburgers every Saturday night. Maybe Sunday night is always breakfast-for-dinner night. Maybe Tuesday is pasta night.

10. **Start a dinner co-op.** You cook dinner for everyone in the co-op one day a week and deliver it. In return, dinner is delivered to your door four days a week. Find four other moms who have similar family sizes, cooking abilities and lifestyles. (If your family tries to

The most remarkable thing about my mother is that for thirty years she served the family nothing by leftovers. The original meal has never been found.

—Calvin Trillin

Bright Idea

It's all too easy to develop a recipe drawer, a catchall that is hard to use because it's so messy. There's a better way. Put your clipped and jotted recipes into a photo album—any type that you can add pages to. Use tabs to divide into sections, and place recipes accordingly. They'll be right at your fingertips, and the plastic will keep them smudge-free.

Dining is and always was a great artistic opportunity.
—Frank Lloyd Wright

eat low fat, you wouldn't want to be in a co-op with families who serve primarily high-fat foods.) Arrange a time to meet to talk about food preferences, food allergies, cooking days, menus, delivery times and so on. Next, purchase sealable, microwavable, dishwasher-safe container sets. Each set should include an entree container, two side dishes and a salad bowl. Each family needs to purchase four complete sets.

11. **Team up with a coworker.** You both cook double portions of what you're fixing for dinner on Monday and Wednesday nights, then take the extra portion in a cooler to the office the following day. You both get Tuesday and Thursday nights off from cooking. Again, this works best if you and your colleague have similar family sizes, tastes and nutritional preferences. It also means you need to have a refrigerator at work to store the food in during the day.

12. **Have a basic repertoire of five main courses that you can vary by switching around seasonings.** For instance, one week you might sauce boneless chicken breasts with crushed tomatoes, grated mozzarella and grated Parmesan; another week you might season it with white wine, lemon juice and thyme; and a third week you might brush it with a mixture of Dijon mustard and honey. An Italian bread crust could be topped one night with goat cheese, chopped black olives, canned artichokes and chopped fresh herbs; the next week topped with caramelized onions; and a third week, topped with cubes of leftover chicken, Fontina cheese, grape tomatoes and fresh mint.

13. **Think outside the box when planning your menus.** If your family loves breakfast, you may want to consider having omelets, quiche or even pancakes and bacon occasionally in the evening. Likewise, if they are partial to pizza and you have leftovers, serve it for breakfast.

FEEDING FINICKY EATERS

I know a mom who, from the time her kids turned three, made sure they ate only fresh fruits and vegetables after 4 P.M. I wish I had learned how to do that! I had to find sneaky ways to get my kids to eat most vegeta-

Schedule a Cooking Day

I'm a great planner, but execution is my weak point. So when it comes to cooking, my husband, Bill, and I work together. Once every month or two, we have a cooking day. We decide on what we're going to cook, then I go to the grocery store and gather all the ingredients. At home, I place everything out on the counter along with the recipe books, the right pots and pans, and utensils. I give Bill his apron, put on some music and, as the sous-chef, wait for him to tell me what he wants me to do. In one big pot we might stew chicken breasts for making chicken enchiladas, chicken spaghetti, chicken divan and chicken noodle soup. In another big pot we might brown lean ground beef for chili, sloppy Joes and meatballs. We put up six or eight meals in the freezer. Then we both clean up.

Not only do we have all those meals prepared ahead of time, but we've spent a leisurely day together. While we're chopping, sautéing, simmering and roasting, we talk about current events, vacation dreams, the kids and a number of other topics we might not have time to cover in the hurry of our usual schedules. Bill enjoys doing something with me, and I don't have to cook. It's a win-win solution.

bles. If you have a fussy eater (or two or three), here are some ideas for getting those nutritious foods in:

1. Make macaroni and cheese using shells. First, cook the shells and rinse with cold water. Hide a green pea in the middle of some of the shells. Gently fold into cheese sauce. Your kids will never know!

2. Let your kids sprinkle cinnamon and sugar on cooked carrots or sweet potatoes.

3. Make your own healthy version of pizza. Buy crust mix or flat bread and add tomato sauce, lean ham or turkey sausage, cheese and your favorite cut-up vegetables. Make it a family adventure to build your pizzas together.

4. Make a meal from baked potatoes and an offering of various toppings: cheese, butter and chopped vegetables.

5. Add finely chopped, cooked broccoli to a grilled cheese sandwich.

6. Ask your child to try peas from pods she opens herself. She might love 'em!

7. Add brown sugar, maple syrup or orange juice to cooking carrots.

8. Buy plastic holders to make eating corn on the cob fun.

9. Make Green Bean Packages. Lay about six long, cooked green beans together. Sprinkle with brown sugar. Tie together using a piece of bacon that has been cut in half lengthwise. Place a bundles in a shallow pan; add ½ cup water and bake at 350 degrees F for ten minutes or until warm.

10. Wrap vegetables in biscuit dough. Bake and serve.

11. Offer a variety of vegetables with ranch dip. Some kids will eat almost any vegetable dipped in ranch dressing or some other favorite dip. For added fun, color the ranch dip with food coloring.

12. Make Cheesy Potato Boats. Bake medium-size potatoes until soft. Slice each potato in half lengthwise, and scoop the pulp into a bowl. Save the shells. Add 4 tablespoons of butter, 4 tablespoons of nonfat sour cream, ¼ cup grated cheddar cheese and 1 teaspoon salt. Mix well, pile back into the shells and bake ten minutes or until very hot. Make paper sails and stick in the potatoes with toothpicks.

13. Add cooked, pureed vegetables to your meatloaf in place of other liquid. Use tomatoes, squash, turnips and other mild-flavored vegetables. Add shredded vegetables such as carrot or zucchini to ground beef and make into patties for burgers.

14. Create friendly names for foods—for example, broccoli trees, bunny salads, mashed potato sand castles.

15. Let your child choose the vegetables he wants to add to homemade soups.

16. For kids over age four, try frozen green peas for a TV-time snack.

17. Fix a shish-kebab meal by arranging bite-size pieces of meat and cut-up vegetables on skewers.

18. Add steamed and pureed turnips to mashed potatoes. Kids usually love mashed potatoes, and turnips are mild enough in flavor that they cannot be detected. You can also add pureed cauliflower.

19. Shred carrots and stir into Jell-O.

20. Add shredded zucchini or carrots to potato-pancake batter.

21. Even kids who don't like spinach will like warm spinach dip. Use the recipe on a package of Knorr Vegetable Soup mix.

In general my children refused to eat anything that hadn't danced on TV.
—*Erma Bombeck*

22. Add extra sautéed onions, bell peppers and tomatoes to chili—homemade or canned. Chop them very fine.

23. Add steamed and pureed carrots and tomatoes to pizza sauce.

24. Add finely chopped and cooked tomatoes and bell peppers to ground beef. Season with taco seasoning. Serve on taco shells or hamburger buns.

25. Place carrot strips in pickle juice for two days in refrigerator. Yum!

26. Buy pasta made from vegetables, such as spinach or carrots.

27. Artichokes are so much fun to eat when each family member gets his or her own along with a little bowl of lemon butter. Snip off the leaf points and cut off the top and stem. Put whole artichokes in a large pot and cover with water. Simmer for about twenty-five minutes, until you can pull the leaves out easily and the artichoke is tender when poked with a knife. Drain. Pluck leaves out one at a time and dip base in lemon butter.

28. Make sweet breads that have vegetables in them, like zucchini-spice bread or carrot-cinnamon bread.

29. Add grated and steamed carrots to cheesy scrambled eggs.

30. Not everything that crunches is a potato chip. Try vegetable sticks. Fill celery stalks with peanut butter or low-fat, flavored cream cheese. Cut carrots into sticks or thin rounds. Experiment with parsnips, zucchini and other crunchy vegetables.

31. Mix grated cucumber and green food coloring into cream cheese and use as a sandwich spread.

32. Let your kids help you cut off the end of a bunch of celery. Place the stalks into red- or blue-colored water (use food coloring). Set in the refrigerator overnight and the next day you will have colored celery to eat!

33. Top pasta with steamed zucchini in tomato sauce.

34. Add grated and steamed carrots to nacho cheese dip.

35. For a healthy, protein-rich snack, spread a slice of turkey sandwich meat with a little mayonnaise or mustard and then wrap it around a celery or carrot stick.

36. Make crazy veggie open-faced sandwiches. Spread a slice of bread with cream cheese pimento cheese, or peanut butter. Create funny

My mother made me eat broccoli. I hate broccoli. I am the president of the United States. I will not eat any more broccoli.
—George H. W. Bush

205

The Ten Commandments for Feeding Fussy Eaters

You shall:

1. Keep it simple.

2. Refrain from feeding them lots of sugary foods and sweet drinks (even too much fruit juice can douse a good appetite).

3. Sneak in the four food groups every day.

4. Never guilt a child into the clean-plate club.

5. Find ways to make mealtimes fun.

6. Involve even the youngest finicky eater as sous-chef.

7. Never use food as punishment or reward for other behaviors.

8. Stock proven favorites even if you get bored.

9. Keep trying to find pleasing foods.

10. Let the choosy eaters help with menu planning.

faces on top using olives, celery, carrot sticks and rounds, radish slices or any vegetables.

37. Kids love crunchy foods, so try drizzling vegetables with a little olive oil, sprinkling with kosher salt and roasting in a 400-degree-F oven for fifteen to twenty minutes.

38. Make a sweet-sour cucumber salad by marinating thin slices in white vinegar that you've seasoned with sugar and salt.

39. Stir-fry carrot slices, zucchini slices and broccoli florets in a little peanut oil, and drizzle with soy sauce before serving.

40. Thaw frozen chopped spinach, squeeze dry and stir into scrambled eggs just before they are set. Tell your kids, if it was good enough for Popeye, it's good enough for them.

Turn Dinnertime into Quality Time

TEAM-BUILDING

There's just something about having a regular dinnertime, especially when everybody's had a hand in getting the meal on the table, that cements family ties. Here's how to make it happen at your house:

1. **Reclaim the family dinner hour.** Decide to eat together certain nights each week—and do it. Decide with your spouse on dinner goals—for example, how many nights you'll eat together—then talk to the kids. They might protest, and you may have to adjust your schedule and give up some things yourself. But remember, you're building for the future.

2. **Beware of the "whining hour."** If you have small children, have some light, healthy snacks such as grapes and string cheese, to tide them over until dinnertime. Try to arrange your dinner prep time so you don't have to start right in cooking the moment you walk in the door from work at night. If you can devote the first fifteen or twenty minutes exclusively to your child, whether to read a story, check homework or just cuddle, she'll probably be less clingy in the long run and go back to her own activities, allowing you to get

started on dinner. You can make the evening less stressful by planning meals that cook without constant supervision, such as crockpot dinners. Or microwave a frozen casserole while you spend the predinner time with your child.

3. **Cook smart.** Develop a repertoire of easy meals, and always keep the ingredients on hand. Don't let complicated recipes and menus limit the time your family can sit around the dinner table and talk about the day. It's more important to eat together than to eat elaborate meals.

4. **Predetermine and post menus.** With tight schedules and double-parent burnout at the end of the day, the last thing you need is disorder and dissension over what to fix for dinner. Decide beforehand and let family members have a say.

5. **Assign everyone a meal-related job.** Cooking and working cooperatively with other family members teaches kids responsibility and important skills they'll use the rest of their lives. Even young children can learn early on that they're part of the family team. A three year old can help set the table, tear lettuce, wash vegetables or just play with "cooking" toys while parents and older siblings prepare dinner. Just keep in mind that it's important they feel included. Kids over the age of eight can be responsible for clearing the table and loading the dishwasher. You may want to have two children alternate nights, and if one is busy on a particular night, with a swim team practice or baby-sitting job, he can switch kitchen duties with a sibling.

6. **Be prepared.** Keep an ongoing grocery list in a prominent spot in the kitchen so everyone can record needs. When you're preparing dinner, have one family member check on staples and add to the list. Create a routine: when someone opens the last bottle or package of an item, he or she immediately adds it to the list.

7. **Create a user-friendly kitchen.** Designate a low cabinet where kids can organize plastic cups and dishes. (Put safety catches on cabinets that store dangerous things.) Keep table accessories—napkins, dinnerware, place mats, salt and pepper shakers—easily accessible to the dinner table.

Bright Idea

Eating dinner together as a family is a great way to nourish and nurture kids—study after study points to the benefits. If your family is hard pressed to find the time, help is just a click away! Many food websites provide timesaving and delicious meal solutions. One of my favorite online resources is DinnerMadeEasy.com, sponsored by General Mills. It's filled with ideas to make dinnertime a cinch, from menu planning to prep to cleanup.

207

8. **Maximize teachable moments.** Think of your kitchen as a classroom where you can enhance your child's intellectual development. Elementary school–age kids can learn that 1 cup does not mean a coffee cup, and a teaspoon is not just any spoon from the drawer. When we double or halve recipes, we can teach math skills. And dinner-prep time is the perfect time to teach children about safe use of appliances and equipment.

9. **Clean up as you go.** When cooking, return used ingredients immediately to where they belong and toss all wrappers and scraps. This saves time and keeps you from forgetting whether or not you added that pinch of salt. Always fill your sink with warm water and soap while cooking. Soak pots, pans and utensils while you're eating for easier cleanup later.

10. **Focus on your family.** Cut off the outside world and break the I-have-to-answer-the-phone" habit. Let your answering machine or voicemail service take charge of calls. To get quality conversations started, ask a question such as, "What was one interesting thing that happened today?" or "What made you feel happy today?" If it's hard to come up with a conversation, try taking turns going around the table and having each family member tell about the best thing that happened to them that day. (Also see "Fun Around the Table," page 209.)

11. **Create a pleasant dining atmosphere.** Don't reserve ambiance for guests or celebrations; serve it with every meal. Adding ambiance doesn't have to be time-consuming or expensive. Use cloth napkins and pretty place mats, light candles and turn off the TV. Replace background noise with pleasant music.

12. **Think (and talk) positively.** Ban critical words and arguing at the table. Avoid disciplinary discussions that could be handled at another time. Dinner's not the time to talk about who's not doing chores, or problems at school.

13. **Show appreciation.** Compliment everyone who helped with the meal. And when it comes to cleaning up, remember it's more important for your family to work as a team than for the kitchen to be spotless. Praise team members for effort—for example, say to

them, "You did an excellent job of washing the dishes, but please try to remember to clean out the sink after you've finished."

14. **Start and finish together.** Make sure everyone who is at home is seated at the beginning of the meal. And even though kids may complain, you're teaching good manners by having them remain at the table until everyone is excused. One way to get everyone on the same eating schedule is to have a family ritual of saying a short prayer or blessing at the beginning or end of the meal.

15. **Plan an ethnic night.** Come up with a simple Chinese, Mexican or Caribbean meal that appeals to the family. Choose appropriate dinner music sung by a person of that culture. Let your children draw scenes of the country you are celebrating, and use these to decorate the dining room. If your meal revolves around Asian food, allow everyone to eat with chopsticks, and brew tea to serve with the meal. If you are celebrating Italy, play an Italian opera while you cook and have a pasta-making party. A Caribbean feast might include reggae or steel drum music, and the dishes could include some interesting produce like plantains and guava.

FUN AROUND THE TABLE: FAMILY CONVERSATION STARTERS

Here are twenty-one ways to get interesting conversation started around your dinner table:

1. What's the best book you've ever read? Why did you enjoy it? If you were to pick the actors for a movie of this book, who would play the leads?

2. Who has been your favorite teacher? What are three things you like about him or her?

3. What is your favorite time of day?

4. If you could own one of the world's most valued collections, which one would you choose?

5. What day of your life would you like to live over again?

6. What is something you've always wanted to learn to do?

7. If you could possess any extraordinary talent, what would like to be able to do?

Take Note

Dinnertime is about more than food. The American Psychological Association published a study in 1997 that underscored the crucial role of dinnertime in the lives of teenagers. The study found that adjusted teens—those with better relationships with their peers, more academic motivation and few, if any, problems with drugs and depression—ate dinner with their families an average of five days a week.

Studies by the University of Minnesota and the University of North Carolina showed similar findings: drug use, sex, violence and emotional stress were less likely in households where the parents were present at crucial times, particularly during meals.

8. If you could be president of the United States for one day, what would you do?

9. If you could be on the cover of a magazine, which one would you pick?

10. What is your earliest memory?

11. If you could spend one whole day with anyone in history, who would it be?

12. If you could witness any event in history, what would it be?

13. What would be a perfect day for you?

14. What's the kindest thing anyone ever did for you?

15. If you could start a business on your own, what would it be?

16. If you were an author, what book would you write?

17. What five things would you like to experience in the next five years?

18. What do you wish you had more time for?

19. What famous person would you like to meet?

20. If you could eat dinner with three people from history, who would you choose?

21. If you could travel any place in the world this summer, where would you go and what would you do?

Building a Better Bag Lunch

Day after day, week after week. Bag lunches can quickly become boring. If you could use a little inspiration, try out these ideas:

- Homemade or canned soup or chili can make a filling, hearty mid-day meal in the cold weather. Microwave a chunky soup until steaming. While it's cooking, fill a thermos with boiling water. Let it stand for several minutes to warm the inside, and then pour the water out and add the soup.

- Meat sandwiches freeze very well. Don't spread the bread with mayonnaise or salad dressing. Instead, use softened butter, mustard or cream cheese. Wrap tightly in freezer-safe plastic wrap and freeze for up to two months. Don't freeze any of the mayonnaise-based salad sandwiches, such as tuna, egg or chicken.

- If you want lettuce and tomato on your sandwich, pack them separately in a plastic bag.
- Put together individual packets of ham or turkey slices and freeze. Then make up the sandwich with the frozen filling. It will stay cold in a lunch box until time to eat. For sandwiches with meat or poultry, slice thin and use several slices, instead of one thicker slice. It makes the sandwich much easier to eat.
- Make peanut butter and jelly sandwiches the night before. Spread both sides of the bread with peanut butter to act as a sealer and put jelly in the middle.
- Break out of the white bread mold by using hard rolls, rye, pumpernickel, cinnamon-raisin bagels or English muffins to hold sandwich fillings.
- If you are really rushed, make sandwiches for school lunches on Sunday and label and freeze in individual zipper bags. Kids can choose a sandwich each morning, then add fruit, chips or vegetable sticks. An ice pack or frozen box of juice keeps the sandwich cold until noon.
- Divide a grape bunch into small clusters after returning from the grocery store. Put individual servings in plastic bags and store in refrigerator.
- Wraps get even better if made several hours ahead. Spread a flour tortilla with softened cream cheese or Boursin cheese, then add thin slices of turkey and either sundried tomatoes or pitted black olives. Cut in thirds, wrap up tightly and refrigerate.
- Stuff a pita bread with tuna salad, chopped tomato and shredded lettuce, then wrap well and take to work. Enjoy with a bottle of sparkling flavored water.
- Pack a container of hummus (sold in the deli case at the supermarket), along with crackers, baby carrots and celery sticks for dipping.
- Pack lowfat cheese cubes, breadsticks, grapes or cherries, along with a thermos of iced tea. You'll feel like you're on a picnic!

Bright Idea

Watching your weight? Freeze a fruit yogurt overnight and take it to work for lunch. To increase your fiber and vitamin intake, add some whole wheat crackers spread with almond or peanut butter and a piece of fruit.

211

CHAPTER 10

You're the Head Chef

A good manager is always learning—always adding information to her store of knowledge. She is also someone who acknowledges her shortfalls and tries to fill in the gaps. In my case, I'm skilled at many things, but as I've said before, cooking is not one of them. Since feeding my family remains a priority, I have had to find a way around my lack of ability in this area. Therefore over the years I have sought the advice and smart tips of cooking experts. Here are some of those tips to make kitchen time productive and—dare I say it—fun!

Secrets for Kitchen Success

MAKE DINNER TASTE BETTER

1. Boil rice or potatoes in broth or bouillon rather than water. You'll get more flavor.
2. Enhance the flavor of reduced-fat ground beef by mixing instant potato flakes into meat before cooking. Or sauté the meat with some chopped onion.
3. Reduce salty flavor in ham by baking it partially, then draining the juice. Pour a small bottle of ginger ale over the ham and return it to the oven until done.

4. If you accidentally oversalt a dish while it's still cooking, drop in a peeled potato. It absorbs the excess salt for an instant fix.

5. Keep parsley in a bowl of cold water in the fridge. Before using it, rinse it quickly in hot water.

6. Cut a garlic clove in half, then rub it inside your stew or soup pot before you prepare the recipe.

7. Roast chicken or other meats on top of celery stalks; they make a moisturizing and flavorful meat rack.

8. Absorb grease from roasts with a piece of stale bread placed under the rack.

9. Add a teaspoon of sugar to cooking peas to enhance flavor and help retain color.

10. When boiling corn on the cob, add a pinch of sugar to help bring out the corn's natural sweetness.

11. Retain flavor: turn cooking chicken with two wooden spoons rather than piercing the meat with a fork.

12. Double the flavor and get moister meat: after stewing chicken, let it cool in the broth, then cube.

13. Use raisin bread for French toast for a change.

14. Add a pinch of cinnamon to a cup of warm honey and use with pancakes or waffles in place of maple syrup.

15. Add a pinch of baking powder to the milk-egg mixture for fluffier French toast.

16. Keep your meat from curling: cut fatty edges with scissors in three or four places before cooking.

17. Save juices from canned fruit to flavor baking ham.

18. Check the age of beef by looking at the bones and fat in the package. In younger beef, the bones are tinged with red and the fat is cream colored and smooth. The bones are less porous in an older animal, and the fat is white and looks brittle.

19. Bake apples, stuffed peppers or tomatoes in a muffin tin. They'll retain their shape better.

20. A teaspoon of baking soda makes mashed potatoes lighter and more fluffy.

A mother stirs a little bit of herself into everything she cooks for her family.
—Marjorie Holmes

Part of the secret of success in life is to eat what you like and let the food fight it out inside.
—Mark Twain

213

You don't get over hating to cook, any more than you get over having big feet.
—Peg Bracken

21. Revive limp celery and carrots by soaking them in cold water and ice cubes in the refrigerator.
22. Thicken soups by adding pureed, cooked vegetables.
23. Don't throw out leftover wine; freeze it into ice cubes for future use in casseroles and sauces.
24. Make perfect rice by sautéing it over medium heat in a little oil. Add water double to the amount of rice, stir and reduce heat. Cover and cook for fifteen minutes. Remove pan from heat and let sit, covered, for fifteen minutes. Fluff before serving.
25. Freeze salad plates for about an hour before use. The greens will stay cooler and crisper this way.
26. Boil corn with a little sugar, not salt. Salt makes corn tough.
27. Use your hands to tear up lettuce, toss salad or crumble cheese on top of a casserole.
28. When mincing more than three cloves of garlic, sprinkle salt on the cloves before starting to cut. Chop briefly, then drag the flat side of the knife blade over the cloves. The garlic will become finely chopped and won't stick to the knife.
29. Prevent stuck-on food by preheating a wok or stainless steel skillet over high heat before you add the oil.
30. Make your own Asian five-spice seasoning: combine equal amounts cloves, Szechuan peppercorns, star anise, fennel and cinnamon.
31. Make your own poultry seasoning: combine marjoram, sage, savory and thyme.
32. Season quicker and cleaner: replace the salt and pepper shakers on the stove with a bowl filled with three-quarters salt and one-quarter pepper.
33. Feel free to substitute one berry for another, or limes for lemons.
34. Use half as much dried herbs as fresh. Crush dried herbs in your hand before adding to recipes, and cook the dish for just fifteen minutes after you add them. Then taste and season additionally as needed.
35. Use heavy whipping cream interchangeably with light cream in recipes, except those where it is supposed to be whipped. Light

Anyone who has never made a mistake has never tried anything new.
—Albert Einstein

Edible Flowers

- Apple, peach and plum blossoms
- Blue borage
- Chive blossoms
- Chrysanthemums
- Daisies

- Geraniums
- Jasmine
- Lavender
- Lilacs
- Lovage
- Marigolds

- Mimosa
- Nasturtiums
- Pansies
- Rose petals
- Violets

cream won't whip up to nice, fluffy peaks the way heavy cream does. Sour cream and yogurt add a zippier taste to recipes but don't boil well as they may separate.

36. Substitute ground ginger for fresh grated ginger.
37. Toss grapes into Caesar pasta, spinach, chicken, tuna, or turkey salads for enhanced flavor and extra punch.

FIXING BLUNDERS

It happens to the best of cooks—and the worst of them. Whichever you are, here are some ways to make a mishap into nobody's business.

1. If there's too much alcohol in punch or other mixed alcoholic drinks, float thin slices of cucumber to absorb the taste.
2. If there's too much fat in stew, soup or gravy, drop in ice cubes. The grease will stick to them. Remove quickly.
3. If a stew or soup tastes too garlicky, simmer a sprig or small bunch of parsley in it for ten minutes.
4. If a dish tastes too salty, boil a peeled, thinly sliced potato until it's transparent, then remove it.
5. If fish is too salty, add vinegar to the cooking liquid.
6. If a tomato dish is too salty, add more peeled tomatoes to absorb the salt. Leave in dish if appropriate.
7. For oversalty soup, stew or tomato sauce, add pinches of brown sugar to taste.

There is no such thing as a pretty good omelette.
—French proverb

215

8. Salvage burned rice. Leaving behind the burned bottom layer, scoop the rice into a new pot and place a single layer of onion skins on top. Cover the pot and let sit for fifteen minutes. The onion skins remove the smoky, acrid taste from the rice. Discard the onion skins before serving.

9. Baked stuffed green peppers in greased muffin tins so they'll hold their shape.

10. Whiten boiled potatoes by putting a few drops of lemon juice in the cooking water.

11. To eliminate strong cabbage odors in the house, put a small tin cup half full of vinegar on the stove near the cabbage. It will absorb the odor.

12. Instead of throwing out stale bread, make bread pudding. Or reduce the bread to crumbs and use as a coating for chicken or a topping for casserole. French toast tastes even better when made with stale bread.

13. Revive limp carrots and celery by placing them in the refrigerator in a bowl of ice water for two hours before serving.

14. Puree overcooked vegetables and add broth or milk along with seasonings, and you'll have a delicious soup.

15. If brown sugar gets lumpy, put an apple wedge in it and microwave on high for twenty seconds.

16. To put out a fat fire, throw baking soda on it. Do not use water.

17. If a soup turns out too thin, cook it longer so that it reduces. Or add uncooked rice or pasta and simmer, covered, until it's completely cooked.

18. Add crumbled egg shells to a cloudy stock, allow to simmer two or three minutes, then lift out the shells and strain the stock. The stock will be clear.

19. If you overcook a roast and can't serve it rare, turn it into hash, chili or potpie.

20. If you overcook fish and it's dry, make a rich sauce for it or mash it up and make fish cakes.

21. If a cheesecake cracks, sift powdered sugar over the top.

22. If a sauce curdles, beat it vigorously with a hand mixer, then add an ice cube and beat it in.

EXPRESS COOKING

Here are twenty tips to save you time in the kitchen.

1. Make your electric stove work like a gas one by running two burners at once—one on high and the other on low. Switch your pan from one to another when you need to change temperatures quickly.
2. Skip the massive cookware sets and buy it by the piece. You need a 1-quart saucepan, a 2 or 2½-quart saucepan, a 10-inch skillet, a 12-inch sauté pan and an 8-quart stock pot.
3. Use kitchen scissors for small jobs such as snipping herbs into salads, cutting cold cuts and cold chicken breast and cutting up pita bread or pizza. Make your life easier by getting a pair that is dishwasher safe.
4. When fruit is in season, make pie fillings. Freeze in covered pie pans lined with wax paper. All you'll need to do for fresh-baked pie is prepare the crust.
5. Make rice as quickly as pasta: boil it uncovered for ten minutes and drain. Stir in a little butter.
6. When clearing the table, don't stack dishes. You'll have to spend more time cleaning off the food stuck on the back of each dish.
7. Save butter wrappers in the freezer and use them to grease pans.
8. Rinse your measuring cup in hot water before you pour molasses or honey.
9. Run your hands under cold water before pressing rice cereal treats in the pan. The marshmallow won't stick to your fingers.
10. The next time you make tacos, prepare an extra meal's worth of seasoned hamburger. You can freeze this in ice-cube trays and reheat it, one cube at a time, for topping baked potatoes or making taco salads.
11. Mix ½ cup flour with 1 cup water. Freeze this mixture in ice-cube trays. When you need to make a quick gravy, just drop two or three cubes into meat drippings.

Take all the swift advantage of the hours.
—William Shakespeare

There is no such thing as a little garlic.
—Anonymous

217

12. Put slightly diluted jelly into a squeeze bottle for cleaner dispersal.

13. Need a quick pastry bag? Put frosting in a self-sealing plastic bag. Cut the tip of a corner and squeeze.

14. When you see bananas on sale, buy extra. Roll peeled bananas individually in plastic wrap and place in freezer. Thaw quickly by microwaving each banana for ten seconds.

15. Prepare extra whenever you chop or shred veggies and cheese.

16. Remold dense salads by softening them first in the microwave, then rechilling in a smaller mold.

17. For fewer spills, cut a small hole in the seal—rather than removing it—on a new bottle of oil.

18. Bake several chicken breasts just for freezing and future use in recipes.

19. Prepare butter balls or curls in advance for entertaining, drop into iced water, then drain and pack in containers to freeze. Remove and thaw at room temperature about an hour before use.

20. Freeze slices of lemon or lime in plastic bags. Add the frozen slices to cocktails.

21. Before a dinner party, scoop ice cream or sorbet balls onto paper-lined trays. Refreeze, ready to serve.

22. Sprinkle a cut with flour to stop bleeding.

23. Brush beaten egg white over pie crust before baking to yield a beautiful glossy finish.

Skinny cooks should not be trusted
—Anonymous

The Skinny on . . .

BAKING

- When baking bread, shiny pans make a light crust, darker pans make a darker crust.
- For a moister cake, add 2 tablespoons of oil to a cake mix, then follow directions.
- To prevent a cake from becoming too brown and drying out, place a pan of water on the top rack of the oven while baking.

- Another way to ensure a moist cake is to place it in the refrigerator immediately after baking.

- Don't overbeat a cake batter. It can cause the cake to crack.

- Spray the beaters of your electric mixer with cooking spray to keep batter from clinging.

- Don't butter and flour the pan when you are making a sponge or angel food cake, because these batters must cling to the sides of the pan if they're to rise to their full height.

- Be sure to carefully flour the sides of a cake pan. Spots left uncovered by flour will prevent the cake from gripping the sides while rising, and force it to slide back down.

- For the same reason, do not use butter to grease a cake pan. Flour cannot cling to it evenly.

- Tired of wrestling with a big bag of flour when you only need to dust a pan lightly? Place some flour in a clean salt shaker and store it in the freezer.

- Chocolate cakes are notorious for sticking. Be extra careful when you grease and flour the pan. Instead of flour, you can dust the pan with cocoa.

- When baking a cake, remove the rack before preheating the oven as the cold cake pan should not be placed on a hot surface.

- Eggs should be at room temperature before beating them to provide the greatest volume. They should also be at room temperature when they are incorporated into butter and sugar in cake batters. Although egg whites will yield more volume if you allow them to reach room temperature first, cold eggs are easier to separate. Therefore, separate eggs while they're still cold, and then allow them to reach room temperature.

- If you don't have time to allow eggs to come to room temperature naturally, you can place eggs that are still in their shells in a bowl of hot tap water for a few minutes.

- Butter creams best when it's at cool room temperature, about 70 degrees F. To soften it more quickly if it's been in the refrigerator, grate the chilled butter into a mixing bowl, using the large holes on

Bright Idea

Add 1 teaspoon vanilla and an extra egg to make a cake mix taste like homemade.

Never eat more than you can lift.

—Miss Piggy

a four-sided box grater. It will be ready to cream in about five minutes. Alternately, cut the butter into small cubes and leave it for about fifteen minutes, at which point it should be ready to cream. As a general rule, don't microwave butter to soften it. It nearly always winds up melted in some places and too hard in others.

- Don't fill a cake pan more than two-thirds full. Use a spatula to spread the batter evenly, then tap the pan on the counter to knock out air bubbles.

- As an extra precaution, fit a piece of wax or parchment paper into the bottom of the cake pan when you're baking a chocolate cake. To fit paper exactly, trace the bottom of your cake pan onto the paper and trim to size.

- If a cake rises too much in the center, you can push it back down by placing a smaller pan on top of the cake and gently applying pressure to the cake.

- Don't apply powdered sugar too soon before serving or it will be absorbed by the cake.

- Slice creamy cakes, like cheesecake, with a long piece of unwaxed dental floss. Hold it taut and pull it down through the cake. This also works for a hot cake.

- To make colored coconut to top a cake, put shredded coconut in a zip-lock bag. Add a little food coloring and shake.

- To prevent a cake from sticking to the platter, sprinkle it first with sugar. The slices will lift off easily.

- Freeze a cake first before cutting it into decorative shapes.

- Cakes with sugar frosting will keep at room temperature for up to three days; seal any cut surfaces with plastic wrap and store in a cake keeper or invert a large bowl over the cake plate.

- Pies and cakes with butter cream or cream cheese frosting or custard filling should always be refrigerated.

- Freeze unfrosted cake layers in plastic wrap overwrapped with aluminum foil for up to four months; thaw one hour at room temperature.

- Store soft cookies and crisp cookies separately in airtight tins.

Successful Substitutions

Certain substitutions are standard in baking recipes, such as margarine or shortening for butter. Substitutions can, however, affect the taste. Butter has an unmistakable flavor and a very creamy texture that margarine just can't imitate. However, in some instances, substituting vegetable shortening for butter pays off. For example, pie crust made with vegetable shortening is extra flaky. And, since vegetable shortening melts at a higher temperature than butter, it's useful for sautéing and frying. Some people like to use it in their cake frostings.

- It's important to remember that substitutions that work in the oven may not work on top of the stove, and vice versa.
- Whenever you make a substitution, keep in mind that baking times may vary, so be sure to check for doneness more frequently.
- Whenever you make a substitution, try to keep the ratio of liquid ingredients to dry ingredients as close as possible to the original recipe.

■ Freeze soft cookies in an airtight container with plastic wrap between layers for up to six months.

■ To prevent cake crumbs from marring the frosting, apply a crumb glaze—a very thin layer of frosting that coats the cake and seals in any crumbs. Allow it to dry, then frost as usual.

■ To be sure you get the right shade, blend colored frostings in advance and allow them to sit. Food coloring intensifies over time.

■ To get perfect results when writing on a cake, first write on the frosting with a toothpick, and then trace over the marks with decorator frosting.

■ When slicing, always slide the knife out, never bring it back up through the cake.

FREEZING

Avoid freezer burn and retain flavor by following these tips:

■ Make it easy-access. Store certain foods on certain shelves, such as meats, desserts, vegetables and fruits, bread and prepared foods.

221

When you become a good cook, you become a good craftsman, first. You repeat and repeat and repeat until your hands know how to move without thinking about it.

—Jacques Pepin

Bright Idea

Place rinsed and dried grapes on an oblong pan and place in the freezer. When frozen, store them in a plastic bag or container. Frozen grapes are a healthy, refreshing snack and can also be substituted for ice cubes in fruit drinks.

- Don't expect miracles. Your 19-cubic-foot freezer will not necessarily freeze 19 cubic feet of food overnight. Your freezer shouldn't be more than 75 percent full to run at peak efficiency.
- Your freezer's temperature should be zero or less.
- Before adding a lot of food, set freezer at its coldest setting.
- Using a permanent marker, label every plastic freezer bag—before you fill it—with contents and date.
- Highlight use-by date on freezer packages. Move items you need to use soon to the front.
- Tape a list of freezer contents on the inside of the kitchen door or a cupboard for quick reference.
- Use freezer wrap liberally. Aluminum foil is not the best material for freezing because it turns brittle in the freezer and doesn't give a secure seal. It's better to use freezer paper.
- Freeze produce immediately. Fruits frozen in syrup will be less mushy and more juicy when you thaw them. To make a light syrup, boil two parts water with one part sugar. Chill this concoction, then pour about ½ cup over each two cups of fruit.
- Delicate fruits such as mangoes, watermelon and papayas don't freeze well.
- Store chips and crackers in the freezer during humid, hot weather. They'll retain crispness better.
- Before finishing the seal on freezer bags, squeeze out every last bit of air.
- Store cereals, rice, flours and noodles in the freezer if your area is prone to bugs.
- Store ground coffee in the freezer to help retain its freshness, then use directly from the freezer as it thaws quickly in boiling water.
- Freeze raw hamburger patties between flattened cupcake liners.
- Store orange and lemon rinds in the freezer to use when a recipe calls for a little grated peel.
- Divide larger batches of food into smaller quantities that you can use at one time. Freeze portions of pesto or tomato paste in ice cube trays, and freeze chicken breasts in pairs.

FOR BEST RESULTS, DON'T FREEZE...

- Cottage cheese and cream cheese
- Hard cheese, unless you plan to use it for melted-cheese recipes as it crumbles when thawed
- Mayonnaise, sour cream and yogurt
- Hard-boiled eggs
- Cream and custard pie fillings
- Meringue
- Carbonated drinks or anything canned (you can freeze juice boxes)
- Fish and shellfish if they've been previously frozen
- Cooked potatoes, though mashed potatoes make good thickeners for stews or soups
- Garlic
- Cucumbers, lettuce and celery
- Pears
- Cream sauces

GRILLING

- You'll have easier cleanup if you line the base of your charcoal grill with foil, which also reflects heat. Don't line gas grills; just keep the catch pan clean.
- Start a quick fire by building a pyramid with your charcoal briquettes. Then saturate them with lighter fluid (never use kerosene, gasoline or other flammable liquids), and light. Wash hands immediately after applying lighter fluid. You can also purchase easy-to-light charcoal.
- If your fire slacks off too early, restart the flames with wood kindling. Never add lighter fluid after your fire is started.
- When coals are covered in a gray ash (about 25 minutes), you're ready to grill. Spread the coals across the grill bottom.
- Add flavor to food by placing fresh herbs—fennel, thyme or rosemary—over the coals minutes before cooking. The herbs will last longer if you soak them in water before use.
- To prevent flare-ups, keep oil in marinades to a minimum, and cut excess fat from chops and steaks.

Bright Idea

Organize your freezer by creating extra shelving by using coated wire racks or stackable baskets.

Take Note

Add only 3 pounds of unfrozen food at a time for every cubic foot of freezer capacity. This allows food to freeze more quickly, deterring the rate of bacterial growth.

223

- Use nonstick spray on the grill before barbecuing.
- For safety's sake when using a charcoal grill, keep a hose or bucket of sand nearby. If you have a flare-up on a gas grill, turn off the burners and step away from the grill.
- Get dinner on the table quicker by microwaving poultry and meat before grilling.
- Add some veggies to your grilled meal: parboil new potatoes for five minutes, place on metal skewers, brush with oil and grill for eight to ten minutes. Always cook fruits and veggies around the edges, on the cooler part of the grill.
- If your grill has no temperature control, sear meats a couple of inches above the coals; raise higher to finish inside cooking.
- For cooking most meats, place the rack 4 to 6 inches from the charcoal.
- The best way to clean a grill rack is with a very stiff wire brush. Be sure to let the rack cool completely first.
- Store fire-starter in a safe place far away from the grill.
- Vents may be adjusted to keep the heat level you want. When opened wide, they let in more air and you'll get a hotter fire. Partially closed, they will give you less heat. Don't close them completely unless you want to extinguish the fire.
- When grilling fish, rub thick slices of potato on the grill rack first. The starch will coat the metal and help to prevent sticking.
- To see how hot your coals are, remove the grid and place your hand, palm down, at grid level. If you can hold your hand there for two seconds, it's a hot fire (best for searing). If you can hold it there for four seconds, it's a medium fire that's good for grilling. If you can hold it there for six seconds, it's a low fire, good for covered cooking.

Restaurant Rules

TIPS FOR PLEASANT DINING

- Make dinner reservations about six hours before you want to eat—cancellations start coming in about then.

Reorganize your kitchen and storage areas a bit for impromptu summer suppers outside.

- Store barbecue tools, charcoal and lighter, apron and hot pad in an easy-access place.
- Keep hamburger/hot dog condiments—ketchup, mustard, mayonnaise, relish—in a plastic tote in your refrigerator.
- Put paper plates, cups, napkins, plastic utensils, unbreakable salt and pepper shakers and a tray in a cabinet near the back door for quick table-setting outside.

Picnic Checklist

- ☐ Food and condiments
- ☐ Beverages
- ☐ Water
- ☐ Ice
- ☐ Paper plates
- ☐ Paper cups
- ☐ Eating utensils
- ☐ Serving utensils

- ☐ Napkins
- ☐ Tablecloth or old quilt to cover a table or spread on the ground
- ☐ Packaged premoistened towels to clean hands
- ☐ Paper towels for cleanup
- ☐ Garbage bag to take care of litter

- ☐ Bug spray
- ☐ First-aid kit
- ☐ Toilet paper if you're in a remote location
- ☐ Flashlights if you'll be out after dark
- ☐ Camera

- If you order fish on Monday, remember that it was probably fresh on Saturday.
- Don't eat out on holidays. You'll pay as much as double for the same meals the restaurant serves daily.
- Establish yourself as a regular customer. You'll get better service.
- Eat out for lunch rather than dinner. You may pay half as much for your favorite entrée.
- Let new restaurants get better; don't try them for at least three months.
- Want friendly service? Be friendly yourself.
- If you're trying to keep your bill down, watch what you order to drink. Soft drinks are typically overpriced, and once you start ordering alcoholic beverages, your tab really increases. If the waiter asks if you want water, tell him "municipal" is fine or you may be surprised to get billed for pricey bottled water.
- Don't be shy about asking for leftovers to be bagged up; tonight's dinner can become a gourmet lunch tomorrow.
- If you're eating out with kids, try to visit a restaurant early. Service tends to be quicker, and the kiddies won't have as much time to get restless before the meal arrives.
- Be considerate of other patrons and don't take the kids to very upscale, expensive restaurants. Other grownups are paying for a child-free night, and they don't want to listen to yours all during a meal.

Fish, to taste right, must swim three times—in water, in butter and in wine.
—Polish proverb

■ If you have a small appetite, consider ordering two appetizers as your main course.

Food Safety

My family sometimes jokes about my cooking; there were times they threatened to put the Poison Control number on speed dial! Maybe I'm exaggerating a little, but no matter what our culinary capabilities, food safety should be on the front burner of our minds. Some simple steps can reduce the hidden dangers present in every kitchen.

■ Eggs. Buy enough for two weeks at a time. Buy them from the lower shelf in the store; they'll be cooler and fresher. At home, store in their carton for maximum freshness. Keep hard-boiled and raw eggs refrigerated. Don't eat raw eggs in anything—eggnog, salad dressing, custards or meringues.

■ Chicken and eggs are not the only food poisoning culprits. Food-borne illness also can be caused by unpasteurized milk, pork and beef and some raw fruits and vegetables. Drink only pasteurized milk, cook all meat—pork, poultry and beef—thoroughly and wash fruits and vegetables (including bananas and melons) well.

■ Put away any mayonnaise-based foods within two hours of use. Chicken, tuna or other protein-rich foods can cause bacteria to grow.

■ If you remove molds from firm foods such as apples, carrots, cheddar cheese, sweet peppers and potatoes, you can still eat them. Softer foods such as jelly and yogurt are spoiled if they show mold.

■ Freezing halts bacteria growth, but it doesn't kill existing bacteria. Be sure to freeze either fresh or freshly cooked food as quickly as possible, and never let it sit around the kitchen for hours before you freeze it.

■ Keep your refrigerator temperature between 36 and 38 degrees F. Freezers should be maintained at a temperature of 0 or below.

■ Don't store very perishable foods such as eggs, milk, meat, poultry and fish in the refrigerator door, as the door temperature is slightly higher than in the main compartment.

- Wipe down the shelves and doors of the refrigerator once a week with a bleach solution or commercial cleanser.
- Don't rinse chicken before cooking. Rinsing doesn't remove all the bacteria, but it can spread it around your sink, which then can cross-contaminate other foods.
- Have separate cutting boards for meat and vegetables. To help you remember which is for which, buy colored ones—maybe green for vegetables and red for meat.
- Wash cutting boards regularly by immersing them in hot, soapy water or a weak bleach solution, then rinsing well with running water.
- Don't use a fork to turn steaks or chicken. The food-borne bacteria are generally just in the surface of solid cuts of meat, which is why medium-rare steaks and chops that are pink inside generally are safe. But when you pierce meat with a fork, you can transfer surface contamination to the inside and make it dangerous to eat. Turn with tongs instead.
- Wash can lids with hot water before opening them.
- Clean your can opener regularly with a bleach and water solution.

WHEN TO TOSS IT

Immediately throw away:

- Cracked eggs as they may contain salmonella
- Dented, bulging or rusty cans
- Jars with loose or cracked lids, especially those containing milky liquids that are normally clear
- A jar of mayonnaise or tub of margarine harboring bits of other foods such as toast crumbs
- Sliced or peeled fruit or vegetables left unrefrigerated and uncovered for more than a few hours
- Bread or cheese with green mold
- Anything that looks or smells suspect
- Any perishable food that's been left out of the refrigerator for more than two hours

Bright Idea

Never guess again. Buy an instant-read meat thermometer. You'll always know when it's done.

227

Safe Food Storage

Type of Food	Where to Store	For How Long
Raw	Refrigerator	1 to 2 days
	Freezer	9 months
Cooked	Refrigerator	3 to 4 days
	Freezer	6 months
MEAT		
All chops	Refrigerator	3 to 5 days
All ground meat	Refrigerator	1 to 2 days
All roasts	Refrigerator	3 to 5 days
Beef steaks	Refrigerator	3 to 5 days
	Freezer	6 to 12 months
Lamb chops	Freezer	6 to 9 months
Pork chops	Freezer	4 to 6 months
Ground beef	Freezer	3 to 4 months
Beef roasts	Freezer	6 to 12 months
Veal, pork roasts	Freezer	4 to 6 months
Lamb roasts	Freezer	2 to 3 months
Cooked leftover meats	Refrigerator	3 to 4 days
	Freezer	2 to 3 months
Luncheon meats		
(unopened)	Refrigerator	2 weeks
(opened)	Refrigerator	3 to 5 days
	Freezer	1 to 2 months
Bacon	Freezer	2 months
	Refrigerator	2 weeks
SEAFOOD		
Raw lean fish		
(cod, flounder, sole)	Refrigerator	1 to 2 days
	Freezer	6 to 8 months

Raw fatty fish		
(salmon, perch)	Refrigerator	1 to 2 days
	Freezer	4 months
Raw shrimp	Refrigerator	1 to 2 days
	Freezer	9 months
Cooked seafood	Refrigerator	3 days
	Freezer	2 months
DAIRY		
Uncooked eggs in shell*	Refrigerator	3 weeks
Hard-boiled eggs in shell	Refrigerator	3 weeks
	Freezer (whites only)	6 months
Milk	Refrigerator	5 days
	Freezer	1 month
Mayonnaise (opened)*	Refrigerator	2 months
Canned fruits (opened)	Refrigerator	1 week
Canned vegetables		
(opened)	Refrigerator	3 days

*Do not freeze.

(Chart based FDA and USDA guidelines.)

Glossary: Food and Cooking Terms

Ever feel like you need an interpreter when you're reading a cookbook? Those of us who are challenged in the culinary department have a hard time deciphering those special terms familiar to skilled and seasoned chefs. Here's a handy glossary to help:

Al dente: Pasta cooked just until firm.

Bake: To cook food in an oven, surrounded by dry heat; when referring to meat or poultry, baking is called roasting.

Barbeque: To cook foods on a rack or a spit over coals.

Beat: To stir rapidly to make a mixture smooth, using a whisk, spoon or mixer.

Blanch: To cook briefly in boiling water to seal in flavor; blanching is usually used for vegetables or fruit, to prepare for canning and to ease skin removal.

Blend: To thoroughly combine two or more ingredients, either by hand with a whisk or spoon, or with a mixer.

Boil: To cook in water that has reached 212 degrees F and in which bubbles rise constantly to the surface.

Bone: To remove bones from poultry, meat or fish.

Bouquet garni: A tied bundle of herbs, usually parsley, thyme and bay leaves, that is added to flavor soups, stews and sauces but removed before serving.

Braise: To gently brown in a small amount of liquid over low heat in a covered pan until tender.

Broil: To cook on a rack or spit under or over direct heat, usually in an oven.

Caramelize: To heat sugar until it liquefies and becomes a syrup ranging from golden to dark brown.

Ceviche: An appetizer of raw fish marinated in citrus juices.

Cream: To beat ingredients, usually sugar and a fat, until smooth and fluffy.

Cube: To cut food into small, even pieces, usually about ½ inch in size.

Cut in: To distribute a solid fat in flour using two knives or a pastry blender in a cutting motion, until divided evenly unto tiny pieces. Usually used in making pastry.

Deep-fry: To cook by completely immersing food in hot fat.

Deglaze: To loosen pan drippings by adding a liquid, then heating while stirring and scraping.

Dollop: A scoop-size blob of soft food, such as whipped cream or mashed potatoes.

Dot: To scatter butter in bits over food.

Dredge: To cover or coat uncooked food, usually with a flour or cornmeal mixture or bread crumbs.

Dress: To coat foods, such as salad, with a sauce, or to clean fish, poultry or game for cooking.

Drippings: Juices and fats rendered by meat or poultry during cooking.

Filet: A flat piece of boneless meat, poultry or fish. Also, to cut the bones from a piece of meat, poultry or fish.

Flambé: To ignite warmed alcoholic beverages, which are then poured over foods just before serving.

Flute: To make decorative grooves or slashes in pie crusts or vegetables.

Fold: To combine a light mixture, like egg whites, with a heavier mixture, such as a custard.

French: To cut a vegetable or a meat into thin strips lengthwise.

Fricassee: A chicken or meat dish that's flavored with wine and made with vegetables.

Frizzle: To fry thinly sliced meat over high heat until it turns curly.

Fry: To cook food in oil or butter over medium to high heat.

Genoise: A versatile, light cake, much like a sponge cake.

Glaze: To coat food with a thin liquid that turns smooth and shiny; also, a glossy coating for hot or cold foods.

Grate: To shred or rub a piece of food against a serrated surface until it becomes small particles.

Gratin: Any dish that is topped with cheese or breadcrumbs, then broiled until brown and crisp.

Grill: To cook foods over hot coals or another heat source.

Grind: To reduce a food such as coffee beans, spices or meat to small particles in a grinder.

Herbes de Provence: A mixture of assorted dried herbs commonly used in southern France; used to season meat, chicken and vegetables.

Hibachi: A small cast-iron portable tabletop grill that gets its name from the Japanaese word for "fire bowl."

Hull: To remove the outer coating or leafy portion of a food to prepare it for eating.

Infusion: The flavor that's extracted by steeping a food such as herbs, fruit or tea leaves in a hot liquid.

Jell: To congeal a food like gravy or sauce, usually by adding gelatin.

Julienne: To cut foods such as vegetables into thin, matchstick strips.

Jus: Fruit and vegetable juices, or the natural juices that come from cooking meat.

Kabob: Small chunks of chicken, meat or fish that typically are marinated, then skewered and grilled.

Knead: To mix and work a dough either with your hands, a food processor or an electric mixer until it is smooth and elastic.

Lard: Rendered, clarified pork fat. This term is also a verb that means to insert long, thin strips of fat such as bacon into a dry cut of meat to make it more flavorful and juicy.

Leaven: To stir a leaving agent like yeast or baking soda into a batter or dough to make it rise.

Liaison: A thickening agent for soups and sauces, typically made with flour, egg yolks or cornstarch.

Lyonnaise: Dishes that are prepared, seasoned or garnished with onions.

Macerate: To soak a food in a liquid such as brandy or rum in order to infuse it with flavor.

Marinade: A blend of oils, acids and herbs that's used to tenderize meat and flavor vegetables.

Marinate: To soak a food in a seasoned liquid in order to flavor and tenderize it.

Medallions: Coin-shaped or round filets, typically beef, veal or pork cut from the most tender parts of the meat.

Meunière: Seafood served with lemon, parsley and melted butter.

Mince: To chop finely.

Mornay sauce: A sauce made with cheese and fish stock.

Newberg: A cream sauce that is thickened with egg yolks and typically baked with shrimp or lobster.

Pâte: A delicately flavored meat paste.

Pot de crème: A pudding that's usually served in small porcelain cups with lids.

Prick: To make small holes in the surface of meat or fish.

Primavera: An Italian phrase that refers to a dish made with vegetables that are diced or cut into matchsticks.

Puree: To whip in a blender or food processor or to put through a sieve to make a thick sauce.

Ragout: A French-style, rich stew of meat, poultry or fish.

Ramekin: An individual baking dish that is usually used to hold a dessert or a savory custard.

Ratatouille: A French dish made with eggplant, tomatoes, peppers, zucchini and bell peppers, cooked in olive oil.

Render: To melt meat or poultry fat over low heat.

Risotto: Rice that is sautéed and then cooked slowly in liquid.

Roux: A mixture of flour and butter used to thicken a stew or a sauce.

Rumaki: Japanese hors d'ouevres made with chicken livers, bacon and water chestnuts.

Sauce verte: A green, mayonnaise-based sauce made with spinach and herbs such as chervil and parsley.

Sauté: To brown in a small amount of butter or oil.

Scald: To heat milk to just below the boiling point.

Scalloppine: Thin slices of meat, usually veal, that are sautéed and served with a topping.

Shuck: To remove the shell from shellfish, such as oysters or clams.

Simmer: To heat to just below the boiling point.

Skim: To remove the top layer from a liquid, such as cream.

Spumoni: An Italian-style ice cream made with chopped candied fruit.

Strain: To pour a liquid or dry ingredient through a sieve to remove unwanted particles.

Sukiyaki: A Japanese-style dish of thinly sliced vegetables and meat.

Tortoni: A frozen Italian dessert made with almonds and toasted coconut.

Truss: To secure poultry with string, pins or skewers.

Velouté: A French cream sauce.

Welsh rabbit: A cheese sauce, often served over toast points.

Zabaglione: A light Italian dessert made with Marsala, beaten egg yolks and sugar.

CHAPTER 11

You're the Event Planner

Enjoy your own party? After you've slaved over the planning, decorations and cooking for weeks, the idea may sound ridiculous. But you know what? Entertaining doesn't have to be that way. Oh, I've been there. Early in our marriage, when we had small children, I used to make myself, my family and everyone within a five-mile radius miserable getting ready for the dinner parties and elaborate Sunday lunches we hosted several times a month. Over the years I learned that I'd better learn to simplify entertaining, or I would end up in a home for the terminally overwhelmed.

Today I have entertaining down to a fine science, and thanks to my good friend and culinary expert Judie Byrd, even my food is delicious. You can do this too. Remember, the idea is not to get a write-up in the society section with elaborate details of your arrangements that cost more time and money than you have. The idea is to enjoy a special meal or occasion with people you enjoy. Planning is more than half the battle. And even that can be fun.

Let's Get This Party Started!

PARTY IDEAS

- **Pasta Potluck.** Invite five couples to bring their favorite sauces; you supply the pasta. (Allow 2 ounces dry pasta per person, and serve a variety.) Serve crispy breadsticks, an antipasto tray, green salad and garlic bread. Create atmosphere by setting up card tables with red-checked tablecloths and green napkins. Raffia tied around old wine bottles makes festive candleholders. String tiny white lights in houseplants and play soft background music.

- **Family Foot Bowl-Game Party.** Decorate with pennants, banners, balloons and streamers. Create a dining table centerpiece with cheerleader pompoms and a basket of mums. Provide plenty of popcorn and peanuts for snacking. At halftime, serve steaming bowls of chili, jambalaya or chowder, and French bread.

- **Dessert Drop-In.** Offer guests seven or eight confections. Include an assortment of tastes and textures—crunchy, creamy, rich and dense. Provide cheese, fruit and nuts for those who don't eat sugar.

- **Beat the Winter Blues Beach Party.** Turn the furnace up just a tad higher. Serve summer foods you might take to the beach—cold fried chicken, potato salad, deviled eggs and fruit punch—or use tropical recipes. Splurge on plenty of flowers, and play music that reminds you of summer.

- **Afternoon Tea Party.** Offer guests three or four kinds of tiny, crustless sandwiches, such as cucumber and watercress-cream cheese, along with scones, jam, miniature pastries and assorted kinds of hot tea.

- **International Cheese Tasting.** Plan to have a variety of different tastes and textures of cheeses from around the world: a French Brie, an English Stilton, a crumbly, tangy farmhouse Cheddar and Swiss Jarlsberg. Crackers and thin slices of a fresh baguette, along with pears, green grapes and apples, make the perfect accompaniments. To drink? Wine, sparkling water and soft drinks.

- **Pizza Party.** Buy a big batch of pizza dough from your local pizzeria or buy frozen balls of dough at the supermarket. Assemble all the toppings: Fontina cheese, sausage, basil leaves, black olives, goat cheese, cooked crumbled hamburger, sun-dried tomatoes and whatever else you like. Let everyone assemble the pizzas and while they bake, everyone sits down for the salad course. Have plenty of cold drinks and beer on hand.

- **Teenager's Party.** Make a 3- to 5-foot submarine sandwich. Line up foot-long sandwich buns on a long piece of aluminum foil. Let the kids layer favorite sub-sandwich toppings and cut the sandwich into serving pieces.

YOUR PARTY PLAN: WHEN TO DO WHAT

Three to four weeks before the party . . .

- Decide on a theme if you want one.
- Make your guest list. If you have a bigger list than your home can comfortably handle for a seated dinner, consider an informal buffet dinner, a Sunday afternoon open house or an early evening wine-and-cheese tasting. Or choose a day when you can be outside. For a large, special-occasion party, don't rely on the weather. Unless you're positive it won't rain, rent a party tent or have the party at another location.
- Send invitations. (Don't forget maps!)
- Plan menu; figure food amounts; make shopping list.
- Plan a cooking schedule—for example, when to bake and freeze or meet with caterer.
- Shop ahead for nonperishables and supplies.
- Tape an envelope for receipts to the front of your refrigerator. This will help you track expenses.
- Take inventory and start gathering equipment. Reserve rentals, if needed.
- Consider hiring a teenager to help during the party and with cleanup afterward.
- Start polishing silver or brass serving pieces during spare minutes.

Two weeks before the party . . .

- Finalize decorating plans.
- Prepare foods you can freeze.

Bright Idea

Have someone take pictures at your party. Write the date and event on the back of each picture and send copies to the guests in the pictures.

- Decide what you'll wear for the party. Mend or take clothes to the dry cleaner if needed, or shop for something new. Be sure to check accessories.
- If you're planning an adult party, make arrangements or plan entertainment for your children.
- Plan music. Assemble CDs and prepare any musical equipment.

One week before the party...
- Organize your kitchen for the party.
- Keep an eye on guest acceptances and regrets. Work on a seating plan. Write names on place cards.
- Store countertop appliances and other items you won't need.
- Clean your oven to avoid "smoking" your food rather than baking it.
- Begin setting up stations for specifics such as fixing drinks, assembling food platters and stacking dishes between courses.
- Clean out your refrigerator to create more space.
- If you're not going to buy bags of ice, make ice cubes every day, and store them in plastic bags.
- Get party linens ready. Press tablecloths and napkins. Store carefully so they won't wrinkle.
- Wash or wipe off plates, glasses and serving dishes, if needed.
- Confirm arrival time for any professionals you've hired or friends you've asked to help.
- Stock the bar. Purchase nonalcoholic beverages as well.

Two to three days before the party...
- Finalize the number of guests.
- Cook food to be reheated or served cold.
- Give bathrooms a thorough cleaning.
- Rearrange furniture.
- Start decorating.
- Clear space for coats.
- Shop for everything except last-minute perishables.
- Make list of jobs for helpers and hired staff.
- Prepare wood in fireplace.

One day before the party . . .

- Wash lettuce and produce; store in plastic bags.
- Set table and label serving pieces with what they will hold. (This will help you remember the vegetable salad that's marinating at the back of the refrigerator.)
- Chill wine.
- Set up music.
- Do last-minute housecleaning.
- Buy ice, if needed, and fresh flowers. Arrange flowers in containers.
- Prepare foods that can or need to be stored before serving.

Day of the party . . .

- Buy any last-minute perishables.
- Fix remaining foods as early as possible.
- Do a quick-clean run-through on your house.
- Freshen bathroom towels.
- Go outside and walk through your front door as if you were the first guest. Are there any last-minute things you need to do?
- Light fire in fireplace.
- Get dressed one hour before guests arrive, but put on an apron.
- Check bathrooms: stock with toilet paper, towels and soap. Turn on a nightlight or leave light on if switch is hard to find.

The final sixty minutes . . .

- Finish hot food in oven.
- Put out canapés and cocktail snacks.
- Turn on music.
- Light candles.
- Set out food and beverages.
- Enjoy greeting your guests at the door.

After the party . . .

- Depending on your style, do only the cleanup necessary to prevent food spoiling or being eaten by pets during the night.

■ Start a special occasions notebook, in which you make notes about what did and didn't work. You can refer to this resource next time you entertain.

DECORATING IDEAS

■ Use a number of smaller flower arrangements and a low centerpiece on your main table. Even though people won't be sitting across the table from each other, they'll be able to chat with those on the other side of the table as they stand in line. And low centerpieces don't fall over.

■ Place lots of votive candles around your dining room and the rest of the party rooms. They won't tip over like tapers might, so they're relatively safe to burn without your constant supervision.

■ When choosing flowers, remember that heartier flowers such as daisies, lilies or alstromeria stay fresh-looking longer.

■ Consider decorating your mailbox to help guests find your house: use balloons, flowers or streamers.

■ Create a glamorous atmosphere on a party table by tying up a small piece of dry ice in cheesecloth and putting it into a bowl of punch. There will be a lot of smoke, but the punch won't be affected.

■ Use nonpoisonous fresh flowers to turn an ordinary cake into a fabulous dessert. Fill small plastic water picks (available at florists) halfway with water and insert flowers. Push them into the top of a frosted cake.

■ For an autumn luncheon, carve out miniature pumpkins and fill them with chicken, tuna or pasta salad.

■ Use tiny American flags to decorate foods if your party is on a patriotic holiday.

QUANTITIES

■ *Hors d'oeuvres*: Expect guests to consume about four per hour. Plan to serve four or five kinds.

■ *Alcohol*: A fifth (750 ml) of wine fills six 4-ounce glasses. Plan on serving half a bottle of wine per person if it's all you're offering. A

Take Note

For a seated dinner make sure your centerpiece is low enough so guests can see each other across the table. Keep your centerpiece under 12 inches.

Outsourcing: Rental Know-How

- Obtain price lists from local rental companies of items they rent.
- Before choosing a company, ask:
  - Does the cost include same-day or next-day return?
  - Are the quantities and styles you need available on your party date?
  - Are delivery and setup charges included in the price?
  - Is there an extra fee for returning dirty dishes, linens or cutlery?
- What is the charge for broken items?
- Place your order early to assure a wide choice of colors and styles.
- Have the items delivered as early before your party as possible.
- When items are delivered, check off each item and make sure it works before the driver leaves.
- Schedule the pickup time after the party.

fifth of liquor serves thirteen 2-ounce drinks. Expect guests to consume about one drink per hour.

- *Ice*: A 10-pound bag will fill about forty 12-ounce glasses. A 20-pound bag will chill twenty-four bottles of wine.
- *Meat*: 18 pounds of bone-in meat or poultry, or 6 pounds of boneless meat or poultry, will feed twenty-four guests.
- *Salad*: A head of iceberg lettuce feeds ten; romaine, eight; Boston, four. For dressing, 3 cups of dressing will serve twenty-four guests.
- *Bread*: A large loaf offers eighteen to twenty slices. A single baguette feeds ten.
- *Butter*: 2 tablespoons will spread seven slices of bread.
- *Cake*: A sheet cake weighing 5 pounds will serve fifty people.
- *Ice cream*: 1 gallon will feed twenty-four people when you're serving cake or cookies as well.
- *Coffee*: For twenty-four cups of coffee, you'll need 18 cups of water and 3 cups of coffee.

Outsourcing: Catering Queries

Interview potential caterers with these questions:

- Do you order rental equipment?
- When will rental equipment arrive? Who will deliver it? When will it be picked up, and by whom?
- Do you charge extra for reserving rentals or other services?
- How early do you arrive?
- How many staff people do you bring along?
- Do you decorate tables? What table linens do you provide? Do you have a variety of fabrics and colors from which we can choose?
- Do you provide dishes and silverware? What kinds do you have?
- Do you run the bar? Do you set it up?

- Do you serve food such as hors d'oeuvres, or set it out on tables?
- Do you suggest a seated meal or a buffet?
- What menu options are available? Do you take requests? What are your most popular dishes?
- Do you offer different dessert options?
- Do you offer coffee service?
- Do you order flowers?
- How many electrical outlets do you need?
- What cleanup do you do? How much time do you think this will take?
- What kind of insurance do you have?
- What is your fee? Do you add a gratuity?

Entertain with Ease

DETAILS

- If you're planning a large party or reception, reserve your location, caterer and entertainment at least three months in advance.
- Invitations should include whether the party has specific hours or is open-ended; if dinner is served and at what time; if it's BYOB and/or a potluck; if a type of dress is expected; if there are any special activities; and if there are any parking directions.
- Be aware of guests' special dietary needs. Plan to have at least one meatless dish that is hearty enough to serve as a main course to those who eschew animal protein. Also be sensitive to recovering alcoholics. Have on hand plenty of chilled sparkling water, fruit juice and soft drinks.
- If children are coming, make sure at least some of the foods are kid-friendly.

241

- If your party will be large and/or noisy enough to be noticeable, be a good neighbor. The easiest way to avoid potential conflicts is to invite the neighbors. In any case, at least inform those neighbors who are likely to be affected by your party, and ask them to let you know if they are having problems with noise or other aspects of the party.

- If you are expecting more cars than your property or adjacent streets can hold, find alternatives, such as nearby public parking or neighbors who will allow people to park on their property. Let your guests know in the invitation where to park. If space is really tight, suggest that they carpool or use public transportation.

- If you have a bartender or other assistant, explain exactly what you'd like him to do. Tell him where to find extra supplies and make sure he can direct guests to the bathroom and telephone.

- Make arrangements for your pets. Some guests may have allergic reactions to animals.

- Be sure to have plenty of extra bathroom tissue. Parties tend to tax plumbing to the maximum, so it's considerate to keep a plunger in a discreet but accessible location.

SIMPLICITY

- Don't put foods on your menu that take a lot of last-minute kitchen preparation.

- For a buffet, choose foods that will look good after sitting out for more than an hour.

- Set out platters the day before to plan how traffic flow will work.

- Make a smaller table work for large parties by cutting a piece of plywood to the shape and size you need. Lay a blanket over your own table, then place the cutout on top, followed by a tablecloth.

- If you're having a large party, let your kids be servers, door openers or coat checkers. Use paint pens to decorate T-shirts to look like tuxedos for them to wear. Buy inexpensive plastic top hats at a costume or toy store.

- Before the party, line several paper grocery sacks with plastic garbage bags and hide them in your laundry room or pantry. They'll be ready to use for quick cleanup between courses.

Get Your Glassware Sparkling

- File down any chipped glasses with a damp emery board.

- Remove sticky labels by rubbing with lighter fluid.

- Soak glassware with water marks in water with a touch of vinegar. Rinse in cold water, drain and dry.

- Set up a drinks table in a different room from the food.
- Serve chunky punches and iced drinks from a pitcher that has a lip to prevent fruit pieces and ice from pouring out with liquid.
- In addition to the main food table in the dining room, place hors d'oeuvres and pickup foods in strategic areas in your living room and family room.
- If you have wet weather, place mats inside and outside the door. Provide a plastic container for holding umbrellas.
- Start a sink of hot water, a squirt of dishwashing liquid and 1 tablespoon bleach after the main course. Soak dinner dishes while you're eating dessert. The bleach will kill germs.

AMBIENCE

- Lower room temperature before guests arrive.
- For a more dramatic presentation, serve canapés on a small mirror instead of a platter.
- Choose music carefully. Keep the volume low so conversations can take place.

• Classical works well for a formal dinner or buffet; introduce guests to your favorite composers, or ask a local music store to help you find selections by Mozart, Beethoven or Vivaldi.

• Country-and-western music adds flair to a casual dinner or cookout.

• Light jazz (George Benson, Peter White) or instrumental music (Jim Brickman, George Winston) are good general choices. And seasonal varieties are appropriate and enjoyable for most any occasion.

• Consider using live music. Call your local high school to inquire about band students who play in string quartets or combos for parties. Student groups are usually inexpensive, but be sure to check on their fee and repertoire of songs before you book them.

• Have an empty flower vase or two standing by. If a guest brings fresh flowers as a hostess gift, you won't have to run around searching for something appropriate to put them in.

243

SHORT-NOTICE PARTY SHORTCUTS

Here are tips to help you be party-ready in minutes:

- Keep colorful paper goods, candles and decorations on hand at all times.
- Surface-clean only the rooms guests will see. Close the doors to others.
- Master a quick-fix appetizer and dessert recipe, and keep the ingredients on hand. For example:

1. Keep an 8-ounce package of cream cheese in your refrigerator. Place the brick of cream cheese on a pretty plate. Then pour a small jar of strawberry jam, jalapeno jelly or fruit chutney over the top of the cream cheese. Surround with interesting crackers.

2. Keep a bag of chips and the makings of a dip (sour cream and dehydrated soup mix) in your pantry.

3. Keep a frozen pound cake, frozen berries and paper doilies on hand. Serve a slice of cake with berries on top on a doily. Beautiful and delicious!

- Keep drinks to serve guests in a place that is off-limits to the kids. Let the kids have their own special place for their beverages. Keep both places well stocked.
- Keep a frozen family-size entrée (such as a vegetable lasagna) and a tube of refrigerated dinner rolls handy. If company drops in and you want them to stay for dinner, you're ready.
- If you keep on hand a canister of air freshener, a bar of nice soap and some decorative paper finger towels, your bathroom will always be company-ready.

WINE KNOW-HOW

- Chill wine well by refrigerating for at least two hours or immersing in ice for half an hour.
- As a general rule, serve dry white wines or light reds with fish; sparkling or white wines, or dry sherry, with appetizers; robust red wines with pasta or cheese; and a lightly acidic white wine with creamy foods.

- If serving champagne, loosen wires before the party so all you have to do is pop the cork.
- An hour before serving, uncork young red wines to get the best flavor.
- Filter (decant) wine by pouring it through an unbleached coffee filter into a pitcher. Decanting is rarely necessary now unless you are serving an older red wine or a vintage Port.
- Warm red wine in a barely warm decanter; don't warm wine directly on heat.
- Only cook with a wine that you would actually want to drink, and avoid any products labeled "cooking wine," which tend to taste inferior. If you cook with wine, use less salt in your recipe. And use dry, rather than sweet, wines to flavor food.
- Have on hand a bottle of dry vermouth, and use it in any recipes that call for white wine. Vermouth will last for a couple of years once opened, as long as you store it in a cool cupboard.
- The type of red wine determines the temperature at which it should be served. The lightest reds should be slightly below 55 degrees F, while very robust reds should be served a little warmer, say at 60 to 65 degrees F.
- If you're using an ice bucket, place a clean kitchen towel around the neck of the bottle to help catch drips when you remove the bottle from the bucket to pour.

Eat not to dullness; drink not to elevation.
—Benjamin Franklin

TEN ENTERTAINING DISASTERS—AND WHAT TO DO ABOUT THEM

Disasters can be big or small, depending on how they're handled. Some of them can be avoided altogether.

1. **Your electrical system blows a fuse, causing a blackout during your party.** A few days before the party, have a trial run to test your home's electrical capacity. Turn on all lights, ceiling fans, music sources, and any extra appliances you'll be using. If you blow a fuse or flip a breaker, decide what can be turned off without disrupting the party. You may need to use appliances at differing times, or use candles as an alternate light source.

245

2. **More guests show up than anticipated.** Make the most of the situation without making your guests feel awkward. Cut food into smaller servings and fill glasses less full. Stretch iced tea by adding orange juice or lemonade. Always keep ingredients on hand to fix an extra spur-of-the-moment hors d'oeuvre or side dish. Enlist an older child or teenager to run the dishwasher mid-party so you don't run out of glasses and plates. Or use your stashed paper plates if you have to. If you can't squeeze extra place settings on your table, use inexpensive bamboo lap trays for creating an additional conversational dining group. Note: Your guests will feel more comfortable and welcome if a host or hostess sits at each location.

3. **Fewer guests show up than anticipated.** Avoid this problem by sending out invitations early—at least three weeks in advance. People are more likely to respond to an invitation that says RSVP than Regrets Only. Also, be sure to mail an invitation back to yourself. If you don't receive it, you'll know to check with the post office to see if a bag of mail was misdirected. If bad weather or unforeseen circumstances arise and guests cannot come, be sure to make those who do come feel welcome. Keep the party on a positive note by not drawing attention to the missing guests.

4. **A guest spills something and stains your carpet.** Clean up the spill with as little fuss as possible. Let the guest help if this eases the embarrassment. If the carpet is treated with stain repellent, most spills will blot up. Douse the spot with club soda and clean it later.

5. **A casserole bubbles over and smokes up your kitchen thirty minutes before the party.** Cover the smoldering drips with baking soda immediately. Open windows and doors and use a portable electric fan to disperse smoke.

6. **Your guests are strangers and conversation is slow.** Get things moving by asking each guest to tell where he or she was when a significant event occurred—for example, where were you when men first landed on the moon? For humor, have each person at the table, one at a time, make three statements about him- or herself, two of which are true. Other guests try to guess which one is false.

Or introduce one of the guests to the group and say how you know him or her. Ask the rest to introduce themselves and tell how they know you.

7. **Someone chokes.** Remove the food from the mouth. Encourage the victim to cough. If coughing fails and person is making a high-pitched wheezing sound, stand behind him and put your clenched fist—thumb inward—underneath the breastbone. Hold the fist with the other hand, and pull firmly upward and inward up to four times.

8. **Someone drinks too much alcohol and starts making a scene.** Gently encourage the person to lie down in one of the bedrooms for a rest. Make a pot of strong coffee. Quietly ask around to see if another guest could offer this person a ride home. Under no circumstances, allow him or her to drive, even if it means taking away the car keys.

9. **You (or a guest) gets hurt.** Keep a first-aid kit handy at all times for such unforeseen emergencies as these. Butterfly bandages work wonders on cuts caused by a slip with a paring knife. Apply ice cold water (never butter) to burns. Apply firm pressure to a deep cut and keep that part of the body elevated until the bleeding stops. If it's obviously a more serious injury and requires a trip to the ER, have another family member accompany the guest. Stay as calm as possible, since your mood is contagious and guests will look to you for a sign as to how to react to a medical emergency.

10. **A dessert turns out truly horrible.** Always keep on hand a quart of premium ice cream and either a bottle of good liqueur or dessert sauce. Paired with some packaged cookies or chocolate, this is a sweet, festive way to end any meal.

ENTERTAINING ETIQUETTE: ATTENDING A PARTY IN STYLE

Here are a few tips to remember when you're attending someone else's open house or cocktail buffet:

- Respond promptly to invitations whether you can go or not. If an emergency disturbs your plans, contact the host with your apologies as soon as possible.

Bright Idea

For an easy, elegant addition to a buffet, thread grapes, pineapple chunks and kiwi slices onto toothpicks. Serve with vanilla yogurt dip.

A Better Buffet

■ **Use varied tableware, food and accessories for an interesting look.**

■ **Put plates at the beginning of the buffet, followed by side dishes, the main course, then salad and vegetables.**

■ **Place relishes, breads, napkins and silverware at the end of the table.**

■ **Serve drinks from a separate table.**

■ **Leave room between food items so guests have somewhere to put glasses or other items.**

■ **Leave space for maneuvering behind a buffet table.**

■ **Tape down all electrical wires for safety.**

■ Arrive on time—not early, not late. It is often more trouble to the hosts if you are ten minutes early rather than ten minutes late. Call from your car if you will be more than fifteen minutes late.

■ Never take an uninvited child or guest to a party without asking your host first.

■ When you're stopping by several parties in one evening, be polite. Let the host know you can stay just a few minutes.

■ It's nice to take a gift to the host or hostess, such as a small book, potted plant, loaf of interesting bread or bottle of wine. If it's a big dinner party, don't take fresh flowers. Your hose will need to search for an appropriate vase. If you want to give flowers, have them delivered the day before. And if you bring your host a bottle of wine, don't expect it to be served that night.

■ When going through a buffet line, never eat anything directly off of the serving table. And don't nibble while you are walking back to your table. If no seating is provided, you can eat while standing up or circulating through the crowd.

■ If you want to sample the food off someone's plate (with their permission, of course), pass your plate to have a small portion put on it for you to try. Don't reach over and eat off of their plate.

■ Never talk with food in your mouth.

Birthdays

Birthday party. Just the mention of these two seemingly harmless little words can send even the most organized moms into a tizzy. I should know—three times a year, the familiar sense of panic sets in just before my three boys' big days.

It's not that I didn't want to give each of my sons a party. It's just that in our go-go lives, fitting anything else on our already full to-do lists can send the stress meter sky high. Especially today. Children's parties are becoming more and more elaborate—from hiring magicians or clowns to settings up backyard petting zoos, having outings at skateboard parks or even booking pizza places with indoor playgrounds. On the one hand, it's wonderful to have so many fun options, but many parents also report feeling pressured to keep up.

In my family's experience, the simplest parties were always the best—a good, old-fashioned birthday party at home. Before the stress of planning your child's next birthday gets to you, keep in mind that most children are happy with the basics: a few presents to open, some friends to share the day with and a special cake just for them.

Regardless of the type of party you're throwing, if you plan in advance, get input from your child and come up with a manageable guest list, than it will be a success. Below are some ideas and inspirations for making your child's day special and some tips for making your job easier. Remember, in the end, your goal is happy children, not impressed adults.

BETTER BIRTHDAY PARTIES

- A great party starts with smart planning. Begin planning a month in advance, especially if you're hiring entertainment or renting equipment. Ask around for referrals from neighbors and friends. A less expensive option may be to hire a teenager or two to amuse your guests. I know of a six year old whose savvy mom paid two high school cheerleaders to teach her daughter's friends some basic cheerleading moves. The girls loved it, and the party cost next to nothing.

- Determine how much you can afford to spend, and how many children your child can invite. The general rule is that the number of guests should equal the child's age, but that doesn't always work. Some children don't enjoy the chaos of a large crowd. In that case, two to three friends may be the perfect party.

- Keep in mind that if you're planning a party for two or three year olds, you'll need to invite a parent, too. This will help the kids feel more comfortable and provide extra hands for games and refreshments, but you'll need to provide refreshments for the adult crowd as well. Between six and eight kids this age are plenty!

- Four and five year olds need lots of energy-busting activities. Eight to ten of them will be all you can handle unless you have help. Since six year olds are fairly independent and capable of helping during the party, you can handle more of them. Invite eight to twelve.

What one loves in childhood stays in the heart forever.
—Mary Jo Pitney

- Plan to have a party assistant—your husband, a friend, an older child—to help with younger children's celebrations. Or hire a responsible teenager to help with preparations, picture taking and cleanup.

- Be sensitive to hurt feelings when putting together your guest list. Don't neglect new children in the neighborhood. If possible, invite a school-age child's entire class. If the class is too large, explain to your child why having everyone won't work out and mail invitations to the guest's home addresses (instead of distributing them in class), so no one feels left out.

- Let your child's age determine the length of the party. The younger the child, the shorter the party. A sixty- to ninety-minute celebration is just right for two year olds. Older kids can handle two to three hours of partying. A length of a party for teenagers might depend on parental tolerance for late hours and loud music. Negotiate the length of the party beforehand with your teen.

- Come up with several themes for the birthday girl or boy to choose from or ask your child for ideas. You can build a party around almost anything your child has an interest in. A favorite color can become a "Ga-Ga for Green" party. A passion for trucks might inspire a "Keep on Trucking" party. (For a fun cake, fill a large, clean, plastic dump truck with "dirt" made from crumbled-up chocolate cake and chocolate pudding.) Does your preschooler enjoy playing Candyland? How about a party spilling over with sweets? Set up a cupcake-decorating station with M&Ms, rainbow sprinkles, Skittles and chocolate kisses. Or buy a cotton candy maker and have the kids make their own to eat.

- Select a kid-friendly location. Home is always a wonderful choice, if you have room to accommodate the guests. It can be the most convenient place since you don't have to transport supplies. The downside, of course, is the preparation and cleanup. But parties outside the home can be pricey. Most places geared to birthday parties start at more than $10 per child and that usually doesn't include goodie bags. Less expensive options worth looking into might include renting a room at your town's library or community center.

A warm-weather party could take place at a public pool or playground.

- Decide what foods to serve. Be mindful of choking hazards for kids three and under (hot dogs, popcorn and grapes are generally considered no-no's). In my mind, the easiest way to do food is to avoid serving a meal by having the party in the late afternoon between lunch and dinner. That way juice, cake, ice cream and a few treats to snack on can make up the menu. I recommend a mid-morning party for two and three year olds, however. That way the party won't interfere with naps, kids are less likely to be cranky and you can serve no-fuss food like donuts, bagels and cream cheese (don't forget coffee for the moms).

- Ask the moms if their children have any food allergies you should be aware of.

- Choose and buy supplies for some simple crafts kids can do while everyone is arriving. Let them draw on the wall. Set out markers and crayons and hang butcher block paper for this purpose. Fashion jewelry from fruit loops or gummy lifesavers and shoestring licorice. Making a place mat is another simple craft that is a hit with kids any age. Make color copies of illustrations from a favorite book and provide precut poster board and glue. Have the kids glue and arrange the illustrations on the poster board, write their names on it and then you, a spouse or helpful friend can protect the masterpiece with a contact paper.

- On party day, make each guest feel special. Put a smiling greeter at the front door to welcome children as they arrive.

- Consider using an instant-development camera to create party souvenirs. Take a snapshot of each guest in the midst of merrymaking and send it home with the child.

- Encourage your child to write thank-you notes to his guests, even if he thanked them at the party. It's a great habit to start for lifelong courtesy.

Bright Idea

Consider making your own invitations. Your son or daughter may enjoy helping with this, and if you have a home computer, it's a cinch. Send them out at least two weeks before the party.

AN AFFAIR TO REMEMBER

Here are some inspirations for a childhood birthday bash they won't soon forget:

TWO TO THREE YEAR OLDS . . .

1. **Little Ladybug Party.** Decorate the party room with red and black streamers and balloons (be sure to place them well out of the children's reach as balloons are a choking hazard for children under three). Buy inexpensive plastic headbands and help kids turn them into ladybug antennae with pipe cleaners and Styrofoam balls painted red. For dessert serve frosted red cupcakes decorated with black jelly beans.

2. **Be a Clown Circus Party.** Face painting is a must for this celebration. Press a neighbor into service or hire an older child to give each guest a clown face—don't forget to add red noses! Then help kids make silly circus hats. Look for the inexpensive plastic variety and decorate by gluing on fake flowers, pom poms and whatever else you find in your craft basket. Create a simple, backyard obstacle course for extra clowning around.

3. **Good Clean Fun Car Wash Party.** If your child has a summer birthday, make car-shaped invitations and invite guests to bring their toddler's cars or trikes over for some squeaky-clean fun. You provide the hose, buckets, suds and driveway. Ask children to come dressed in swimsuits and serve the food outside.

4. **Go Zoo-y Animal Party.** Ask guests to arrive dressed as their favorite animal or have them bring a stuffed zoo animal from home. Round up all your lions, tigers and bears and have the kids take turns playing zookeeper. When the animals get cagey, calm them down with a zoo-themed picture book—for example, my favorite is a delightful little book called, *Goodnight Gorilla,* by Peggy Rathmann. Serve a birthday cake decorated with animal crackers or plastic zoo critters. Animal crackers (in the classic box, of course) also make cute party favors.

KIDS FOUR AND UP...

1. **Pretty as a Picture Painting Party.** Ask parents to dress their kids in old playclothes and shoes that will be okay to get messy. Purchase a roll of butcher block paper, attach it to the wall or an outside fence (weather permitting) and set out enough acrylic paint and paint-brushes for the little artists to create a beautiful mural. If the group is small and theatrical they might have fun using their mural as scenery or a backdrop for a show they put together during the party. Another way to entertain with paint is to set out lots of paper and a variety of household objects to apply the paint with. Old toothbrushes are fun to use and, believe it or not, corn on the cob makes really interesting designs. Plain old string is fun to work with, too (dip it in and spread it across the paper). You can also cut apples in half, dip the flat side into the paint and use the painted fruit as a stamp.

2. **Out of This World Party.** I know a family who converted a back-yard jungle gym into a space ship with cardboard, tin foil and paint. They took photos of the kids peeking out from the round windows of the rocket and had the kids make stars and planets to hang from an oversize homemade mobile. The winner of the "Guess How Many Moon Rocks Are in the Container" game (you can use donut holes) took home the party mobile as his prize.

3. **Tea Time Party.** What little girl wouldn't love to don her prettiest dress and attend a fancy tea party? Pour tea into a few teapots, set out some sugar cubes and creamers and let the girls drink from real tea cups. (Don't use your best china, and be sure to remind them that glass is breakable.) Remove the crusts from white bread and make mini tea sandwiches. Tuna fish, cream cheese and cucumber and peanut butter and jelly usually go over well. Arrange on pretty dishes. After tea, let the girls convert a plastic headband into a beau-tiful hairpiece with cloth ribbon and silk roses.

4. **Backwards yadhtriB ytraP.** Send invitations written backward and ask guests to wear their clothes inside out or turned around. Play favorite games backward or change the rules—for example, instead of playing "Duck, Duck, Goose" play "Goose, Goose, Duck." When it's time to sing to the birthday boy, attempt to do it in reverse.

253

OLDER KIDS...

1. **Play with Your Food Party.** (Note: Kids six and up love this theme but it can get a bit messy, so plan it for the backyard or basement.) Play games with food.

   • Give each guest a piece of bubble gum and have a contest to see who can blow the biggest bubble.

   • Have an Eggceptional Relay Race using a plastic spoon and an egg. Divide the kids into two teams and give each child a spoon. The first person on each team starts with the egg on her spoon, runs across the yard to her teammate and then carefully passes the egg from her spoon to the next runner's (no hands allowed!). The first team to cross the finish line with its egg intact wins!

   • Play Popcorn Toss. Pop a few big bowls of popcorn and have each player toss a piece over her head and attempt to catch it with her mouth. The person who catches the most wins a prize (a box of unpopped popcorn to take home).

   • Hold a Lemon Walk. This one always gets them laughing. You'll need two lemons and two empty containers (coffee cans work well). Divide the kids into two equal teams. Set up each container approximately two body lengths in front of each team. The first player on each team puts a lemon between his knees, runs to the container and drops the lemon into it. Then he picks up the lemon, runs back to the start and passes it off to the next player who continues the relay. If a player drops the lemon or tips the container over, she must return to the starting line and begin again. The first team to finish wins.

   • The Twisted Pretzel Pass is fun and challenging, too. Have everyone sit in a circle and put one end of a coffee stirrer into his mouth. One child starts with a pretzel on the stirrer and tries to pass it to his right without using his hands. If the pretzel is successfully placed on the next stirrer, that player continues to play by passing the pretzel to his right. Anyone who drops the pretzel or touches it with his hand is out. The person left with the pretzel wins.

2. **Step Back in Time Party.** Preteens and teenagers love dressing up in clothes from bygone eras, especially if they're from their parents'

Games They'll Go For

1. **Bottoms Up.** Blow up a few dozen balloons and corral them into two garbage bags. Divide the kids into tag teams and line them up opposite the bags of balloons. Two at a time, have players race to the bags, grab a balloon, pop it and return to tag a teammate. The team who pops the most balloons in ten minutes wins.

2. **Freeze Dance.** For a super-easy game that most four to eight year olds find hilarious, play music and instruct the party guests that when the music stops they have to freeze in whatever position they are dancing in. That's it.

3. **What Am I?** Put the names of persons, places or things on index cards and tape them to the back of each party guest. Then have guests walk around asking other guests for clues to their identity. Questions must have yes or no answers—for example, "Am I a person," "Am I a place," "Do I eat people food?" and so on.

4. **Find the Penny.** Hide pennies in a stack of hay and set a timer. When the buzzer sounds, the person with the most pennies wins. Believe it or not, twelve year olds enjoy this one as much as two year olds do. For a warm-weather party you can set up a few kiddie wading pools and put a few handfuls of change in each one (be sure each pool has the same amount of money in it). The person who collects the most money in one or two minutes wins a prize and gets to keep the change!

5. **Pin the Tail on the Donkey.** This is always a hit with the younger crowd. And it's easy to change the game to reflect the theme of your child's party. For instance, play "Pin the Bright Red Nose on the Clown" or "Pin the Spot on the Ladybug."

generation. Invite the kids to come dressed up in clothes from their favorite decade or pick one—for example, the 1950s, 1960s, 1970s and 1980s all have fun possibilities—and plan accordingly. During the party play top music from that decade. Shop garage sales and secondhand stores for themed party favors.

OTHER ENTERTAINING IDEAS

1. Do you have a friend with a special talent or hobby? See if she'd be willing to lend her talents to a birthday party. I know of a Family Manager who is a stamping enthusiast and makes herself available

for **stamping parties.** At the party she shows the guests how to create pretty cards, notepads and even T-shirts with her extensive collection of rubber stamps and different-colored ink. Each guest goes home with a stack of homemade stationery.

2. A good cook might help you with a **cooking party.** Invite guests to make and eat their lunch with the guest of honor. Homemade pizza (using premade crusts) or make-your-own tacos are always easy and kid-pleasing. For younger children, make grilled cheese sandwiches with a twist. Use three different cheeses and grill it on rainbow-colored bread (available at bakeries or specialty shops). Children's cookbooks may inspire other ideas. Investigate away-from-home cooking parties by contacting kitchen stores, cooking schools or even gourmet grocery stores. Many places that teach cooking have birthday party packages. If your child enjoys baking, invite a few friends over to bake birthday cookies. Buy some inexpensive aprons that guests can decorate with fabric paint. At the end of the party, give the kids their aprons to take home as a party favor.

3. Host a **hair and nail party** at a local hair salon. Many shops open their stores during off hours for birthday parties. They provide the staff. You provide the eager girls. First, second and third graders really get into this one. Hairstylists may also be willing to come to your home.

4. Is there a **homemade candy shop** in your area? I know of a small chocolate store in New Jersey that does chocolate demonstrations and then allows children to make their own chocolate lollipop. Yum!

5. **Paint-your-own pottery** places are springing up all over the country. Many will allow groups to come in and pick out a premade mug, dish or other decorative object. The kids paint them at the shop and, after the party, the staff glazes and fires the works of art.

6. Is your child an animal lover? **Small zoos and pet shops** may have birthday party packages. Call a local stable to inquire about backyard pony rides or petting zoos.

7. I've never known a little boy who wasn't crazy about **fire trucks.** If this sounds like your son, contact your local fire department. Some departments may be willing to bring a fire truck to your party and

show off the equipment and special clothing fire fighters wear to battle blazes. The kids may even be allowed to sit in the driver's seat for photographs. Be sure to offer a donation when you call.

8. A **birthday outing** can be fun for a child who isn't keen on having a party. When a friend's daughter turned five she purchased tickets to the Broadway production of *Beauty and the Beast*. Due to the expense of the gift, the birthday girl was allowed to invite just one other person along. The child chose her aunt, and the family spent a truly special day together. A less expensive option might be a local theater's production of a play or musical geared toward children or taking a few friends to a new movie and a casual meal.

FAMILY BIRTHDAY TRADITIONS TO START

- Create a keepsake your child will treasure. Each year write a birthday letter to your son or daughter describing the events of the preceeding twelve months. Include details about the child's interests, friendships, disappointments, accomplishments and other family news (births of siblings or cousins, marriages or deaths of relatives). Store the letters somewhere safe and present them to the child on his or her eighteenth birthday. Turn this into a family project by getting input from siblings. Ask brothers and sisters to tell you what they love best about the birthday child or to share a funny or special memory. Record that in the yearly letter, too.

- One mom I know, on the morning of her kids' birthdays, looks at them very carefully and reports that something is different (hair is longer, feet are bigger, clothes look smaller, and so on). Then she tells them it looks like the work of the Birthday Fairy so perhaps it is their birthday. They get a huge kick out of this and the little game has gotten years of mileage.

- During the week of your children's birthdays, allow them to arrange and display their collections in the family room.

- Decorate your child's bedroom on a special day with streamers, balloons and small hidden presents.

- One family I know plants a tree when they have a child. Each year, on that child's birthday, a photograph is taken of the child standing

Take Note

When it comes to having young children open gifts at their own party, my advice is don't do it. Young children are likely to make insensitive comments like "I already have this" or "I wanted the purple one." Besides, it's not much fun for party guests to watch gifts being opened. Instead, after the guests have gone home, have your child open her presents and then promptly send thank-you notes.

next to his/her tree. The photos are kept in a special Family Tree Album.

- Two grandparents use basement support poles to chart the growth of their grandchildren. When a child has a birthday, he or she stands next to the pole and grandpa accurately measures the child and marks the height on the pole. The kids love to race to the basement on their birthdays for the annual ritual and to marvel at how they've grown over the years.

- Baking a cake from scratch is another Family Manager's way of marking her children's birthdays. She has a few no-fail family recipes, and the birthday child gets to pick which one she'd like Mom to bake.

- I have a friend who was born in August. Instead of making a cake, her mother always bakes her a fresh peach pie since that time of year is the height of peach season in her native Maryland. Perhaps there's a way to start a similar tradition in your family using the family member's birthday season as inspiration.

- A former neighbor had a clever idea. For her son's first birthday she bought a guest book with space for a few hundred entries. At his annual birthday party she'd set out the book and encourage each party guest not only to sign his name but to record a special message. In the book she also records a description of the party and a list of the gifts.

- An elementary school teacher told recently about a sweet gesture from one of her students on his birthday. Instead of sending cupcakes, this thoughtful first-grader's mother sent the class a gift for them all to enjoy. Ahead of time she asked her son's teacher for a wish list of items she wanted for the class—books, craft supplies and computer software topped the list. Her son picked the present he wanted to give the class from the list and opened the wrapped gift when he got to school on his birthday.

- For no-fail fun and decor, rent a tank of helium and blow up dozens of balloons. Use 1-yard lengths of curling ribbon and tie one balloon to the back of each chair. Then place them in bunches around the perimeter of the party room or cover your entrance hall ceiling with balloons letting the curling ribbons hang down. Kids love this!

■ Sing a rousing chorus of happy birthday to the birthday child at the exact time of his or her birth. For children who arrived during the wee hours of the morning, set your alarm and wake the rest of the family for an unforgettable experience.

BIRTHDAY WEBSITES

The Internet can be a good resource for ideas, how-to's and—if you're really pressed for time—party supplies, too. A number of websites deliver complete party packages (coordinating plates, cups, tablecloths, goodie bags—even candy-filled piñatas) overnight. As you can imagine, the convenience can be pricey. Here are my three favorites:

■ **www.Familyfun.com.** This is the website of a wonderful magazine called *Family Fun* that is published by the Disney corporation. The site is easy to navigate and loaded with recipes, ideas and real mom (read time-tested) advice and tips.

■ **www.orientaltrading.com** This is best known for its reasonably priced party favors and craft kits.

■ **www.birthdayexpress.com** This website has coordinating products as well as party ideas, themes, recipes and links to related sites.

For more options, use a search engine such as www.google.com or www.yahoo.com. Search with the words "birthday parties" for literally hundreds of sites.

PART III

Taking Charge of Your Family's Money

Every Family Manager must be smart about money. This includes knowing how to stretch limited dollars, spend responsibly, choose the right investment vehicle, establish a retirement plan, create a will, plus a host of other important issues. If that list gives you goosebumps, don't be intimidated!

I am pleased to announce a hard-won and deeply comforting truth: you don't have to be a Wall Street wizard to effectively manage the finance department. I should know. I never even heard the word budget until I married Bill Peel thirty-two years ago. Up until that point, my parents provided everything I needed. When I was a teenager, I had my own checking account, but I never bothered to balance it. I had no clue how much money was in it and it

If a man has money, it is usually a sign too, that he knows how to take care of it; don't imagine his money is easy to get simply because he has plenty of it.
—Edgar Watson Howe

didn't matter. If I ran short, our banker would call my mother and she'd deposit the additional funds right away. Yes, it was a sheltered life.

Financial reality set in during my first few years of marriage. All of the sudden, the money wasn't always there. I'd wasted much of what we had on food we didn't eat, clothes I didn't need and unimportant knick-knacks to decorate our cinderblock apartments. This was a painful experience.

Bill attempted to show me the error of my ways, but I got defensive. To me, money was for spending—not saving. That changed! Finances came front and center when we had a family. Very soon, we had to think about and plan for things like life insurance and college. I wasn't going to blow that for my kids. So I decided to learn about money. At first, it wasn't easy, but eventually I learned that bank statements aren't written in a foreign language and that balancing a checkbook is just simple addition and subtraction.

I want you to relax about money. In this section you'll learn how to get your financial house in order. Even today I don't think of myself as a numbers person, but I've learned to safely navigate the rough seas of money management, with only a few dunks overboard. And many times, I have empathized with the woman who announced, "I have enough money to last me the rest of my life, unless I buy something." But here you'll learn how to buy what you need—and come home with change.

CHAPTER 12

You're the Accountant

Your Personal Financial Philosophy

Philosophy means a particular system of principles for the conduct of life. It's a word we seldom use in our day-to-day dealings with family management issues. But whether we're aware of it or not, we live out our philosophies of life all day, every day. It's important that we understand what our philosophy of money is, because this will influence our priorities, our plan and our procedures.

All of us were influenced to some extent by the way our parents handled finances and what they valued. So when two people unite in marriage, they bring with them a philosophy of money and a lot of standards they think are perfectly normal. It is important, therefore, to think about the following questions:

■ What are your views regarding money?
■ What are your husband's?
■ Have your two views brought conflict? How?

Take some time to sit down with yourself (if you're a single parent) or your husband and clarify your philosophy toward money. Consider these six principles when honing your philosophy:

1. Be responsible.
2. Be productive.
3. Be honest.
4. Be generous.
5. Be yourself.
6. Be realistic.

Determining Your Financial Priorities

Once we have our philosophy pretty well nailed down, we need to set our priorities. Unless we've made some decisions about our priorities, it's easy to lose perspective about what's really important to us and end up making impulsive decisions. We spend money we shouldn't which makes us feel worse than we did before we tried to make ourselves feel better. Or if we can't spend any money, unless we've decided what we value in life, we can easily feel insecure, discontent and unable to enjoy the blessings of life that we do have.

Have you ever stopped to think about financial priorities for your family? Now is probably as good a time as any. Do it by yourself or together with your spouse. Include older children if it's appropriate—however seems best for you. Use these questions and fill-in-the-blanks to guide you in developing your priorities.

ACTION STEPS

1. List five things that you value most about your life today.
2. List five things you want that money can buy.
3. List five things you want that money can't buy.
4. How much is enough? I'll feel okay about money when we have _____ amount in the bank. I'll be content when we have _____.

5. List the causes you'd like to give money to. How much would you like to give?

6. Where would you like to be financially in twelve months? In five years? In twenty years?

7. How do you feel about going into debt? About getting out of debt?

8. Given the choice between a job you'd love for less money and the job you have now and dislike at your current income, which would you choose? If you want a job you love, what can you do to either cut expenses or increase income in other ways?

9. Complete this sentence: If I had more money, I would spend it on _____." Sometimes looking at what we want to spend money on and where we actually spend money can help us do some shifting without increasing the amount of money we spend.

10. Fill in the blank: If we suddenly found ourselves in a financial crisis, I could do without _____.

11. If you were suddenly blessed with wealth, do you know how you would react? How would your priorities change?

Taking first things first often reduces the most complex human problem to a manageable proportion.
—Dwight Eisenhower

Developing a Financial Strategy

Once you've decided on your philosophy and your priorities, you need a strategy to make those things happen. Because each of our situations is different, I can't tell you exactly how to create a financial plan for your family. I can tell you, though, the issues we all need to deal with as we formulate a personalized strategy for our families' financial well-being.

- You need a budget.
- You need a savings plan.
- You need an easy, organized way to keep important records.
- If in debt, you need a strategy for reducing that debt.
- You need to know what your insurance covers—and what it doesn't.
- You need to have a plan for making major purchases.

- You need to file tax returns.
- You need to plan a way to meet children's college education costs.
- You need to know when you'd like to retire and what you plan to live on when you do.

Creating a Spending Plan

I don't like the word budget—it sounds so cheap and negative. Instead, I prefer thinking of a budget as a spending plan that details exactly where all your money needs to go. You don't go to the grocery store without a shopping list and you don't want to face a stack of bills and expenses without a plan to pay for them. Here's how to develop that plan.

1. **Determine your monthly income.** Figure out your family's monthly earnings after taxes.
2. **Calculate your monthly expenses.** These could include the following:

   - Child-care
   - Credit card and other loan payments
   - Drugstore items and cosmetics
   - Entertainment
   - Food
   - Health-care and insurance
   - Housing
   - School tuition and supplies
   - Transportation costs and car loans
   - Other miscellaneous expenses

3. **Determine what the numbers indicate.**
   - Subtract your total monthly expenses from your total monthly income.
   - If your monthly expenses are less than your monthly income, you are holding your own. You might consider saving more money, but only if you have no outstanding high interest debt.

• If your monthly expenses total your monthly income, then you're cutting it too close. You need a spending plan that helps you spend less of your monthly income.

• If your expenses are more than your income, you face a difficult choice. Either increase your income or reduce your expenses.

4. **Create a mandatory savings plan.** After all credit card debt is paid off (see page 274) start a savings plan. Or, use this plan as a goal toward eradicating credit card debt. Review these points below and determine the minimum amount you need to save:

• Write down your financial goals—both short term (being able to pay bills in full, paying down credit card debt) and long term (buying a house, saving for retirement)—and consider what kind of spending plan helps reach those goals.

• Put at least three to six months' salary in a savings account for emergencies.

• Set aside at least 5 percent of each paycheck in an individual retirement account (IRA), a pension fund or a 401(k) plan.

• To pay for major purchases, figure out how much you can save each month. Pay for the item once the money is available—don't buy on credit.

Now subtract the minimum amount you need to save to meet these goals from your monthly income after taxes. You may be left with a small number. Don't be discouraged. If it seems absolutely unreasonable, revisit your savings goals. But also keep an eye on where your money goes.

5. **Track how your money is spent.**

• Keep a spending diary for one month. This will give you the most accurate picture of your spending patterns. It's always a revealing process.

• Split your expenses into two categories: fixed (mortgage, car payments, insurance premiums) and variable (clothing, credit cards, entertainment).

Whatever you have, spend less.
—Samuel Johnson

There is no dignity quite so impressive and on independence quite so important as living within your means.
—Calvin Coolidge

267

• Concentrate on reducing the variable expenses.

• Sometimes it's necessary to reduce fixed expenses. Consider buying a smaller house, refinancing your current one or trading down to a less expensive car.

6. **Put your plan into action.**

• Create a worksheet or spreadsheet to track your spending plan.

• Each month, fill in actual expenses and savings next to the projected numbers.

• Compare the two columns to see how well you've stuck to your plan.

• Revise the spending plan as your income and expenses change.

Choosing a Bank

Choosing a bank these days is more complicated than it used to be, because more options and services are now available. It's easier to evaluate all the options if you first determine your needs and then compare the costs at different financial institutions. For example, credit unions, which are member-owned, offer many of the same services as a bank, but with lower costs. If you have this option, look into it.

DETERMINING WHAT SERVICES YOU NEED
Answer these questions about your banking use:

- How much money is in your checking account monthly?
- How many checks do you write a month?
- How much money is usually in your savings account monthly?
- Do you frequently use local ATMs?
- Do you often use ATMs in other cities?
- Do you bank by telephone or online?
- Is having combined checking, savings and credit card accounts useful?
- Is having a human bank teller important?
- Does your employer have a preferred banking partner that offers you lower rates or extra service?

EVALUATING A BANK'S SERVICES AND FEES

- Is the bank FDIC insured, which protects your deposits up to $100,000?
- Are minimum monthly account balances required?
- If you open multiple accounts, including credit card and mortgage, are lower fees offered?
- What are the interest rates on the savings accounts?
- Is a direct deposit service available?
- What are the ATM fees?
- If using another bank's ATM, does your bank charge you?
- If you write just a few checks monthly, is no-frills checking available?
- What monthly fees or per check charges are involved for checking accounts?
- What charges are incurred for telephone and online banking?
- Can you speak with a representative twenty-four hours a day, every day?
- Are the branches conveniently located?
- How much is the annual fee for a safe-deposit box?
- Are investment and estate planning services available?

CONDUCT AN ON-SITE EVALUATION

- How many people are staffing the information desk?
- Are there long teller lines?
- Do you see an ample number of customer service representatives?
- Do the employees look approachable and friendly?

There are many banks to chose from, so do shop around. Remember, you are the customer and it's most important for you to get what you want out of a banking relationship. If at any point you're unhappy, say something. Banks want to keep their customers satisfied and are often willing to waive charges, reduce fees or make other compensations to keep your business at their institution.

If you know the value of money, go borrow some.
—Benjamin Franklin

Make all you can. Save all you can. Give all you can.
—John Wesley

269

GLOSSARY: BANKING TERMS WORTH KNOWING

Annual Percentage Yield: The amount of interest earned on an account over the course of a year.

Balance: The exact amount of money in an account.

CD: The abbreviation for certificate of deposit, which is a type of savings account in which the money is deposited for a specific time at a specific interest rate.

Compound interest: Interest on top of the interest already earned; accounts that are compounded (or added to) more often earn higher amounts.

Debit: A decrease in an account—for example, a debit card that decreases money in a checking account.

Deposit account: Any account with deposited monies in it, like a checking or savings account.

Interest rate: Percentage of an amount of money paid for the use of the money.

NSF: Nonsufficient funds, usually in reference to a check written for an amount greater than what is in the account.

Overdraft: When a check bounces the bank charges the overage to an interest-bearing credit account.

PIN: Personal identification number, which is a personal code for accessing ATMs and other personal accounts.

Revolving credit: An amount of money borrowed for a specific period of time.

Paying the Bills

Everyone has bills to pay each month. It's a part of life. But you need to keep track of the bills and make sure each is paid on time.

THE BILL PAYING PROCESS

- Two types of bill payers seem to exist: those who pay the bills the day they arrive and those who file them away and set up a bill paying day or evening. Either method is fine, as long as your pay-

Money is like promises—easier made than kept.
—Josh Billings

ments arrive on time and there is money in the bank to cover the checks.

- If you're not paying your bills online, either through your bank or a software system like Quicken, consider trying it. It's easy to learn and greatly simplifies the chore of paying bills by setting up files for every payee and by balancing your accounts. You can even arrange for the system to make automatic payments, so you'll never miss a rent or mortgage payment.

- Try and make the bill paying experience more pleasant. Play some music, have a favorite movie playing in the background or sit outside on a sunny afternoon. Unless you can't avoid it, never pay bills when you're in a bad mood. You're guaranteed to feel worse!

PRIORITIZING THE BILLS

If you're unable to pay all of your bills one month, it's important to know which unpaid bills generate what consequences. Remember that you need to keep your credit rating intact. Should you find yourself continually falling short every month, then revisit your spending plan.

Here's what happens when payments are skipped:

- If rent payments are more than two weeks late, eviction proceedings can begin, although the process takes several months. Make this payment a priority.

- Mortgage payments are also a top priority. The foreclosure process only starts if several payments are missed, but late fees and marks on your credit record happen immediately.

- Bank cards also report missed or late payments immediately. Attempt to pay at least the minimum amount due each month.

- Insurance payments for cars and houses are usually paid in advance and include a thirty-day grace period, so some lag time is permissible. Health insurance, however, must be kept current or you risk losing the coverage.

- Car payments may allow a late or partial payment if your prior payment history is strong. Repossession happens only after several months of nonpayment.

- Utilities are usually forgiving, allowing the occasional late or skipped payments.

IF YOU'RE REALLY STRAPPED FOR MONEY

- Call the creditors and explain the problem. Taking the initiative and working out a payment plan is better than avoiding or not returning their phone calls.
- Try to make minimum payments. Some payment is always better than no payment, and creditors always appreciate your efforts.
- For professional advice, visit a local debt consolidation service for free tips on contacting creditors and structuring payment plans.

BORROWING MONEY

When you need to borrow money for whatever reason, make sure you follow these guidelines:

- Always borrow what you know you can repay.
- Completely understand the conditions of the loan.
- Research all your options before signing anything.
- Repay the loan promptly to retain a good credit history.

What kind of loan is available to you depends upon your collateral, loan history and existing relationship with a lender. These are the major loan sources:

- **Borrow from a friend/family member.** If you have a friend or family member willing to lend you money, only accept their generosity once you've both signed a formal IOU. Writing out the terms of repayment, the interest rate and any other specifics of the loan insures against any confusion in the future. Nothing sours a relationship faster than a disagreement about money, so enter into this type of loan agreement carefully.

It sometimes happens, even in the best of families, that a baby is born. This is not necessarily a cause for alarm. The important thing is to keep your wits about you and borrow some money.

—Elinor Goulding Smith

- **Borrow from a bank or credit union.** Most loans from these institutions start around $1,000 and usually require some tangible item like real estate, a car, investments or personal possessions for collateral. Interest rates vary significantly between lenders so investigate thoroughly.

- **Borrow from your investments.** Creating a margin account allows you to borrow up to 50 percent of a stock's value with a reasonably low interest rate. Understand that if the stock's value decreases, then you must either sell shares or add funds to the account to cover the difference in the changed value.

- **Borrow from your retirement account.** You can borrow from your IRA once a year, provided that money is rolled into another IRA account within sixty days. From a 401(k) retirement account, you can borrow up to $50,000. The usual repayment period is five years and you must pay interest into the account.

- **Borrow against the value of your home.** Home equity loans allow you to borrow the difference between the current market value of your home and the outstanding amount on your mortgage. Usually the borrowing limit is $100,000 and your home is the collateral. The interest paid is tax deductible, which is why home equity loans are so popular.

- **Borrow from an insurance policy.** Depending upon the type of insurance policy you own and how long you've paid premiums into the account, you can borrow against the cash value of the policy. This amount is then repaid or the borrowed amount is deducted from the policy's death benefit payout.

- **Borrow on your credit card.** You can borrow cash from a credit card. However, this is among the most expensive ways to borrow money as credit cards usually charge steep interest rates.

If only God would give me some clear sign! Like making a deposit in my name in a Swiss bank account.
—Woody Allen

Pay as you go is the truest economy.
—Farmers' Cabinet

Keeping Your Credit Clean

Guard your credit carefully. Having a good credit record is necessary for obtaining mortgages and other types of loans. If any problems with your credit record arise, you need to fix them as soon as possible. Here are some important things to know:

1. **Establish credit.** Starting a good credit history is mandatory and relatively easy to do. Open a checking account with an overdraft protection. This ensures that any bounced checks are covered up to a specific amount. Then you are billed for the overage amount. If you bounce a check, make sure to pay this overage amount in full. Utility bills, placed in your name and paid on time, are another step to good credit.

   Department store credit cards or gas company credit cards are usually smart choices for those beginning a credit history, as this type of card usually has low limits and can be paid in full each month.

   For widely used cards, like MasterCard and Visa, shop around for the right card for you. If you usually carry a balance each month, then search for a card with a low interest rate. Cards with higher rates are fine, if you pay the outstanding balance in full every month. Consider a secured credit card if you're opening an account for another family member or if you have a bad credit history. These cards, drawn down against a prepaid amount, are almost like a checking account—for example, you deposit $500 and then when that amount is fully charged on the card, you deposit more funds.

2. **Understand your credit report.** If you have ever been denied credit, it was probably due to information on your credit report. This report is supplied by credit bureaus to lenders like banks and credit card companies. Credit bureaus serve as clearinghouses for information about consumer debts and bill paying habits. They profile creditworthiness and tell prospective creditors if an applicant is a good or bad credit risk.

   If you have been denied credit during the past sixty days, you can receive a free copy of your report from any of the following bureaus. Residents of some states can request a free copy of their credit report each year. You should request reports from all three credit bureaus so you can make sure they are all correct. To request a report, contact each company to see what information is required from you.

TransUnion
2 Baldwin Place
P.O. Box 1000
Chester, PA 19022
800-888-4213
www.transunion.com

Experian
P.O. Box 2002
Allen, TX 75013
888-397-3742
www.experian.com

Equifax Credit
P.O. Box 740241
Atlanta, GA 30374
800-685-1111
www.credit.equifax.com

Carefully review each report when you receive it. If you find any errors, follow these two steps:

1. **Contact the credit agency.** Photocopy your report, note the errors on it and return it, along with an explanatory note. The law requires the agency to follow up on a consumer complaint. If the agency can't prove you wrong within thirty days, it must remove the disputed information from your report.

2. **Determine who made the mistake.** If the mistake is the fault of one of your creditors, say a department store or gas station which incorrectly reported information to a credit bureau, then you'll have to go straight to that company and have them correct the mistake. It's then the responsibility of the company to notify the credit bureaus of the error. In a case where you have had a long-standing argument with a creditor, it's best to settle the dispute before ordering your credit report.

3. **Know your credit bureau bill of rights.** All of your dealings with credit agencies are governed by the provisions of the Fair Credit Reporting Act. These are your rights under the act:

- To learn the name and address of the consumer reporting agency whose report impaired your application in connection with a credit or job application.
- To discover on request the nature and substance of all information, except medical, that a credit agency has on file about you.
- To know the sources of such information, except investigative sources.
- To get the names of all people who have received reports on you within the previous six months, or within the previous year if the report was furnished for employment reasons.
- To have all incomplete or incorrect information investigated, and if any information cannot be found or is found to be inaccurate, to have that information deleted from your file.
- To have your side of any controversy included in a creditor's report, if the difference with that creditor cannot be resolved.
- To have no information sent out that is more than seven years old (ten years if you have been bankrupt), with two exceptions: if you are applying for an insurance policy over specified limits, or if you are applying for a job with a salary over specified limits.

4. **Understand your debt situation.** Consumer debt continues to rise at an alarming rate in the United States. Most of the debt is on credit cards. If your debt is growing, now is the time to reduce it. By carefully understanding how much you owe and what your payments are, you can set about eliminating it.

Answer the following questions honestly. If the answer is yes to any of them, then you've got debt issues.

- Do you pay just the minimum amounts due?
- Are you frequently late with your payments?
- Are you unsure about how much principal you owe?

- Are you unsure about how much interest you owe?
- Have you reached the credit limit on one or more cards?

5. **Create an action plan.**

- Write down all your credit card debt, including all bank, credit, department store and other cards. Note the amount due and the interest paid for each.
- Make paying down this debt a financial priority by adjusting your monthly spending plan. Spend less on variable expenses and more on getting out of debt.
- Leave the credit cards at home and start using just your debit card or cash.
- Direct any windfalls, like tax rebates, tax returns or bonuses, to paying off the debts.
- Think of these payments as the way to vastly improve your financial situation.
- If you own your home, consider a tax-deductible home equity loan to pay off the debts.
- Where possible, condense all the higher interest cards onto lower interest cards.
- Stick to the plan and reevaluate it after six months.

A NOTE ABOUT BANKRUPTCY

This is the last resort for those with outstanding debts they are unable to pay. Sometimes circumstances like a medical problem, job loss or divorce create unexpected financial difficulties. Bankruptcy is a legal process that liquidates outstanding debts with the assistance of a court-appointed trustee.

Usually the payment schedule is spread out over four to six years. This proceeding is serious, with significant long-term ramifications. Before considering this option, investigate any debt consolidation services in your community. This service is free and helps gather all outstanding debts into a manageable payment schedule.

Downsizing

If you or your spouse loses a job, the shockwave runs through the entire family. You have bills to pay and need to find another source of income. If you're now eligible for unemployment, collect it. While it may not replicate your previous salary, it is some money for the checking account. Then get an action plan in place to minimize spending until the next job comes along.

HOW TO TIGHTEN YOUR FAMILY'S FINANCIAL BELT

- A critical first step is to talk with your children about the change. Involve them in dealing with it. They may welcome ideas for earning money for extras themselves.

- Tighten the budget now, not when money runs out. Take a long look at your spending plan and see what adjustments are possible. Be tough as the resources are limited.

- List some free or inexpensive activities your family can do. Free videos from the local library, community events and stargazing are all good family time entertainment.

- Don't dip into the savings. Every family needs a safety net, so leave your savings intact. Make an effort to set aside $1 each day and put your loose coins into a piggy bank. Similarly, resist the urge to charge on your credit cards.

- Schedule an old-fashioned date with your spouse. Just listen to each other and omit all criticism. Working together as a team is important, especially now. Keep a positive focus on each other and about finding work. Create action plans for preparing a revised résumé, networking and interviewing toward a new position.

- Begin searching for a new job immediately. Think of your new job as finding the right new job. Don't think of this as vacation time. But do take time to be thankful for a good interview or a networking session by rewarding yourself with a Friday afternoon off or a long morning walk—something you couldn't do while working at your old job.

- Consider counseling if family stress becomes too great. Talking to a minister, therapist or social worker about the situation often lessens family tension and anxieties. Payment, if any, is usually on a sliding scale and insurance often reimburses a portion of the cost.
- Be flexible in your plans and tell everyone you're looking for a job. You never know who will have the next great job in an unexpected industry that's perfect for you.

Some expenses are essential to the welfare of your family and better left untouched. Here are the payments you *must* maintain.

1. **Medical and dental insurance.** Your entire family should be covered by the working spouse's insurance plan.
2. **Rent or mortgage.** You have to have a place to live.
3. **Life insurance.** Consider increasing the value of the working spouse's life policy.
4. **Medications.** Dropping your blood pressure medication may save you a few dollars today, but the long-term consequences could be devastating.
5. **Food.** Stick with nutritious meals—products, grains, fruits, vegetables and meats. Eliminate convenience and junk foods.

Teaching Money Management for Kids

One of the most important aspects of our children's education is a healthy perspective about money—and they won't learn that in school. Bill and I learned that the best way to teach good money values to our kids was to simplify the financial principles we live by and look for everyday opportunities to apply them to our kids' lives.

GUIDELINES FOR TEACHING KIDS ABOUT MONEY

- **Be responsible.** Make sure your kids know that you will not automatically replace items that get broken, destroyed or stolen because of their irresponsibility.

> *Lending money to your children is comparable to a bank lending money to a Third World country: You never get the interest back, let alone the principal.*
>
> —J. L. Long

279

■ **Be productive.** As soon as children can help around the house, they need regular chores. Even two year olds can fold dishtowels and pick up toys.

■ **Be honest.** Kids need to know about stealing nonmaterial things, such as time from an employer, credit for something someone else accomplished and someone's talent or services they used but didn't pay for.

■ **Be generous.** Young children can be taught to share their resources and time with others. As kids get older, get them involved with religious organizations, local charities and not-for-profits. Become a family of givers.

■ **Be yourself.** Kids need to understand that they are not what they own, wear or drive. Each of us is valuable as a unique human being.

■ **Be realistic.** Kids need to know that none of us always get what we deserve, but most of the time, we will have more than we need. We need to nurture contentment with what we have.

ALLOWANCES FOR A JOB WELL DONE

At our house, each family member is responsible for certain household duties. If you decide to give allowances to your kids, consider their ages and skill levels and how well they do their assigned chores. Here are some basic guidelines for determining allowances:

■ Give an allowance to kids age six and up, depending on their ability to count and their understanding of money. Consider giving $.50 or $1 for every year of your child's age.

■ Children should have the opportunity to earn a few dollars each week. Whether they earn it is up to them.

■ Establish spending rules up front about what their allowance can or cannot buy, and when they will need to spend their own money to purchase something.

■ If kids don't fulfill their responsibilities, suspend their allowance. When they're grown, if they haven't learned the importance of fulfilling their responsibilities, they won't have the privilege of getting a paycheck.

- Pay only for jobs that are completed. Half-done jobs do not earn half an allowance.

- Encourage them to save part of their allowance. If they want to buy a more expensive item, help them set goals for saving. Consider matching their savings dollar per dollar.

- Provide opportunities for kids to earn extra money by taking on extra jobs—for example, cleaning out the garage or basement or washing the car or windows. Post Help Wanted ads on your bulletin board or refrigerator that list kids' opportunities to earn extra cash.

EVERYDAY ECONOMIC LESSONS FOR KIDS

There are all kinds of daily situations that you can use as a springboard for discussing financial matters. Here are a few:

- The next time you use an ATM or cash a check, take a few seconds to explain that the machine isn't printing money. The money is coming out of your account. This is a connection your child won't make without your help.

- In the grocery store, show your child how to use the unit-price tags, and she can help you shop for the best deal in the cereal or soft drink aisle.

- Let your child cut and file coupons from magazines and newspapers, then collect the savings.

- At home, make money a game—literally. Getting the whole family together for Monopoly, Life or Payday is a fun lesson in taking out mortgages, paying bills, saving for college or buying stock.

- When you pay bills, get your children involved so they see how much things cost. Emphasize that family finance is a family topic and not for everyone else to know about.

- When your children want to spend more time shopping, give them a clothing allowance.

- If you buy something in a store, and the clerk mistakenly gives you back too much change, let your child see you return the extra money you received.

There are times when parenthood seems like nothing but feeding the mouth that bites you.
—Peter De Vries

281

■ Do you have anything in your home that you should be paying for, but aren't? Extra cable channels that you get by mistake? A neighbor's magazine subscription that comes to your address? Turn the situation into a teaching opportunity by correcting it and telling your child it's wrong to accept something without paying for it.

JOBS FOR KIDS

Start by brainstorming about the types of services or products your kids can offer. Check with local government offices to see if a business license or permit is needed. Then create an advertising flyer or a business card to distribute to homes or post on public bulletin boards. Here are some ideas:

■ Aid the elderly—for example, do their shopping or run errands.
■ Baby-sit.
■ Bake and sell homemade bread and cookies.
■ Be a birthday clown.
■ Caddie at the golf course.
■ Clean carpets, houses and swimming pools.
■ Clear away old junk and trash.
■ Clip and organize coupons in envelopes for Mom. (Let your children keep the refunds.)
■ Distribute flyers for local small businesses.
■ Groom pets.
■ Help neighbors move, pack and clean up.
■ Hold a garage sale.
■ Iron clothes.
■ Make and paint signs.
■ Move furniture.
■ Mow lawns.
■ Paint outdoor furniture, fences, dog houses, porches, decks, storage sheds.
■ Paint house numbers on curbs with stencils.
■ Pet-sit for working pet owners and out-of-town neighbors.
■ Plan and host birthday parties for smaller children. Older children

can dress up like a party-theme character, help with crafts, organize and oversee games, pass out food, pick up trash and help watch for small guests who might wander off.

- Plant a pumpkin patch in the spring and sell the pumpkins in October.
- Produce a backyard carnival and sell tickets for the games and refreshments.
- Publish a neighborhood newspaper or newsletter.
- Pull weeds.
- Put on a backyard day camp.
- Rake leaves.
- Repair bikes.
- Run an errand service, including grocery and dry-cleaning delivery.
- Start an odd-job service.
- Sweep porches and driveways.
- Tend and entertain younger children.
- Tutor younger children in reading.
- Type/word process.
- Wash cars. Kids can go door-to-door carrying cloths, buckets, window spray, hand brushes, and a portable mini-vacuum.
- Wash windows.
- Water plants and yards for vacationing families.

Bright Idea

Make a big deal out of your child's first paycheck. Have a copy made of it, and put it in a frame.

TEACH KIDS HOW TO INTERACT WITH ADULTS AS ENTREPRENEURS

Be sensitive about what kinds of jobs your kids will feel comfortable performing. An outgoing child won't mind going door-to-door, drumming up business from neighbors. But a shy child may feel threatened at the thought of talking to an adult one on one. Teaching your children some simple communication skills can bolster their courage and help them make a good impression on potential customers.

- **Have a neat appearance.** An adult is more likely to want to hire a child with clean clothes and neatly combed hair.
- **Make good eye contact and shake hands firmly.** Have your child practice looking directly into your eyes while talking. People are

more likely to trust someone who will look them in the eye. Practice a firm handshake. This sends the signal that your child has a good self-image and takes his or her business seriously.

- **Give a clear, concise message describing services or products.** Help your child write down exact words. Pretend you are the customer and role-play the situation until your child has memorized the lines and feels comfortable saying them.

- **Smile and be courteous—even if you get turned down.** A person who says no to a service today may buy another product next time.

- **Celebrate a job well done.** Whenever big or small goals are met, celebrate their success with a special dessert or some other family recognition.

Tipping

HOW MUCH IS APPROPRIATE?

How much to tip for a service is often confusing. Try following the guidelines below as parameters for tipping. These are average amounts for average service. If you've received outstanding service, then increase the tip to show your appreciation. Undertipping is appropriate when the service is bad. But remember that if the food in a restaurant is poorly prepared or a long time coming out of the kitchen, don't take your frustration out on the wait staff by leaving a small tip. Instead, take it up with the manager.

Here is a list of suggested tips:

- Airport red caps: $1 per bag
- Airport wheelchair operators: $5
- Airport cart drivers between gates: $2
- Bartender: 10 percent of the bill
- Caterers: $20
- Delivery person for furniture or appliance: $10 per person
- Dog groomer: 15 percent of the bill
- Hair salon cutter: 15 percent of the bill

- Hair salon shampooer: $2
- Hotel bellhop: $10 if showing you to your room and carrying luggage; less if just opening room door and turning on lights
- Hotel concierge: $10 for a few requests; more for many requests
- Hotel doorman: $2 if helps with unloading car; none for opening doors
- Hotel maid: $3 per day; more if room cleaned twice a day
- Limo driver: 15 percent of the bill
- Manicurist: $2
- Parking garage attendant: $1
- Party entertainers: $20
- Pizza deliverer: $2
- Restaurant coat check: $1 per coat
- Restaurant counter waiter: 15 percent of the bill
- Restaurant maitre d': $20 or more if you're a frequent patron or have a special request
- Restaurant waiter: 15 percent of the bill
- Taxi driver: 15 percent of the fare
- Tow truck: $5 depending on service

CHAPTER 13

You're the Financial Planner

"About the time we think we can make ends meet, someone moves the ends." I think Herbert Hoover said it all. In this chapter you'll find ideas to help stop those ends from moving, by helping you make sense of insurance, investments and more. Get ready to be your family's financial planner with confidence!

How to Purchase Insurance

Think of insurance as a protection plan against any problems with your car, home, and health. It's important to take the time to understand how much and what types of insurance your family needs.

AUTO INSURANCE

Although auto insurance is not required in every state, all states require drivers to have the financial means to reimburse other drivers or passengers if they are injured or if their cars are damaged. Purchasing auto insurance is the simplest way to indemnify yourself and your family in case these events happen. Check the requirements of your state before you start shopping for auto insurance, so you'll know what you need.

Types of Auto Insurance

Familiarize yourself with the six basic types of auto insurance, before you start shopping. All are fairly self-explanatory and straightforward:

1. **Bodily injury liability.** This policy protects you against legal costs and claims should your car injure anyone and covers members of your family and those who drive your car with your permission.
2. **Collision.** If you car collides with another car or object, this covers all the repairs to your car no matter who caused the accident.
3. **Comprehensive physical damage.** Should your car be damaged by theft, fire or any other events, this policy covers the repairs.
4. **Personal injury protection.** If you and your family are either injured in your own car or while riding in someone else's car, this insurance pays your medical expenses.
5. **Property damage liability.** Should your car damage someone else's property, this coves all legal and claim costs, excluding any repairs to your car.
6. **Uninsured motorist.** If you or anyone in your car is in an accident involving an uninsured or unknown driver, like a hit and run, this covers medical costs and repair expenses.

How to Start Smart

- Consult insurance agents and agency and insurance industry websites, and talk with your friends to see what types of packages and rates are available.
- Set up a folder or notebook to collect information from the various agencies and sources you'll be checking.
- Determine how much of each kind of coverage you need. For example, liability insurance is required in many states, so buy that. But if you drive an old car worth less than $1,500, then skip the comprehensive physical damage policy.
- Figure out how much you can afford for premiums. Usually lower premium costs are available if you're willing to pay a higher deductible.

Lowering Your Insurance Costs

Luckily, there are several ways to lower your insurance costs. Knowing what's available before you buy may save you money.

- If you own several cars, ask about a multi-vehicle discount.
- Some insurance companies provide home and auto insurance as a package deal.
- Owning what is considered a low-risk car usually qualifies for a discount. A listing of low-risk cars is available on the National Insurance Crime Bureau website.
- Cars with low annual mileage are cheaper to insure.
- Cars built with anti-lock brakes, anti-theft devices, airbags and automatic seat belts often qualify for a discount.
- Drivers with no accidents in several years and those over the age of fifty usually receive discounts.
- Some reductions are often available to students with good grades and those who have completed driving courses.

Before You Sign the Policy

- Get a minimum of three quotes and make sure the insurance companies providing the quotes are financially reputable. The websites for the National Association of Insurance Commissioners, Standard & Poor's and Moody's Investor Services all provide this information.
- Never pay cash for premiums and make the check payable to an insurance company, not an individual.
- Always get a copy of the policy you're considering in writing. Go over it carefully and make certain all the details are correct and agreeable to you.
- Clearly understand what is not covered under a policy. For example, are rental car costs included? If not, consider purchasing supplemental insurance to cover this expense.

Take Note

Make sure your selling agent is reputable. If you don't see an agent license number, or the agent can't provide this and you suspect fraud, then contact your state's insurance bureau.

After You Sign the Policy

- Keep a copy of your insurance card in your car's glove compartment. Put the original in your safe-deposit box.
- Revisit your coverage and costs at least every other year, as rates change frequently.
- If you file a claim, make sure you keep detailed records about the accident, interaction with the insurance company and costs of the repairs. Also, request detailed backup materials for all repairs and review the charges carefully.

Glossary: Auto Insurance Terms to Know

Conditions: Detailed descriptions of what your responsibilities are and what the responsibilities of the insurance company are, explained in the policy.

Coverage: An explanation in the policy of the specific circumstances that qualify you to file for the policy's benefits.

Declarations: The components of your particular coverage. This includes the premiums, the policy number and information about you and your car.

Deductible: The amount you must pay before receiving any claim benefits from the insurance company.

Exclusions: An explanation of what is not provided under the policy.

Liability: Your financial responsibility incurred because of an accident.

Premium: Your cost for the insurance policy.

Rating: The set of statistics and facts about you, where you live and your driving habits that determine your insurance costs.

Supplemental payments: All additional costs, usually related to legal expenses, which you may need to pay for additional coverage.

LIFE INSURANCE

Talking about life insurance means talking openly and calmly about you and your spouse's death, specifically either of your premature deaths. If that were to happen, how much money would it take to pay the mortgage, send your children to college, make the payments and stay out of financial trouble? With careful planning, life insurance can cover those expenses by preparing for the worst.

"Whoever created the name life insurance had to be the sales genius of all time.
—Robert Half

289

Determining How Much You Need

The standard rule is to purchase life insurance equal to between five and ten years of your annual salary. An alternate estimate is two-thirds of your current monthly income when your children are living with you and then half the monthly income amount when they move away from home. But circumstances between families are different. Ask yourself the following questions to assess your needs:

- How much money do you spend a year on housing?
- What are your annual food and clothing costs?
- How old are your children? Younger children require care for more years.
- What primary and secondary school expenses are forthcoming?
- What amount of college tuition bills do you expect?
- Do you have other savings and investments to offset any of these expenses?
- What is an appropriate amount set aside for any medical situations or emergencies?

Types of Life Insurance

You will choose between three types of life insurance policies: term, permanent and variable.

Term Insurance

Term life insurance lasts for a specific term or period and contains no savings component. There are five kinds of term insurance:

- **Renewable term.** Permits you to renew at the end of each term without taking a medical examination. Premiums increase as you age.
- **Convertible term.** Allows a switch from term to permanent without a medical exam. The premiums are slightly higher than the renewable term.
- **Level term.** Provides a fixed premium cost for a specific period of time. Premiums will increase significantly when the level term expires and a new policy is issued.

- **Decreasing term.** Over time the death benefit payout amount decreases, while the premium remains constant.
- **Increasing term.** The death benefit increases every year, along with the premiums.

Permanent insurance is usually provided for the length of your life. Premiums remain the same, making it usually more expensive than term insurance. The insurer invests your premiums into its investments, so this insurance has a cash value, or a savings component, and pays dividends. You may borrow against this amount. Interest is charged and the loan is usually deducted from any death benefits. The four types of permanent insurance are:

- **Whole life.** The policy has a fixed rate and guarantees a cash value.
- **Universal life.** Allows for changes in death benefit and premium payments.
- **Variable life.** More of an investment option, with the amount of any payout equaling the performance of a preselected portfolio or investments.
- **Variable universal.** A combination of variable and universal.

Choosing Between the Types of Insurance

- Term is usually better for young families, because the rates are lower and the coverage dates are flexible. For example, you can easily buy just enough term to cover all your children's tuition expenses.
- Term has no savings component. As you get older, the premiums increase, as does the probability of a medical exam before granting coverage.
- Permanent offers a lifelong constant premium rate and should be considered as a long-term investment tool.
- Permanent usually requires no medical examination past any initial one.

Buying the Policy

- Obtain at least three quotes before making a decision.
- Compare rates online, from insurance companies directly and from independent insurance salespeople.
- See if memberships in any clubs or professional groups entitle you to less expensive insurance.
- Determine if your selected insurer is financially sound by contacting a state or national rating agency as described in the auto insurance section.

After Selecting the Policy

- Make sure you and your spouse each understand all the specifics of the policy.
- Store the policy in your safe-deposit box.
- Review the policy occasionally and determine if more or less coverage is appropriate based on your current situation.

Glossary: Life Insurance Terms to Know

Cash value: For permanent policies, this is the portion invested by the insurance company in its investment portfolio.

Death benefit: A payment made at the time of death. An accelerated death benefit is sometimes available if the insured person requires long-term medical care or is terminally ill.

Policy loan: A cash loan against the cash value of a permanent life insurance policy.

HOME INSURANCE

Every house needs a homeowner's insurance policy against theft, fire and other hazards. If you rent, purchase a comprehensive renter's insurance policy that insures the replacement of your possessions in case of any damage. Additional insurance, for disasters like floods and earthquakes, is also worth getting in areas prone to these types of natural disasters.

Selecting a Policy

- Secure at least three quotes to compare a range of rates.
- Ask if adding any home security devices would lower your premiums.
- Make sure your home has no underlying problems that would cancel the coverage.
- Consider combining auto and home policies with the same provider and lower the premiums for both policies.
- Be clear about whether you're purchasing straight replacement cost or cash value coverage. Cash value is less expensive but is limited to the amount of the policy and may not reflect the fair market value of your home.

Glossary: Home Insurance Terms to Know

Additional living expense insurance: A reimbursement of expenses when living away from your home while it is repaired.

Broad form: Policies that provide higher coverage for disasters like fire and theft.

Debris removal clause: For additional costs, this clause provides removal of downed trees, shrubs, and so on after a disaster.

Full reporting clause: When a property owner is required to report the market value of the insured property.

Named perils: A listing of all the disastrous events covered by the policy.

Personal property: Possessions like furnishings, cars and clothing, not including real estate.

Schedule: A list of items covered by a policy.

Umbrella policy: A policy that covers a variety of hazards.

Warranty policy: A policy written by an insurance company in good standing.

Understanding Investments

If you don't already, most likely at some point you will soon own some stocks, either outright or indirectly through a mutual fund or retirement

How to Read Stock Tables

A. 52-Week High, Low: Highest and lowest price during preceding fifty-two-week period.

B. Dividend: Annual payment per share.

C. Price-to-Earnings Ratio: Derived from dividing the company's stock price per share by its earnings per share.

D. Weekly High, Low, Last: Stock's highest, lowest and final price per share for the previous day. Closing figures must be converted to dollars and cents to determine price.

E. Yield: The dividend as a percentage of the stock price, computed daily.

F. Volume: Number of shares sold during the day, in thousands.

G. Change: The difference between yesterday's closing price and the closing price for the day before that.

STOCK TABLE

52W high	52W low	Stock	Ticker	Div	Yield %	P/E	Vol 00s	High	Low	Close	Net chg
52-week high, low, highest and lowest price during preceding 52-week period		Name of stock	Stock abbreviation	Annual payment per share	Yield: the dividend as a percentage of the stock price, computed daily	Profit-to-Earnings Ratio: price of a share of stock divided by earnings per share for a 12-month period	Number of shares sold during the day, in thousands	High, Low, Last: stock's highest, lowest and final price per share for the previous day. Closing figures must be converted to dollars and cents to determine price		Closing price or last sale of the day	The difference between yesterday's closing price and the closing price for the day before that

BOND TABLE

Issue	Coupon	Maturity date	Bid $	Yld%
The company or government issuing the bond.	The fixed interest rate that the issuer pays the lender.	The year when the borrower will pay the investors their principal back. Typically, only the last two digits of the year are listed. For example, 25 means 2025.	Bid Price: Price someone is willing to pay for the bond. It is quoted in relation to 100, no matter what the par value is. For example, a bid of 92 means it is trading at 92% of its par value.	The yield indicates annual return until the bond matures.

plan. While the stock market is fairly complicated, understanding a few key terms and tables can eliminate some of the confusion.

THE BASICS YOU SHOULD KNOW ABOUT STOCKS

A *share of stock* represents ownership in a corporation and is either one of two types: common stock or preferred stock. *Common stock* (or equity) usually entitles the owner to vote in the election of a board of directors and other stockholder issues. Dividends, which are cash payments made from the company profits, are usually paid on this class of stock. Companies like DuPont and Wal-Mart pay dividends, while most technology companies do not. *Preferred stock* is another form of ownership. This stock has no voting rights but guarantees a fixed dividend, which is paid before common stock dividends. If dividends are paid, they are paid to preferred stockholders first. *Blue-chip stocks* are companies that are consistent money makers and category leaders, such as IBM and Coca-Cola. The name refers to poker's blue chips, which have the greatest value. The Dow Jones Industrial Average is the average of the prices of thirty blue-chip stocks on the New York Stock Exchange and used as a barometer of trends in the market.

BONDS

Unlike stocks, bonds provide a guaranteed income, as the seller of the bond, usually a corporation, government, state or city, pays a specific amount of interest at defined periods of time and then the value of the bond when it matures. A bond is not a ownership stake; instead bond owners are creditors of the bond issuer. The three major types of bonds are government, corporate and municipal. Usually only government bonds and corporate bonds are fully taxable, while municipal bonds are tax-free.

MUTUAL FUNDS

A mutual fund is a pool of combined monies used to purchase stocks, bonds or a combination of both. Mutual funds can specialize in types of stocks, such as technology and international, or types of companies, like growth companies and value companies. Owners purchase shares in the

> *The only absolutely safe way to double your money is to fold it once and put it in your pocket.*
> —*Kin Hubbard*

fund, which collectively owns the individual holdings. All gains and losses on the underlying investments are spread proportionately based on the number of fund shares owned.

TYPES OF FUNDS AVAILABLE

Since most investing is done through mutual funds, you'll have to make a decision about what type of fund is right for you, based upon how much of a risk-taker you are and if you need income from the account.

- *Bond funds* invest in bonds of corporations and government agencies. The risk is usually low and the return is relatively low, but guaranteed.
- *Stock,* or *equity funds,* purchases, based on stock shares of companies. There is more risk than in bond funds. No income is guaranteed, and the value of the underlying investments could increase or decrease over time.
- *Growth stock funds* generally invest in companies that are growing rapidly. *Value stock funds* purchase stocks perceived as undervalued, or a good deal. Typically both types have some risk.
- *International funds* invest in common stocks of companies located outside the United States and are recommended for investors looking to diversify beyond the usual domestic mutual fund opportunities.
- *Balanced funds* incorporate both stocks and bonds. These are best for those who like the best of both investing worlds—some income from bonds and some growth in their investment from stocks.
- *Tax-exempt funds* invest in tax-free municipal bonds, making the interest earned tax-exempt in most cases.
- *Money-market funds* are made up of short-term securities, like government treasury bills. This is the safest type of investment, but also has the lowest expected return.
- *U.S. Government income funds* invest in government securities, including treasury bonds, federally guaranteed mortgage-backed securities and other government notes. This is another safe investment option.

> One of the funny things about the stock market is that every time one man buys, another sells, and both think they are astute.
> —William Feather

Outsourcing: When to Hire a Professional Money Manager

If you've got over $100,000 to invest, you should work with a financial professional who can provide information on growing your investment and managing your tax liabilities. Work with someone who makes you comfortable and is knowledgeable. Clearly understand all the fees involved before committing and read your statements monthly. If you ever feel pushed into purchasing certain investments, don't hesitate to move your business. Inertia is a leading cause of poorly performing portfolios.

Other life-changing events should also trigger a visit to professional. These include:

• Receiving an inheritance over $25,000.

• Receiving a damage award in a lawsuit.

• Selling a business.

• Retiring and needing to decide about pension fund payouts.

There are many money managers in business today. Choose one with fewer than a hundred clients, or you risk not receiving any personalized attention. Also ask where they receive their financial information. You need someone with access to specialized research from the top investment houses, industry publications and personal contacts. Here is a list of questions to ask when interviewing prospective money managers:

• Do you specialize in specific types of investments or business sectors?

• Have you been doing this type of work for longer than three years?

• Do you review my portfolio quarterly?

• Is there an annual review of your performance?

• How will you meet my family's unique needs?

• How many clients do you have?

• What are your sources of financial information?

• May I contact some of your clients to discuss your capabilities?

• How frequently can I make withdrawals or change the investments in my portfolio?

For all types of mutual fund, be sure to read the prospectus carefully. Pay close attention to Part B, which spells out fees and charges. Expenses should be no more than 1 percent of the amount you invest.

HOW TO CHOOSE AN INVESTMENT

Ask yourself the following questions when determining what type of investment is right for you:

- How quickly will you need the money you are investing? If you can invest for many years, consider the stock market. If you may need the money sooner, than a money-market fund is a wiser choice.
- How comfortable are you with risk? Choosing a high-risk stock fund that invests in companies just starting out might pay off substantially, or you may lose it all.
- Are you comfortable with letting someone else choose your investments? If you are, then go with mutual funds exclusively. If you prefer picking your own investments, open a discount trading account in addition to your mutual fund accounts.
- How much do you want to pay for someone to manage your money? Again, managing your own money is free, but does require a significant amount of time to research, evaluate and track your investment choices.

Simplifying Your Taxes

Taxes remain a perpetual headache for most families. It comes around every year and wreaks havoc leading up to the April 15 deadline. But there are ways to simplify the process and organize the paperwork, and eliminate that last-minute rush.

GETTING ORGANIZED

Keeping organized tax records throughout the year makes tax preparation much easier. Make separate file folders or large envelopes for each category of deductions. Then toss in receipts, bank statements and other doc-

The hardest thing in the world to understand is the income tax.
—Albert Einstein

uments during the year. If there is any question about saving some document or throwing it away, always save it. Try organizing according to these categories:

- **Charitable contributions.** Keep all cancelled checks for any donations. For donations over $250 you need a receipt from the organization acknowledging your donation. When you donate noncash items, like clothes, your old car or unused furniture, to a charity, submit an itemized list with an appropriate value and have someone from the organization authorize the receipt. Remember to keep track of any transportation and mileage costs you incur traveling to perform any volunteer work. This is deductible.

- **Business- and job-related expenses.** Depending on your type of business, several items are deductible. These could include uniform costs, magazine and newspaper subscription costs and course fees. When you're looking for a new job, all of those costs are deductible as well, such as travel costs to interviews. Also, moving expenses to start a new job are allowed. Home office and expenses are somewhat more complicated, as only a percentage of some costs are deductible. Consult a tax guide or CPA for clarification before filing.

- **Dependent care.** All the expenses you incur to care for your dependents, such as child-care, alimony, medical care and any special costs incurred to care for disabled dependents, comprise dependent care. Many of these expenses are deductible, based on whether or not you work and the age of your dependents.

- **Income sources.** Each year you'll receive statements from all employers who have paid you for work in the prior year. Also keep all dividend and interest statements together, as those are also taxable income sources. Real estate sale and rental information goes in this folder also.

- **Investment expenses.** All costs of purchasing accounting software, all fees to prepare your taxes and the cost of the safe-deposit box are deductible. Keep careful track of the sales of all investments, so your profit and losses from these transactions are accurately calculated.

Outsourcing: When to Consult a Certified Public Accountant

Taxpayers with simple returns—those eligible to use Form 1040EZ or TeleFile—can prepare their own returns without the fear of making costly mistakes. Even if something is submitted incorrectly the government will double-check the math and fix any errors.

However, professional tax advice from a CPA is sometimes a good idea. A good barometer for making this decision is asking yourself if it is worth risking a mistake. Could the cost of the visit be less than the cost of the mistake? If the answer is yes, see the CPA. If the answer is no, and you're comfortable and willing to do the tax research yourself, then go ahead. But, whenever any of the following situations arise, call in outside assistance:

- **If you've sold investments.** If you sold securities, real estate or other investment property in the previous tax year, make sure the profit or loss is accurately calculated.

- **If you are a sole proprietor of a business.** Taxes are often complicated for sole proprietorships and owners of "S" corporations.

- **If you have received an IRS notice.** If you receive any communication from the IRS that you don't understand or wish to contest, outside tax counsel can clarify the issues. This is mandatory with any tax evasion or criminal charges.

■ **Medical expenses.** Each dependent is allowed a specific deductible for all medical expenses during the course of the year. Expenses above this amount are then itemized on the tax forms. For every family member, keep a separate folder of all medical bills, including drugstore charges.

■ **Mortgage expenses.** At year-end, your lending institution will mail you a summary of the interest you've paid on your home. All of this interest, along with any interest from any home equity loans, is deductible.

AVOIDING THE AUDIT FLAGS

Tax audits are fewer than before, thanks to recent overhauls at the IRS. But they still exist and you'll want to avoid one. The types of inconsistencies and issues listed below almost always raise a red flag and an auditor's curiosity:

- Illegible, hard-to-read returns.
- Reporting several dependents.
- Deductions not appropriate for your type of business.
- Deductions that are greater than your income.
- Inconsistent reporting of income on state and federal returns.
- Major reductions in income compared to the prior year.

A NOTE ON REFUNDS

If you're one of the families that celebrate getting a refund every year, rethink your partying. A refund means the government has had the interest-free use of some of your hard-earned money during the year. Avoid this free loan situation by balancing your withholdings so they equal your deductions at year end.

GLOSSARY: TAX TERMS TO KNOW

Deduction: An expense you may deduct from your tax bill.

Dependent: A person you support, whose care entitles you to a dependency exemption.

Earned income: Salary and other wages for work you've done.

Estimated tax: If you are self-employed or have no taxes withheld from your salary, you may have to pay a quarterly income tax on your earnings.

Gross income: Your total income before any deductions.

IRA: An individual retirement account, which allows annual tax-deductible contributions.

Keogh plan: A retirement plan for self-employed individuals that allows for tax-deductible contributions.

Lump-sum distribution: The payment of a pension fund or profit sharing plan.

Personal interest: Non-tax-deductible interest on credit cards and car loans.

Reimbursement account: A nontaxable account to pay for medical and child-care expenses funded by money diverted from your salary.

Rollover: A tax-free transfer of money from one IRA account to another.

Tips for Preparing Your Taxes

- **Write clearly.**
- **Include your social security number and sign the returns.**
- **Attach all relevant documents and schedules.**
- **Meet all filing deadlines.**
- **Report all income for all sources.**
- **Be honest about deductions and dependents.**

Roth IRA: A savings account that allows for tax-free withdrawals after age fifty-nine-and-a-half, although it taxes contributions made into the account.

Standard deduction: An automatic deduction given to every tax filer.

Taxable income: After all allowable deductions, the income upon which your tax rate is based.

Unearned income: Income from interest, investment and dividends, all nonsalary earnings.

Withholding: The amount deducted or withheld from your paycheck to pay for your income and social security taxes.

Wills and Estate Planning

Dying without a will creates a confusing and expensive situation for those you leave behind. They, along with lawyers and other court officials, have to try and figure out what to do with your property, other investments and belongings. Eliminate all of this confusion by taking the time to create a will that details exactly what you want to happen after you die. Now is the time to start—not when you're older and not when you're richer.

BEGINNING THE ESTATE PLANNING PROCESS

Asking yourself some tough questions about your family is the first step in assembling an estate plan:

- If children are young, who should care for them?
- If a child is handicapped, how is that planning process different?
- If your children are older, should they inherit money immediately or wait until they're older?
- How do you care for stepchildren?
- Who would care for any older relatives?
- What would happen to your husband or ex-husband?
- If you have a family business, how would that continue?

Outsourcing: Seeking Professional Assistance

Preparing your own will is easily done, however, you may make costly mistakes or use packaged materials that are out of date. So using a professional is recommended. There are many qualified professionals who can help you develop an estate plan. The key person is usually a lawyer, ideally one who specializes in trust and estate law. Depending upon your situation, additional expertise from CPAs, trust officers from a bank or other financial advisers may be helpful. In addition to using a will to carry out your desires, wills can eliminate some after-death legal fees and taxes.

Outsourcing: When to Hire a Lawyer

Lawyers are handy people to know and undoubtedly you'll need one on several occasions.

Find a lawyer who specializes in what you need. Referrals often come from friends, bankers, physicians, real estate brokers or others, depending upon what type of transaction is required. For any of the following actions, consult a lawyer:

- Buying real estate.
- Selling real estate.
- Starting a business.
- Writing a will.
- Getting married, if you or your spouse have children.
- Getting divorced.
- Being sued.
- Received a summons.
- Accused of a crime.
- Injured in any sort of accident.
- Feel harassed or discriminated against.

When you meet with a lawyer, make sure you understand exactly what services are provided and how much it will cost. The fee structure may be project based, hourly or dependent upon the outcome of the case, as in personal injury suits. Ask for references from previous clients and follow up with those clients. Determine who will work on your case and how often you will meet with the attorney. Above all you want to feel comfortable and confident with your choice of lawyer. If you don't fee secure, find another. There is no shortage.

Now look at your financial picture:

- What would happen to your house?
- Who should inherit your investments?
- How should your possessions and family heirlooms be distributed?
- How can estate taxes be avoided or minimized?
- How can probate fees be avoided?

Also ask the difficult questions about death and dying:

- If you become incapacitated, do you want life-sustaining measures administered?

> **The minute you read something you can't understand, you can almost be sure it was drawn up by a lawyer.**
> —*Will Rogers*

- If you become senile, who would handle your affairs?
- What sort of funeral and burial do you want?

POWER OF ATTORNEY DOCUMENTS

In addition to preparing your will, ask your lawyer to prepare a Durable Power of Attorney, a Healthcare Directive and Medical Power of Attorney.

The *Durable Power of Attorney* allows for someone else to act on your behalf when you are alive. Should you become unable to care for yourself, this person could sign your checks, make decisions on taking care of you home and so on. It just involves signing a simple document. Legally, the person designated with this responsibility must act with your best interest, so choosing someone you know and trust is essential.

A *Healthcare Directive*, also known as a living will, states your wishes about medical treatment if you are unable to communicate. This often includes specifics on when to administer or withhold life-saving measures.

The *Medical Power of Attorney* allows for someone to make medical decisions on your behalf. It is similar to the Healthcare Directive, and is recommended to ensure that your medical decisions are followed. Again, choose someone you trust and someone who is familiar with your decisions about these issues.

THE SPECIFIC COMPONENTS OF A WILL

While wills vary in complexity, most include the following items:

- Specifies any organ donation or use of body for medical research.
- Details all burial and funeral instructions.
- Names an executor, often a spouse or child, who will administer the will.
- Names a guardian to care for young children.
- Provides a way to hold assets until children reach maturity.
- Makes bequests of items to whomever is designated.
- Details any trusts established for specific care and tax savings.

THE PROBATE PROCESS

After someone dies, the probate process begins. This is a legal proceeding that proves the validity of the will, identifies and distributes all the property in the estate and pays the taxes. The process can take two years to complete and the cost is usually 2 percent of the total estate. Many states have laws exempting some amount of the estate from probate. If your estate's value is greater than $100,000, consider avoiding probate by establishing a joint tenancy, which automatically transfers property to a survivor, usually a spouse. Life insurance policies also avoid probate.

TRUSTS OVERVIEW

Creating a Living Trust also effectively avoids the time and expenses of probate. A Living Trust is a legal entity that contains all the assets of your property and states specifically what to do with those assets. It also maximizes the Unified Credit, a law passed by Congress that allows a $1 million shelter from estate taxes. A Living Trust is relatively simple to set up and easy to administer, with the aid of an attorney. Other trusts may also be established for the care of special needs children, for the ongoing care of older parents and for the education of younger children.

UPDATING YOUR ESTATE PLAN

Reconsider your will and other estate documents when any of the following events occur:

- You get married or remarried.
- You get divorced.
- You have children or become a step-parent.
- Your health changes.
- You inherit a significant amount of money.
- The value of your assets significantly increases.
- When any of your beneficiaries marry, have children or die.
- If any federal or state laws change.

GLOSSARY: ESTATE PLANNING TERMS TO KNOW

Administrator: The person or company that oversees an estate of someone dying without a will

Beneficiary: Someone receiving some portion of an estate.

Codicil: An amendment to a will.

Estate: The assets of a deceased person.

Executor: The person or company who oversees the estate of someone with a completed will.

Guardian: An adult who is responsible for an underage child or a handicapped adult.

Heir: Someone inheriting from an estate.

Intestate: Dying without a will.

Probate: Legal process overseeing how property is distributed in a will.

Testate: Dying with a will.

Testator: Someone who writes a will.

Trustee: A person or company who administers a trust.

GLOSSARY: GENERAL LEGAL TERMS TO KNOW

Because there are some many instances when a lawyer's help is needed, there are many legal terms worth knowing.

Affidavit: A statement made under oath.

Alimony: Monies paid between the two parties in a divorce.

Appeal: A request to overturn the ruling of a lower court.

Arraignment: In criminal cases, an initial appearance before a judge.

Bail: Money paid for a defendant to guarantee a future court appearance.

Beneficiary: Person named in a will or insurance policy to receive property.

Caveat emptor: A Latin phrase meaning "buyer beware," meaning it is the buyer's responsibility to inspect all goods before purchasing.

Chapter 7 bankruptcy: When a person sells all his assets and the proceeds are distributed among his creditors.

Chapter 13 bankruptcy: When a person keeps his assets and pays his creditors by following a court-approved plan of repayment.

Class action suit: A lawsuit in which a group of people make a similar claim.

Community property: The property purchased jointly during a marriage.

Contract: A legal agreement between two people.

Deed: A legal document defining the outline of a property.

Easement: The right of one person to cross another's property.

Felony: A crime whose punishment is at least one year in jail.

Foreclosure: When a borrower stops making payments on a property and the property owner decides to sell it.

Grand jury: A jury that decides if a suspect should be tried as a felon.

Immunity: Exempt from prosecution.

Indictment: The formal accusation of a felon.

Infraction: A minor offense, like a speeding ticket.

Joint custody: After a divorce, when both parents retain custody of a child.

Just cause: A viable reason for an action.

Legal custody: The parent who has the right to make all decisions about raising a child. May be one or both parents.

Malpractice: Wrongful behavior by a professional, like a doctor.

Misdemeanor: Crime punishable by imprisonment for less than a year.

No-fault divorce: When neither party is blamed in a divorce.

Open adoption: An adoption plan that grants the birth mother some involvement.

Perjury: The act of lying under oath.

Physical custody: A type of custody in which the parent lives with the child.

Plaintiff: Someone who starts a lawsuit.

Plea bargain: A negotiated agreement between the defense and the prosecution in a criminal case.

Power of attorney: The authorization for one person to act for another.

Prosecutor: A government lawyer who tries criminal cases.

Public defender: A government lawyer who works for clients unable to pay for their own lawyer.

Settlement: The resolution in a civil lawsuit.

Slander: Hurtful statements.

Subpoena: An order to appear in court.

Verdict: A formal decision reached by a jury.

Visitation right: The right of a parent or other relative to visit a child.

Warrant: An order authorizing an arrest.

Witness: A person who delivers evidence in court.

Worker's compensation: A benefit received by an employee after suffering a work-related injury.

CHAPTER 14

You're the Real Estate Agent

Moving can be an exciting experience, but handling all the details can be exasperating. Whether you're moving cross-country or across town, the tips in this chapter will help you perform your job as your family's real estate agent with as little stress, and as much success, as possible.

Selling Your House

CHOOSING AN AGENT

As soon as possible before you want to put your house on the market, meet with prospective real estate agents. Get references from friends, your banker or colleagues. Ask the prospective agents to visit your home, and watch their reactions. When you've narrowed your choices to two, ask:

- Can you give me some comps (information comparing the sales price per square foot) of similar homes in the area that have recently sold?
- Can I see a copy of your selling contract? What is your commission? Is it flexible at all?

Take Note

If you constantly hear that you're in a seller's market, you may not really need to paint every room, repave the driveway or recounter the kitchen. If your agent recommends that you update the bathroom or kitchen, get a second opinion. Remember, though, that some cosmetic changes can make the sale.

■ Is there anything we need to do to this house to maximize its selling potential?

1. **Create curb appeal.**

• Trim overgrown shrubs to a height near the bottom of the windows. Remove any ivy growing on the side of the home.
• Prune branches hanging low in the yard so that no one will walk into them when surveying the property.
• Clean out flowerbeds; create a distinct border between the beds and the yard. Depending on the season and where you live, invest in a few flats of flowers to beautify the appearance of your home. Put a blooming flowerpot or two on the front porch.
• If you paint nothing else, at least give the front door a fresh coat of paint.
• Attend to the "small" stuff. If the doorbell is broken, replace it. Clean the mailbox. Keep the porch swept. Get an attractive mat for people to wipe their feet on.

2. **Make your house a must-have.**

• Air out the house. Because you are the last person who will notice any peculiar odor, ask a friend to give you an honest opinion, then search for the offender. It may be a litter box, a dog bed or a mildewed shower.
• Wash all the windows, inside and out. While you're at it, clean the windowsills and the bottom of the window jams. Clean blinds or shutters.
• Have the carpets cleaned. Bare floors should also be waxed or polished.
• Buyers like bright and cheery, so keep drapes and shades open during the day, even if you're not in the habit.
• Put bright lightbulbs in lamps.
• Clean out all closets, cabinets and built-in drawers. Be ruthless; the idea is to make storage space look as if it has enough room to hold additional items. Box up off-season clothes and store, along with shelf clutter, elsewhere. Get everything off of the floor.

• Be sure there is not too much furniture in a room. Even though it may be inconvenient, select the pieces that look best and put the others in the garage, basement or, better yet, storage. You can usually rent space at a mini warehouse very reasonably.

• Go over your kitchen like a health inspector. Clean the oven and keep it that way (you may need to eat out more). After cleaning the range, put new drip pans under the burners—or at least cover the old ones with foil. Clean around the seal of the door to the dishwasher.

• Clean and organize items under the sink. Straighten cabinets and drawers.

• Bathtubs, showers and sinks should be freshly caulked. All the grout should be clean and in good condition. There should be no leaks in the faucets or traps.

• Put fresh towels out in the bathrooms and replace the shower curtain if needed.

• If you have limited counter space in the kitchen, be sure to keep unnecessary items put away.

• Keep children's toys out of the front yard and off the sidewalks and front porch. Talk to your children (of all ages) about the importance of keeping the house looking good while it is on the market. Take down posters until the house is sold. Fill in holes and paint over.

• Clean the ashes out of the fireplace during the season that it isn't being used.

• Make sure that the pull-down staircase is screwed together and strong enough to be used safely.

• Be sure there is a light in the attic.

3. **Show off for a good cause.** Small touches mean a lot when your house is being shown.

• Open all the doors between rooms to give an inviting feeling.
• Turn on all of the lights, including lamps.
• Turn the TV off; tune the radio to some quiet, elevator-style music.

- Pick up any newspapers or magazines and other clutter that may be lying around.
- Make sure dirty dishes are in the dishwasher.
- Take out the trash if needed.
- If you have pets, get them out of the way. Not everyone may share your love for animals, or potential buyers may be allergic to them.
- The beds should be made and clothes picked up. Bathrooms should be clean and the toilet lid down.

TIPS FROM THE PROS: LOW-FARE FLAIR

A few relatively inexpensive touches can make a world of difference to a buyer.

- Consider changing the wallpaper in the entry way, kitchen or bathrooms.
- Replace light fixtures that are dated or ugly.
- Install practical and attractive ceiling fans.
- Newer appliances in the kitchen can make the difference between selling or staying.

SAVE A STEP: THE PRECONTRACT PROFESSIONAL INSPECTION

A professional inspection is usually paid for by the buyer and conducted after you have successfully negotiated a contract. To save time, order an inspection when you're preparing to sell. The benefit: you will find out early if there is anything that needs attention. Many times an inspector will do these precontract inspections for less than his or her normal rate. You will have time to get a second opinion and find a reputable and reasonable contractor to make the repairs. And later, if the buyer's inspector finds something your inspector didn't, there is now room for a difference of opinion.

Bright Idea

Always leave your house "showing ready." You never know when the right person is going to look at your home.

Buying a House

HOW MUCH CAN YOU AFFORD?

Buying a house is a big deal—in a lot of ways. Before you make the important step of buying your first home and before you move on to a larger home, carefully determine how much you can afford based on your current income and household expenses.

The Federal National Mortgage Association recommends that your monthly mortgage payment, including all property taxes and insurance, should not exceed 33 percent of your gross monthly income. Similarly, your total monthly debt obligations, including the mortgage, should not exceed 38 percent of your gross monthly income.

Most new home buyers need a loan, so try prequalifying for one. Scan the business section of your local paper and compare the mortgage rates of local banks and savings and loans. Then call your lending institution of choice and ask to speak with a loan officer about a mortgage. Explain that you'd like to determine how big a mortgage you would qualify for. Usually this is quickly arranged over the phone, online or in a short meeting at the lender's office. Be prepared to answer questions about your annual income, credit and job history. Once you know how much you can borrow, you'll know the limits of your house price. Sometimes this is done more formally by written application, which can produce a loan approval letter. You'll have to pay something—usually the cost of the credit report—but a seller will know you are a truly serious shopper who can buy quickly, which can strengthen your bargaining position.

HOME BUYER CHECKLIST

When visiting a prospective home, always pick up the description sheet and sketch a floor plan on the back as you walk through. Also consider bringing a camera along. If you're looking at lots of houses, this helps you remember what you saw. Store all of your research in a folder, along with the real estate agents' cards and your own agent's office, cell phone number and pager number.

As you're going through the house, or soon after you leave, complete this handy checklist so you can equally compare all the property you see.

Let us keep our mouths shut and our pens dry until we know the facts.
—A. J. Carlson

313

HOME BUYER CHECKLIST

Address:			
Asking price:			
Taxes:			
School district:			
Construction material:			
Year built:			
Availability date:			
Lot size:			
House total square footage:			
Number of bedrooms:			
Number of bathrooms:			
Dining room?			
Family room?			
Laundry room?			
Other rooms?			
Porch or patio?			
Garage with room for how many cars:			
Type and age of plumbing:			

Type and age of wiring:			
Type and age of heating and air-conditioning systems:			
Insulation in floors, walls, ceiling and roof?			
Condition of basement and foundation:			
Condition of roof:			
Driveway:			
Condition of interior and exterior paint:			
Number and type of windows:			
Condition of appliances:			
Size of yard:			
Any landscaping features:			

Then jot down a couple of notes about your first impression of the house, because that's always important, and write a few lines about what's required of this house to make it the right home for you. Be specific.

QUESTIONS TO ASK BEFORE MAKING AN OFFER

After you've decided on a house, you'll need answers to specific questions about determining the value and financing options for the home. Gather all the information available about the property, the neighborhood and the financing options from the realtor, then make your offer. Good realtors will gladly provide all this information. Don't be shy about asking for clarification if anything looks confusing. Be sure to ask:

- Is a property disclosure statement available for review?
- What type of property financing is available? Is there a quote sheet?
- Has there been a recent appraisal of this house?
- What are comparable prices for recent sales in the area?
- Are there any issues that might affect the value now or in the future?
- How much would it cost to do any necessary repairs before moving in?
- What are the estimated closing costs?
- What are the approximate house payments?

Home Protection Plan

As an additional benefit, some sellers provide a home protection plan for the buyer. With a home protection plan, the new owner pays a nominal service fee for repairs while the bulk of the repair costs are covered by the plan. This coverage is good for one year on selected items such as central heating and the air-conditioning system, interior plumbing, built-in appliances and electric pool equipment.

If the home you choose does not have a home protection plan, you can usually purchase coverage from a home insurance company. Annual coverage costs are about $300. Most pre-existing conditions, like a leaky roof or an air-conditioning system that's been problematic for several years, are usually not covered, so read the policy carefully.

ITEMS NEEDED FOR A MORTGAGE APPLICATION

As you apply for a mortgage, you'll discover that financial institutions want a lot of information about you. In order to analyze you as a financial risk, they need a complete understanding of your financial situation. If you've kept all your tax return information, banking and credit card statements handy, then the process is fairly easy. Be prepared to fill out many forms. It's a time-consuming process, but worth the effort to get the mortgage you need for the home you want. Below is the information you will need to provide:

If employed . . .
- Addresses for two full years
- Gross monthly income
- W-2s, if available
- Proof of pensions, retirement, disability or social security
- Proof of income from rental property and any other sources
- Proof of child support or alimony paid/received
- Year-to-date pay stub

If self-employed . . .
- Two years 1040 tax returns
- Current-year profit-and-loss statement

Creditor information . . .
- Each creditor's name, address and type of account
- Account numbers
- Monthly payments and approximate balances
- Amount of child-care expenses

Banking information . . .
- Names and addresses of saving institutions
- Account numbers for all accounts
- Type of accounts and present balances

317

Miscellaneous...

- Listing of principal assets in stocks, bonds, and land
- Life insurance cash value (documented if used as cash down payment)
- If applicant is selling a home, a copy of sales contracts
- Social security numbers for all parties
- Certificate of Eligibility and DD-214 for veterans
- Cash or check to pay for application fee

Property information...

- Copy of sales agreement
- Copy of property listing

MOVING TOWARD THE CLOSING

Once the buyer accepts your bid, then the process of transferring the property begins. The final step is the closing, in which all the legal documents are signed and you take possession. Although this depends upon how quickly your mortgage company can process your application, the usual closing schedule is four weeks. The week-by-week timetable below is a guide for the different steps in the home-buying process. Again, if any questions or concerns arise during the process, contact your realtor immediately. They only get paid when the house sells, so it's in their best interest to keep you happy.

First week...

- ☐ Sign contract and write earnest money check. (Your real estate agent should know the appropriate amount. It will be based on the cost of the house and customs in the area.)
- ☐ Make loan application.
- ☐ Pay for appraisal and lock-in fee.
- ☐ Arrange for property inspection.
- ☐ Arrange for exterminator inspection.

Second week...

- ☐ Make property inspection.
- ☐ Make exterminator inspection.

☐ Make repair request to seller.

☐ Make sure all the information the mortgage company requested has been submitted.

☐ Arrange for movers.

Third week...

☐ Call to find out if repairs have been completed.

☐ Call to find out if mortgage company needs additional information.

Fourth week...

☐ Walk through to verify completed repairs.

☐ Arrange for settlement and signing of papers.

☐ Arrange for transfer of utilities.

☐ Arrange for the exchange of keys and personal items.

Moving

COUNTDOWN TO MOVING DAY

Six weeks before...

☐ Get at least three competing bids from professional movers. Ask friends or the Better Business Bureau for recommendations. If possible, visit the moving company's location. If they don't have helpful staff, and you can't see that they have clean and well-maintained trucks and quality storage facilities, scratch them off your list.

☐ Decide if you want to have the moving company pack you, or you want to pack yourself. If you pay them to pack, they will be liable for broken crystal, chipped furniture and so on. Ask for a break-down of the cost difference between their packing some fragile items and your packing everything else. If you do pack yourself, use lots of high-quality packing material.

☐ If you decided to buy full replacement value insurance on your belongings, determine the replacement value of everything you own.

☐ Get a signed copy of the bid you accept. Make sure the price is guaranteed or if there are any conditions.

319

☐ Make a checklist of everything you need to do before and after the move.

☐ Start collecting boxes.

☐ Talk with your kids about the move. Let them voice fears and expectations.

☐ If you haven't already, plan a trip to hunt for housing in your new city. Take the whole family if you can.

Four weeks before...

☐ Designate a packing room on each floor of your house. Keep all your packing materials—boxes, two pairs of scissors, wrapping materials, tape, felt-tip markers—in there.

☐ Pack the packing room first, then, one room at a time, start packing the things you won't need in the next few weeks. Even if you pack only three boxes a day, they really add up over time!

☐ Put plastic trash bags in every room. If you always have one nearby, you won't be tempted to pack things you really should toss.

☐ Arrange to transfer funds to a new bank and establish credit.

☐ Arrange for insurance for your new home or apartment.

☐ Arrange for the transfer of your children's school records.

☐ Arrange with doctors, dentists and eye doctors to have your records and prescriptions transferred or to take them with you. Make sure you have enough prescription medicine to get through a week in a new city.

☐ Notify the post office of your move and fill out change of address cards.

☐ Order address labels for your new home. You can use these to leave your new address with friends or businesses.

☐ Contact utilities, insurance agencies and other businesses you regularly deal with to let them know you're moving.

☐ Check on auto licensing and insurance requirements if you're moving to a new state.

☐ Close local charge accounts.

☐ If you'd planned a garage sale, have it now.

Bright Idea

Eliminate everything you don't want to move—and don't want to pay to have moved! Start boxes for charity or a garage sale.

☐ Use up canned goods, frozen foods and other household supplies. Buy small quantities when you run out of something.

☐ If you're flying to your new city, buy plane tickets and reserve hotel rooms.

Two weeks before...

☐ Arrange to connect utilities at your new home.

☐ Make family farewell visits to parks and other favorite sites.

☐ Have an informal going-away party, an open house or a potluck. Keep arrangements simple so you can spend time with friends.

☐ Let your kids see their friends often.

☐ If you're driving to your new city, have the car serviced.

☐ Take pets to the vet. Make sure ID and rabies tags are securely attached to their collars. If your pet will be flying, get the required certificate from your vet for the airlines.

☐ Return any items you've borrowed from friends and books to the library. Collect all items remaining at the repair shop, dry cleaners and gym or club lockers.

☐ Arrange for a cleaning service to clean your home after you've moved out.

Three days before...

☐ Pack suitcases with clothing and personal items you'll need on your first day in your new home.

☐ In a special carton, place items you'll need the first hours in your new home—for example, soap, toilet paper, towels, coffee, cooking pots, sheets, pillows and so on. Mark the carton "Load Last, Unload First."

☐ Label any boxes you do not want to be loaded on the truck.

☐ If you haven't made arrangements with your movers to do this, take down shelves, mirrors, the TV antenna or dish and any other installed items you're taking with you.

☐ Make activity packs for the kids to play with on the drive or the plane, or at their new home. Include a favorite stuffed animal or blanket, healthy snacks and moist towelettes.

Ease the Pain of Moving for Your Children

■ *A fun good-bye.* Have a farewell party for your children and their friends. Let kids decorate moving boxes with sponges, brushes, fingerprints and footprints and even help pack up their toys and books.

■ *Mail from home.* Give your child's teacher your new address and enough stamps and envelopes so she can have each former classmate write a letter to your child after you've gone.

☐ Reserve a baby-sitter's services for moving day. See if a close family friend or relative can take younger kids somewhere for part of the day.

☐ Get traveler's checks and cash.

☐ Make sure drawers don't contain any spillable or breakable products.

☐ Dispose of all flammables.

☐ Empty the fridge and freezer at least twenty-four hours before you go.

☐ Arrange for accommodations—at home with everything packed, with friends or family or in a hotel—the night before the moving truck comes.

☐ Pack a "first night" kit for your new home. This should include things such as paper plates, plastic silverware, toilet paper, notepad and pencil, nonperishable food, can opener, bottled water, linens, towels and toiletries.

☐ Put together a small tool kit. You'll need this often as you unpack.

☐ Verify packers' or movers' arrival time. Confirm your truck reservation and when you'll pick it up.

The day before...

☐ Get ready for the packers. Be around so the packers can ask questions.

☐ If you're packing yourself, finish it all well before your truck comes. Packing dishes and other last-minute items will use up most of a day. Double-check closets, the garage, the attic, and the basement for forgotten items.

☐ Finish packing personal belongings. Leave out an alarm clock.

☐ Plan a simple breakfast for the next morning.

Moving day...

☐ Be available to answer movers' questions and sign forms. Make sure everything is loaded and that the truck driver has your new home's address.

☐ When the truck is loaded, pack the phone and other last-minute items.

☐ Do one last check. Are the windows closed and locked? Has anything been left behind? Are the furnace and lights turned off? Have you arranged to disconnect or transfer utilities? Leave a note for the new residents, along with any extra house keys, with your new address and phone number.

How to Pack for a Move

- Label boxes by the importance of their contents: mark essentials with a 1, necessary but not essential with a 2 and low priority with a 3. This makes unpacking simpler.
- Newsprint leaves ink; instead, try wrapping items in unprinted newspaper, available from moving companies.
- Consider placing color-coded stickers on the boxes to distinguish between, for example, kitchen and bath items. Keep a list of what color indicates what room.
- Small plastic bags are handy to hold screws, picture hooks, small parts and so on. Tape them securely to the inside of drawers so you can find them easily once you're in your new house.
- Pack light; try not to make boxes heavier than 45 pounds. Using lots of smaller boxes rather than fewer big ones helps.
- For items like TVs, VCRs and computers, pack them in their original boxes whenever possible.
- Use wide packing tape with its own dispenser to make the job easier. When you seal a box, make sure the tape extends at least halfway down each side.
- Put a layer of crumpled paper at the bottom of each box, with additional cushioning in the middle and on top.
- Don't pack breakable items with heavy items.
- Use "Fragile" to mark the outside of appropriate boxes.
- If a box must be kept right side up, write boldly on the outside of the box, "This end up," and draw an arrow.
- Once at your new home, don't let everyone randomly choose boxes to unpack. Plan who should handle what room, and set a few ground rules such as, empty a box completely before you start on another.
- Arrange furniture before unpacking boxes.
- Put bedrooms or kitchen together first; you'll need both throughout the unpacking process.

Bright Idea

Label boxes boldly on all sides so you won't have to move them around to know what's in them.

GLOSSARY: TERMS TO KNOW WHEN BUYING AND SELLING PROPERTY

Appraisal: A professional estimate of the value of a house based on its construction, amenities and property. The estimate always includes the comparable value of several similar properties.

Closing: When the property is officially transferred between owners and when the new owner signs all the mortgage papers and assumes the property's title.

Closing costs: All the fees paid by either the buyer or the seller at closing.

Conventional mortgage: A mortgage not insured by the government, such as a Federal Housing Authority or Veterans Administration loan.

Deed: The document that transfers the title from the seller to the buyer.

Down payment: The amount of the final purchase price of the house that is paid in cash and not financed by the mortgage.

Earnest money: Money paid by the buyer to the seller at the time an offer to purchase the home is presented.

Escrow: An independent and interest-bearing account that holds monies for third parties.

First mortgage: A mortgage that is a first lien on the property pledged as a security.

Fixed mortgage rate: A constant rate of interest charged for a defined period of the mortgage loan.

Good faith estimate: A written estimate of all the expected closing costs, provided by the lender to the buyer.

Home inspection: A survey of the house to determine if any structural or mechanical problems exist.

Lien: A legal claim on a property.

Lock-in: A guarantee from the lender that the mortgage rate is valid for a specific rate of time.

Mortgage: A legal document using property as collateral for repayment of a loan.

Mortgagee: The lending institution as stated in the terms of the mortgage.

Mortgage broker: A service that matches buyers and lending institutions, for which the buyer pays a fee.

Mortgage note: A pledge to repay the mortgage loan in a timely manner as set forth in the mortgage.

Mortgage rate: The interest rate on the loan.

Offer to purchase: A written contract that states how much a buyer will pay for a property, contingent upon several clearly stated factors.

Origination fee: A fee charged by the lender to process all the paperwork of the mortgage.

Periodic rate caps: The limit of interest rate increases for adjustable rate mortgages.

Personal mortgage insurance: Insurance to repay the mortgage, often required if a mortgage exceeds 80 percent of the property's assessed value.

PITI: Principal, interest, taxes and insurance that comprise all components of a monthly mortgage payment.

Points: One point equals 1 percent, or one one-hundredth, of the total mortgage amount. The lending institution sometimes charges points to the buyer.

Qualify: To meet a mortgagee's lending requirements.

Term: The amount of time to repay the mortgage.

Title: The right of ownership and possession to a property.

Title insurance: A policy that protects a buyer against problems regarding the right of ownership of the property.

Up-front charges: Any expenses such as inspection and appraisal costs incurred before the contract is signed.

Variable mortgage rate: A interest rate that changes during the life of the loan depending upon factors outlined by the lending institution.

CHAPTER 15

You're the Personal Shopper

A professional shopper saves her clients legwork by gathering the best products at the best prices. In much the same way, this is what we do for our families. Cutting costs doesn't have to mean eating macaroni and cheese five nights a week. Nor does it mean depriving yourself of all life's joys. Instead, just by making some simple, realistic changes and adopting some new shopping strategies in your day-to-day living, your family can net hundreds—possibly thousands—of extra dollars every year. Try all of these strategies and write down how much you save every month.

Savvy Savings

HAVE MORE FUN FOR LESS MONEY!

- **Be gym-savvy.** Look into purchasing a family membership at your local YMCA or community recreation center instead of joining a fancy health club. Ys and community centers often provide the same facilities and services for a lot less money—and also offer lots of programs for kids, from swimming lessons to art projects.
- **Love the library.** Before buying new children's books or renting videos, head over to the library with your kids to see if they're available there first. After you've checked

them out, write the due dates on your kitchen calendar to avoid paying late fines.

- **Take advantage of the great (and free) outdoors.** Get up early with the kids, watch the sun rise and have breakfast at a local park—or go on an easy nature hike together. Your local parks department can also provide you with info about inexpensive programs and activities that everyone will enjoy.

- **Reduce restaurant bills.** Drink water instead of ordering soda, juice or other beverages when dining out, and easily lop $5 off each tab. Ask the server to put a paper umbrella or an orange or lemon slice in the water to make it more fun for kids. Also, try splitting entrees if the portions are large.

- **Brown bag it.** Decorate lunch bags and put personal notes inside for a lunch that's way more entertaining than cafeteria food. If you and your kids take sack lunches to work and school every day, you'll save hundreds of dollars a year.

BE A SMART SHOPPER

- **Cut appliance costs.** When shopping for pricey appliances, such as vacuum cleaners or dishwashers, ask to buy floor models at a reduced price.

- **Identify your priorities.** Make a list of the items you need or want the most. When considering a new purchase, ask yourself, how many of our priorities would this purchase fulfill? Priorities will help you to think of purchases as trade-offs, making financial decisions easier.

- **Use plastic wisely.** Use your bank debit card instead of your credit card to avoid accumulating debt through costly finance charges.

- **Save on sporting goods.** Purchase a demo racket instead of a new one and save up to $100. If you just need a casual hiking shoe instead of a waterproof, rugged one, that choice is $75 cheaper. Always buy skiing equipment in August, when prices are lowest.

BE SMART ABOUT GETTING MONEY BACK ON REFUNDS AND CREDITS

- **Keep receipts for a year.** Save grocery receipts for a month. You never know when you'll need a proof of purchase.

> *Ask thy purse what thou should spend.*
> —Scottish proverb

- **Leave tags on clothes.** Until you try them on at home and make sure they fit, leave the tags on for easy return.
- **Return products nicely.** Remind the store clerk that you are a steady customer, smile and respectfully ask to see the manager if necessary.
- **Understand the refund policy.** Learning a store's refund policy *before* you purchase something and getting it in writing simplifies any return headaches.
- **Pay with a credit card.** Using a credit card, provided it's promptly paid off, or debit card makes it easier to process refunds and usually covers against any warranty issues.

BE A SMART INTERNET SHOPPER

- **Comparison shop.** The Internet is ideal for comparison shopping for commodity goods like airline tickets, hotel rooms, brand name clothes, books, music, office supplies and toiletries.
- **Know the return policy.** Make sure you fully understand how returns work before pressing the buy key.
- **Monitor personal information.** Look for indications that the website is secure when detailing your credit card information. If you feel nervous, exit the site immediately.
- **Say yes to e-mail sale notices.** Agree to receive e-mail notices from websites you like. These often include special sales and free shipping notices.

BE A SMART CATALOG SHOPPER

- **Consider shipping and handling costs.** These can significantly increase the cost, so comparison shop before you order.
- **Know the refund and return policies.** A reputable company will promptly handle your returns so they can get your future business.
- **Keep records.** Know what you ordered and what you were promised.
- **Inspect carefully.** Check out mail-order products upon delivery.
- **Keep everything.** Store all paperwork and packaging should you need to return the merchandise.
- **Buy with your credit card.** Use your credit card, only if you can pay

A penny saved is a penny earned.
—Benjamin Franklin

Entertainment Coupon Books

They're ubiquitous: a school team or class sells them every year. Not only can you support someone's cause by buying one, you can also make the most of the savings they offer. Here's how:

- As soon as you buy the book, go through it and identify the deals you want to try. Either mark the pages with sticky notes or list on an index card the most appealing offers.

- Browse the whole book before selecting specific deals; prices on oil changes and the like can vary dramatically.

- Keep the book in a central location so any family member can take advantage of it when going out.

- Always read the small print before you cash a coupon.

- When planning to use a coupon, check with the vendor to see if they're offering something even better than the coupon deal.

- Store fast-food coupons in your glove compartment or rubber-banded to your visor for easy, immediate access.

- When using a restaurant coupon, give it to the waiter before you order.

- Don't use coupons on holiday meals. Restaurants may charge up to twice as much for meals on special days, so even with a buy-one, get-one-free coupon you're paying full price.

- Tip the waiter according to the full price you would have paid.

the balance within thirty days, or use your debit card for easier and faster returns.

BE A SMART HOLIDAY SHOPPER

- **Start early.** Start as early in the year as you can stand it and keep an eye out for gifts on sale.

- **Keep a list.** Having a list makes the process easier. Add ideas for each person on the list throughout the year, especially when you hear them mention something they'd like to have.

- **Set a spending limit.** Know how much you can spend for holiday gifts and stick to the spending plan.

- **Buy in quantity.** If you can buy the same gift for a teacher and a soccer coach, do it.
- **Gifts of time and service.** Remember the value of donating your time and service in lieu of a box to unwrap.

SAVE ON SERVICES

- **Get cheap cuts.** Try family haircuts at a beauty or barber school instead of a salon, and you can save about $10 per cut.
- **Become a D-I-Y family.** You can save a lot of money by learning to do a lot of household chores, like plumbing and furniture refinishing, yourself. Check out how-to videos from the library to build your home improvement skills and save money at the same time.
- Use entertainment coupon books.

SHARE COSTS WITH NEIGHBORS

- **Toy-swap with other families.** Trade the toys your preschooler doesn't mind living without for a couple of weeks. The kids will love having different toys more often, and you'll save money by not buying new ones.
- **Share magazines with neighbors.** Instead of spending $100 every year on subscriptions, you and your friends can each order a few different magazines, then swap when you're done reading them.
- **Host a swap party with your friends.** Decide on a theme such as videos, tools or kids' clothing. Each partygoer brings a few of these items along. At the end of the event, everyone will have new, no-cost stuff.

Buying Big-Ticket Items

APPLIANCES

Out with the Old, In with the New

When it's time to buy a new home appliance:

- Do your research. Talk to friends about their experiences with various brands, and check *Consumer Reports* (available at your local library) for product evaluations.
- Decide what capacity or size you need and what special features you want.
- Measure the space where the appliance will live. And don't forget to measure the door and hallway clearance for delivery.
- Ask the dealer to show you the care manual for the appliance you are interested in. Look it over before you buy and check to be sure special cleaning products aren't required.
- Ask about the warranty. Find out what is covered and for how long. Divide the cost by the number of months in the life expectancy of the appliance. Sometimes good warranties cost just a few dollars a month and are worth the investment, especially if service calls are unlimited.
- Ask about delivery charges and service availability. I know a couple who has saved hundreds moving appliances and furniture themselves by renting trucks from Home Depot. Of course it helps to have teenage sons or strong neighbors who don't mind flexing their muscles once the item arrives.

Get the Best Deal on Any Appliance

Don't resign yourself to paying full price. Take advantage of these savvy strategies for getting a significant discount or some useful extras:

- **Ask.** You could save as much as 15 percent just by showing yourself to be a smart and worthy customer. If you've seen the item on sale

Bright Idea

If you see a floor sample or slightly damaged appliance marked down, sometimes a store manager is authorized to further reduce the price of the item to move the merchandise out of the store. It never hurts to ask.

Repair or Replace?

The age of an appliance helps determine its longevity. According to the National Association of Remodeling Industry (NARI) and Sears Home Central, here are average life spans of some of the appliances in your home:

- Washing machine: 13 years
- Dryer: 13 years
- Refrigerator: over 15 years
- Stoves (gas or electric): 17 to 20 years
- Microwave oven: 16 years
- Furnace replacement: 15 to 30 years

- Water heaters: under 12 years
- Room air conditioners: 12 to 15 years
- Central air conditioners: 11 years
- Basic sewing machine: 24 years
- Dishwasher: 10 years
- Garage door opener: 10 years

Remember, these are just averages and every appliance is different. Some can live long past their life expectancy.

elsewhere for a lower price, or you are a regular customer who plans to tell others about the store, say so!

- **Know your stuff.** Check all of the ads, especially the ones appearing from Friday to Sunday, for the appliance you need. Clip the ads and take them with you to a store with a "lowest price guaranteed" promise. If initially you don't get the price you want, show the salesperson the ads. You could save as much as 20 percent.

- **Get freebies.** Say you'll take the appliance if the salesperson throws in free disks (for a computer sale), free video head cleaner (for a VCR) and so on. Salespeople want to close the deal, and such additions don't cost the store much.

- **Buy the next-to-latest model.** Purchasing last year's model in a closeout sale can get you discounts from 10 to 25 percent. If a store doesn't have closeout items, choose an appliance from "older" stock and ask politely for a discount—you may get 15 percent off.

- **Become a "preferred customer."** These special patrons receive invitations for private sales held usually two to four times a year in which special discounts (not offered to the general public) are available. Ask a salesperson how you can get your name added to this list.

Words to the Wise

Repairing appliances is not a fun thing to spend your money on. A few simple strategies can help stretch the life of your appliances and keep them in tip-top condition.

■ Once the appliance is in your home, try each feature and control. Most defects show up during the first few uses.

■ Read and follow all manufacturers' instructions.

■ Never inspect or work on an appliance until it is unplugged. Disconnect from the wall outlets before unplugging the cord from the appliance.

■ Keep small appliances unplugged when not in use.

■ Use a separate grounded electrical circuit for each major appliance.

■ Use a three-ring binder or accordion file to keep all of your appliance manuals together. This makes them easily accessible, plus it's a good selling point if you put your house on the market. Read the manuals to find out what kind of maintenance is required to keep appliances performing at maximum. On each booklet, jot down the date and store where the purchase was made, as well as the salesperson's name. Staple your receipt to the booklet. Refer to this record when deciding whether to keep or toss an aging appliance.

■ Buy the best washing machine hoses you can afford. Inspect the ones you have, since after three years the rubber ones tend to be more brittle and prone to breaking. Stainless steel mesh is best. (Turn off the taps to your washing machine when you leave for an extended period of time.)

■ Consider regularly turning off the water taps to the machine if you can incorporate it into your routine or if your machine is in a basement or garage where you don't see it every day.

Bright Idea

Keep appliances looking good for years. Apply a coat of automobile paste wax to the appliance exterior to help protect against moisture and dirt. Apply touch-up paint to scratches as soon as you see them. (Check with appliance or auto dealers for touch-up paint.)

Bright Idea

Attach a magnetic dry-erase board on the side or front of your refrigerator and deep freeze. Keep a running list of leftovers and the date you saved them.

Fridge and Freezer Facts

- Consider buying a new refrigerator instead of repairing your old one. Many times the new one will pay for itself in energy savings and, depending on the problem, repair work can cost as much as the cost of a new fridge.

- A family of two needs 12 cubic feet of food storage. Add an extra 2 cubic feet for each additional family member. Add more if you entertain guests regularly.

- A family of two needs 4 cubic feet of freezer space. Add 2 cubic feet for each additional person. Increase the freezer space if you stock frozen products or shop infrequently.

- Top and bottom fridge/freezer configuration offers the most storage flexibility. Side-by-side models have more total storage space, but it's often difficult to store large items—for example, pizzas, boxes of pies and cakes and family-size containers of pasta dishes such as lasagna—in them. One advantage of the side-by-side model is it's easier to see what you have on hand at a glance and less digging is required since they aren't as deep as the top/bottom style.

- If possible, place your refrigerator away from heat sources like stoves and even sunlight. Extra heat will cause it to work harder to stay cool.

- Placing your refrigerator on coasters will allow you to easily move it to clean behind it.

- If your refrigerator has wire shelves, buy sheets of acrylic or plastic at a home and garden store or a hardware store. Cut the sheets to fit on the wire shelves. This will help prevent smaller items from tipping over, and cleaning will be easier, too.

- Clean condenser coils quarterly—more often if you own a dog or cat. Clean underneath your refrigerator once a month. (Be sure to flip the switch and unplug the unit before cleaning.)

- Keep the door seal clean. These often need to be replaced because of excessive mildew, and that can be expensive. Clean gaskets with soap and water—never with bleach, which can cause them to become brittle and crack.

- Analyze your shopping and cooking habits before deciding which refrigerator to buy. If you shop more often and eat more fresh than frozen food, you'll want proportionally more refrigerator than freezer space.

■ Clean the lint trap on your dryer before every load. Heavy lint buildup can cause a fire to start.

Extended Warranties

When shopping for appliances or electronics, you will likely be asked by a salesperson to purchase an extended warranty that provides coverage above and beyond the traditional manufacturer's warranty. Before purchasing one, consider the following:

■ Most products don't break down that often, and those that do may well be covered by the original warranty.

■ What are the terms of the manufacturer's warranty? If it covers labor and parts for a number of years, you really don't need a second policy.

■ Find out if your credit card has a warranty policy that extends the manufacturer's warranty for no charge.

■ Check out the *Consumer Reports* ratings for the item in question. Usually you can learn the expected life span of the product, which you can compare to the length of the warranty. If the item is likely to last a very long time, consider purchasing the extra warranty.

■ If you decide to go with the extended warranty, check the terms and conditions carefully. Find out if the repair is paid directly by the company or if you're required to file a claim first. What's the average length of time for processing a claim? How high is the deductible?

■ Ask the salesperson if there are any less expensive warranties available as he or she may only be offering you the most expensive option. Realize that you can always shop around—for example, contact the warranty company directly to see if they have a better deal.

CARS

Thanks to the Internet, luckily the process of buying a car and dealing with car salespeople is much easier today that it was years ago. Now buyers can research new cars, gather quotes from multiple dealers and learn

> *The only way to solve the traffic problems of the country is to pass a law that only paid-for cars are allowed to use the highways.*
> —*Will Rogers*

335

the trade-in value of their current car all before stepping foot in the dealership. Of course, this doesn't mean the process is completely demystified. Newspaper ads can still be pretty confusing, so it's important to take the time to do the research and make yourself an educated buyer before purchasing this major item.

How to Choose the Car That's Right for You

1. Set a maximum price you can afford and stick to it.
2. Write down your specific requirements.
3. Talk to friends about what they like and don't like about their cars.
4. Research the models you like.
5. Familiarize yourself with each model's options.
6. Test drive your top three choices, without committing to any dealership

Covering the Cost

1. Determine the monthly car payment you can afford.
2. Order your credit reports and see exactly what the dealer's finance department will see.
3. If you're trading in your old car, find out the trade-in value.
4. Consider selling your car if it's easier and more profitable than trading it in.
5. Familiarize yourself with the terms of a financing agreement.

Dealing with the Dealer

First visits to dealerships are usually to test drive, not to buy. You might get a better deal shopping later in the month, when some dealers are concerned about meeting a monthly sales quota. The best months to buy a car are in September and October, late in the model year, and December, when most people are buying gifts, not cars.

Don't be pressured, intimidated or exasperated by a dealer; if you ever feel uncomfortable, take your business elsewhere. Beware of add-ons once you agree on a price. Stay away from overpriced and often unnecessary features, such as rustproofing, paint sealer or extended warranties.

Finally, once you are comfortable with the car you are purchasing, never leave a deposit until a dealership approves your offer in writing.

How to Negotiate a Price for Your New Vehicle

1. Determine the dealer cost by consulting online and hard copies of automotive directories and start negotiating from that number.
2. Decide on your price before starting any negotiations, and remember that price all through the negotiation process.
3. Check the volume of unsold cars of the model you're seeking in automotive trade magazines. If the supply exceeds sixty days, you have much more negotiating leverage.
4. Ask for a clear explanation of all ongoing incentive programs.
5. Obtain quotes from at least three dealerships, and get each offer in writing.
6. To close the deal, pay for a down payment with a credit card, not a check, in case any problems or disputes arise. Proceed to the finance office with the credit report in hand. Take delivery of the vehicle.

Financing Your Vehicle

Always compare dealership financing with the finance terms of other loan sources. Home equity loans or a line of credit may be cheaper sources of financing than a new loan.

If the dealership won't release a completed finance contract to compare with other loan sources, don't finance with the dealer and never inflate your income or misrepresent your financial situation, as it will be verified by creditors.

When to Lease Instead of Buying

The most popular lease is the closed-end kind. You lease a car for a given number of months at a given monthly charge—say, thirty-six to forty-eight months—and at the end of the term, assuming the car is in good condition, you either walk away from the lease with no further responsibility, or you buy the car at the price agreed on at the time you signed the lease.

The advantages of the closed-end lease are the following:

> *Never lend your car to anyone to whom you have given birth.*
> —*Erma Bombeck*

337

- Usually the monthly payments are lower than payments on a car loan.
- Up-front payments are smaller with a lease.
- You always get new cars every thirty-six to forty-eight months.

The disadvantages of a closed-end lease are the following:

- Mileage limits on the lease make it more expensive if you drive long distances.
- Customized additions like a stereo or a paint job are prohibited.
- You never own the vehicle outright.

HOME COMPUTER

Possibly the most confusing purchase for your home office will be the family computer. Somehow it makes the buying process a bit easier if you can accept the fact that whatever system you purchase, it will become slightly obsolete in three to four years. The good news is that prices continue to fall, meaning that you get much more for your money than you used to.

The Necessity of a Home Computer

If you're not working from home and consider the purchase of a home computer an unnecessary expense, think twice. Computers are a huge time-saver for all aspects of family management. Because there are so many ways computers and technology can simplify your life, and because it's now easier than ever to purchase and install a computer system, there's no good excuse for not joining the online generation and getting up to speed. Plus, if you're already using a computer at work, then you've already got the know-how. Just imagine the applications it can have at home:

Home and property...

- Maintain a current and complete home inventory to prevent hours of rummaging and calculating in the event of burglary, fire or natural disaster.

There are only two kinds of computer users: those who have lost data in a crash, and those who will lose data in a crash.
—Bob LeVitus

338

- Keep car information in one place and up to date, including repairs, oil and air-filter changes, mileage records and insurance information. Store a current copy in the glove compartment for quick reference in case of accidents or breakdowns.
- Create a digital photo sheet of your house if you're selling it yourself. For houses you're looking to buy, a digital spreadsheet for each house you like makes the comparison process easier with less bulky papers to track.

Food...

- Have several different weekly menus on file that you can use every month or two.
- The Internet allows for easy comparison of lots of recipes, menu options and sites to order specialty food items.
- Cooking software gives you the choice of thousands of recipes, provides a handy cooking glossary and translates old, rich recipes into healthier ones.

Family and friends...

- Maintain an accurate record of each family member's medical history, allergies, doctors' visits and vaccinations to pull up in the event of a health crisis or problem. Software programs for recording your family's medical history allow you to make charts and graphs of just about anything, including day-to-day changes in your blood pressure.
- Consult one of the many online doctors to diagnose the common cold, flu and other easily treatable viruses or ailments. The information you quickly receive from the Internet saves wasted time at the doctor's office for less complicated medical situations.
- Allow the computer to cut your time as your child's tutor in half. Use programs for teaching grammar, spelling and math to supplement your tutoring and free you up for an hour. (A word of caution. If your children use the Internet, monitor where they go on the Internet and how much you're spending on their accounts. Investigate if a parental control system, which restricts websites from your kids, is available from your Internet provider.)

■ Keep in touch with friends and family using e-mail. This saves so much money on telephone calls and is much simpler and faster than regular mail. Plus you can send photographs, maps and all sorts of documents digitally all at the same time. It just takes some practice.

■ Keep your address book on your computer. It's the easiest way to collect, sort and quickly change contact information, and it's hard to lose a computer.

Finances . . .

■ Install an online banking program for paying bills, balancing your checkbook, preparing year-end tax information and tracking all your investments.

Special projects . . .

■ Use the Internet to plan your family's vacation. Research destinations, compare airline ticket prices and investigate various hotel options. Create driving maps, get prices and hours of operation for local attractions and even check local weather information.

■ Create a holiday card file for all addresses and set up a separate birthday card calendar. Use software to create your own greeting cards, invitations, picture books, calendars or certificates of merit. This will keep kids busy for hours.

Time and scheduling . . .

■ Shop online for clothes, household appliances and just about anything else you can imagine. Almost all nationally recognized merchants have online sites as do smaller specialty stores. Comparison-shopping has never been easier or faster.

■ Use personal information manager software to check your family's schedule and print a weekly copy for everyone. That way everyone knows what's happening and conflicts are fewer.

■ Keep grocery and household shopping lists on file and print one out before you go shopping.

■ If you have overtime work from the office, suggest to your boss that you will do it at home and then leave on time.

Personal...

- The computer can save you hours of work and, as a result, give you more time for other tasks. Use the time for your own personal growth, relaxation or rest.
- Read your favorite magazine and newspapers online
- Keep a log of your daily intake of fat grams and calories.
- Track your exercise regimen.

Glossary: Computer Terms to Know Before You Buy

You don't need to become a complete computer geek, but understanding a few key terms about a computer's inner workings and knowing what the different components are called makes the purchasing and using process easier for you and those who are trying to help you.

CD recorder: A device that allows you to create and play your own compact disks.

CD-ROM: A data storage disk, containing significantly larger amounts of data than a floppy disk.

Disk drive: An internal or external device for storing data and programs.

Floppy disk: A flat, thin disk that stores information for the computer to read, like a backup of all your word processing documents. Floppy disks are used less today as CDs hold more data.

Graphics card: This component controls all the graphics for applications like games and high-quality computer-aided design. Some graphic cards connect to a TV allowing you to play a DVD through your computer on the TV screen.

Hard drive: This device stores many of the programs and data inside the computer.

Memory (RAM): How quickly your computer responds to the software is measured by its random access memory and expressed in a number of megabytes (MB). A higher RAM is desirable.

Modem: The communication device between the computer and the Internet. The higher the modem speed, the faster your computer retrieves information from the Internet.

Monitor: The computer's display screen. Pixels measure the clarity of

Quick Tips on Choosing a Computer System

- **Choose a computer with at least 128 MB of RAM.**
- **Purchase as large a hard disk as you can afford, at least 10 gigabytes.**
- **Pick a monitor with a resolution of 768 × 1024 and a dot pitch or .28 or lower.**
- **Only purchase software that you know you'll use.**
- **Purchase a laser printer if high-quality printing is necessary.**
- **Choose video cards with a minimum of 4 MB of video RAM.**
- **A modem should be at least 56K.**

341

what you see on the screen and the dot pitch measures the sharpness. Higher numbers for each means a higher-quality visual.

Multimedia: A program like a game that incorporates both audio and video components.

Network card: A device that links two or more computers together. This is useful if two people are using two different computers at home at the same time.

Operating system: The software that communicates with the processor, handling all the different applications of the computer. Windows is the most popular operating system.

Processor: This chip inside the computer is the center of the entire system and is measured by its speed. The faster the processor the faster all of the computer's actions happen.

Software: These are the applications or tasks that your computer runs, like word processing, a bill paying system, surfing the Internet and organizing your address book.

Sound card: This component of the computer controls all the sound on the computer. A higher quality one means DVDs are clearer to hear.

Video RAM: A connection between the monitor and the computer that enhances computer games and how some Internet sites are viewed. A higher VRAM means the computer displays the information faster.

How to Shop for Computer Equipment

■ Shop for a computer like you shop for a car. Learn the language and talk to friends and colleagues about what computers they use and like. Don't buy at the first place you visit and see if purchasing several products together lowers your cost.

■ Look through several computer magazines to familiarize yourself with brand names, features and new trends in the marketplace.

■ Choose between Mac and Windows PC based upon your needs. If you use more graphics and creative applications, Mac may be better. For most word processing, a Windows PC is better. Be consistent with whatever system you use away from home or whatever your children use at school.

■ Determine your needs after you've gained some understanding of the options available. Are you building web pages? Just using the computer for word processing? Are you working with photographs, site plans or other documents requiring extensive manipulation? Do you or your children enjoy playing computer games that require good-quality speakers? Do you need a large screen or small screen to view your work? Is a lower-quality printer acceptable or is high resolution a top priority?

- If portability is important, consider a laptop instead of a desktop model. There are a few disadvantages to a laptop: it's more expensive, upgrading to install new components is more difficult and the screens are smaller.

- Prepare to spend somewhere between $1,000 and $3,000 for all the equipment, including the computer, monitor, software, keyboard and mouse, zip drive for storing your data, additional memory capacity, printer, modem, speakers and scanner.

- Investigate discounts on equipment that might be available from your children's school, your company or your spouse's employer. Often these discounts save you hundreds of dollars.

- Visit both online retailers and computer stores for price comparisons. Online purchases usually exclude sales tax and returns are easily arranged. But determine what twenty-four hour help lines are available. Take your online retailer quotes into computer stores and see if they'll match the online price and service. If not, understand completely what services or extra features might justify spending more.

- For first-time buyers, consider purchasing name brand equipment. Often those manufacturers provide better service and repair. Store brands or new entrants on the market usually lag by comparison.

- After you've selected your system, carefully read the instructions before assembling the components, or hire someone to do this for you. Once it's installed, invest in some online or offsite training to get the most from your new purchase.

> ### Extend the Life of Your Computer
>
> - **Buy and use a virus protection system. It's invaluable.**
>
> - **Backup your data often and thoroughly.**
>
> - **Save all the paperwork for any repairs and upgrades.**

FURNITURE

Secrets for Buying Furniture That Lasts
Furniture buying can be tricky, but it doesn't have to be. Just because one sofa costs three times as much as another sofa doesn't mean it's necessarily worth the price. Learning what quality components distinguish fine furniture from the junkyard variety will save you money in the long run.

The Distinctions of Wood
Understand what types of wood are used in making furniture. A piece described as "all wood" is often built with cheap particleboard or plywood. "Solid wood" indicates that all the outside pieces are made of real wood, but some synthetic substances might be used in less visible areas, like underneath the seat. "Wood veneer" is a slice of wood that is usually glued to a plywood core, providing a more stable surface with less chance of cracking. "Laminate" looks like wood but is completely synthetic.

Examining the Construction of Chairs, Chests and Drawers
- Ensure the piece sits squarely on the floor with all legs equal in length.
- Gently push the sides and top corners, checking for stability. If you feel any movement or slipping, don't buy it.
- Chairs' and chests' back panels must connect securely to the seat or base. Rock it slightly to see how the joint holds.
- Run your hand along the back and sides checking for bumps or rough spots.
- Turn all chairs upside down and examine the legs carefully. Look for stable joints and corners secured with wood not metal.
- Drawers should move smoothly and quietly. Look for dovetail construction, which connects the sides and back of the drawers and is stronger than nails.
- Panel doors on armoires and entertainment centers should swing evenly and without sticking.
- Bookshelves for heavy books require supports at several points along the length to prevent sagging.

Dream-furniture is the only kind on which you never stub your toes or bang your knee.
—C. S. Lewis

Checking Out Upholstered Furniture

- Ideally, the frame should be made of a hard wood, although metal is acceptable.
- The webbing holding the springs should be interwoven and closely spaced.
- Eight-way, hand-tied coils are still the most desirable type of springs, although flat or sinuous wire springs are almost as good and significantly less expensive.
- The frame should be completely covered and well padded, so you don't see or feel the frame.
- Cushions made of heavier materials feel more comfortable and last longer. Lift cushions to feel their weight.
- Cushions should look evenly filled and bounce back quickly after sitting.
- Cushion fill material should be self-contained and not covered just by the upholstery.
- Choose the most comfortable filling and fabric you can afford. Seating on hard, scratchy cushions is unpleasant.
- Make sure the pattern is centered on the furniture and matches at the seams.
- For leather furniture, choose full-grain or full-top grain quality.
- Check the underside of leather cushions and see if the color is uniform, meaning the leather is "aniline dyed."
- If a piece is advertised as "hand-rubbed," that means it has a high-quality finish. If you love the piece and it isn't hand-rubbed, buy it anyway and do this at home with a mixture of boiled linseed oil and turpentine.
- Wood-stained furniture should have a water-resistant coat. A few drops of water placed on it should bead, not puddle. Again, you can do this process at home.
- Study the color of the finish in bright, natural light, by a window or outside, to make sure it's the right color.
- Rub the surface for cracks or bubbles in the protective coat. If it's not smooth to the touch, don't buy it.

Sleep fast, we need the pillows.
—*Jewish proverb*

Pampering Your Pillows

Dry clean down and down-and-feather pillows every six to twelve months. You can usually wash synthetic pillows; read the label. Some people use pillow protectors; in that case, you need to wash your pillows just once a year.

Pillow Types and Sizes

- Standard (20 × 26 inches)
- Queen (20 × 30 inches)
- King (20 × 36 inches)

BETTER BEDDING

Busy Family Managers take note: according to the National Sleep Foundation, 63 percent of American adults don't get the recommended eight hours of sleep needed for good health, safety and optimum performance. If you have small children, you're probably not surprised. Be this as it may, you should do yourself the favor of making the time you *do* sleep as beneficial as possible.

Picking the Best Pillow

Pillows serve for more than comfort; good ones help keep your spine aligned with your head in the same way as when you are standing. When purchasing a pillow, make sure you buy one that offers the support you need, as well as the softness, thickness and firmness you consider comfy. The different types include:

- **Down.** Filled with small goose or duck feathers. These supply spectacular comfort, last a long time and offer adjustability. But they're also usually expensive and need to be fluffed frequently. They may cause allergic reactions in some people.
- **Down-and-feather mix.** Soft but not luxurious. These offer the comfort and resilience of down along with feathery support. If you can't afford down, the mix is a less expensive alternative.
- **Feather.** Goose feathers are the best; duck feathers are the second best. These may cause problems for people with allergies.
- **Synthetic fiber.** Long-lasting and relatively cheap. Generally, these polyester-puffed pillows last as long, and are as comfortable as, down. If allergies are a concern, these are a great alternative.
- **Latex.** Less expensive, more resistant to mildew and dust mites.
- **Foam rubber.** Inexpensive and hypoallergenic. You can sculpt these to match your comfort level. Because these are extra firm, people who like sinking into their pillows won't like these.
- **Buckwheat hulls.** Moldable. But these are usually smaller than regular pillows, and they can be noisy—and irritating—to use.

Comforters and Duvet Comforters

Comforters can be filled with cotton, down, silk, wool or hypoallergenic synthetics; they do not have removable covers. Duvet comforters are made to be encased in a duvet cover. Think about the following when buying a comforter:

- Choose wisely. Unless you are allergic, consider a down comforter; if cared for, it will last eight to ten years. Goose down is your best choice because goose feathers fluff better.
- Get the correct thickness. Try to get one with a fill of 600 to 700.
- Cover carefully. Your duvet shell should be made of ticking. Make sure down filling doesn't bunch up in places.
- Clean regularly. Dry clean comforters at least quarterly, unless they are machine washable.

The Lowdown on Sheets

- Thread count describes how many threads are woven into each square inch. The higher the thread count, the more comfy the bed linens. Muslin sheets have a thread count of 140 to 180; percale, 180 and up. Choose sheets with a thread count of at least 200.
- Be aware that sheets with a thread count of 300 to 400 feel great, but don't last as long.
- Sheets made of a 50/50 blend of cotton and polyester tend to be stiff. A 60 percent cotton blend with 40 percent polyester offers more softness.
- If you live in a cold-weather climate, consider buying silk satin sheets, which hug heat to your body. They're expensive though, and must be dry-cleaned.
- If you live in a hot-weather climate, try linen sheets. They're expensive but they last. Another breathable fabric for sheets is cotton jersey knit—the same material T-shirts are made in. But beware of deep colors in jersey as they often fade.

Take Note

Sleep experts say that most people need seven to eight hours of sleep a night to function optimally. Some people need nine.

Sheet Sizes

- **Twin flat: 66 × 96; Twin fitted: 39 × 75**
- **Full flat: 81 × 96 (to 100); Full fitted: 54 × 75**
- **Queen flat: 90 × 102 (to 106); Queen fitted: 60 × 80**
- **King flat: 108 × 102 (to 106); King fitted: 78 × 80**
- **California king flat: 102 × 110; California king fitted: 72 × 84**

347

A well-spent day brings happy sleep.
—**Leonardo da Vinci**

Mattress Matters

- Flip your mattress once a year to spread out the wear.
- Invest in an extra-thick mattress pad to add as much as three years of use.
- When purchasing a new mattress, always check out the lesser known brands. You may get as much comfort and wear from these as from the super deluxe mattresses, and you'll save at least 25 percent.
- The coils in a bed maintain its shape. Expect a good king-size mattress to have at least 450 coils; queen size, 375; and full size, 300.
- Be brave: lie down on every mattress you're considering and roll around on it. Just sitting on it won't tell you anything about comfort. If it sways or you hear creaks, keep looking.
- Beware of the temptation to buy an extra-thick mattress. If it's 3 to 5 inches thicker than your old mattress, you'll have to buy new sheets, which is an added expense.

Everyday Savings

CLOTHING

Tips for Savvy Shopping

When the going gets tough, the tough go shopping—or so some women say. If this is your mantra, keep in mind that you're more likely to get your money's worth by spending a little extra on well-made clothing, but a designer label or famous brand doesn't always ensure that you're getting a built-to-last garment. Whether you're spending $15 or $150, check out these clothing details:

- ☐ **Is there extra fabric at the seams?** Cheaper manufacturers cut corners by not leaving any room to let seams in or out at the waist, seat or sides.
- ☐ **Do patterns match?** Patterns should match uniformly, especially on the back and around all pockets. Check that plaids, stripes and checks match at the seams. Armhole and crotch cross-seams should also match up. If they don't, it's a sign of poor quality.

☐ **Are the hem seams visible?** Skirts, pants and jackets should all have invisible hem seams. Garments of real quality have silk threads, which won't fade after years of dry-cleaning. Hems should also be straight.

☐ **Is the color uniform throughout?** Fabric shouldn't be faded anywhere in the garment. If the color is darker or lighter in any areas, don't buy it.

☐ **Does the fabric have backing and quality lining?** Make sure there's a felt backing underneath the collar of a sport coat or better-quality jacket. Most good-quality suits have lining throughout the entire piece—not just in portions of the jacket.

☐ **Is the waistband reinforced?** Look for a single-piece waistband in pants. It should be reinforced to prevent rolling or bunching.

☐ **Are lapels properly shaped?** Lapels should be gently rounded and drop into place smartly when you tug on them.

☐ **Are shoulder pads secure?** If the shoulder pads bunch up or fall out of place, it's a sign of cheap merchandise.

☐ **Do jeans have double rows of stitching?** Look for the same features on tailored shirts: You don't want rips at stress points such as the armholes.

☐ **Are trim items secure?** Snaps, buttons and buckles should be neatly secured with enough thread to keep them from falling off.

☐ **Are zippers properly sewn in?** They should be sewn in straight, lie flat and dyed to match the fabric of the garment.

☐ **Are buttonholes reinforced?** Buttonholes that are sewn through both sides of the fabric hold up especially well.

☐ **Is stitching neat, straight and even?** Small, close stitching usually means a garment will hold up well to washing and wearing. Lots of strings hanging down from a garment indicate poor quality and workmanship.

☐ **Are seams and darts flat?** Even slight puckering at the seams should be avoided.

☐ **Is fabric evenly woven, with no flaws?** Some natural fibers have small flaws that do not detract from the garment. Other flaws (especially in synthetic fibers) should be avoided.

Beware of enterprises that require new clothes, and not rather a wearer of new clothes.
—Henry David Thoreau

349

Man does not live by bread alone, but he also does not live long without it.

—Frederick Buechner

☐ **Are pockets flat?** Pockets should be flat with reinforced corners and should be large enough to use comfortably.

Find Your Style

- Shop around in stores you like and find a personal shopper or sales-clerk you sense is honest and pleasant to be around. Stick with her. Or go shopping with a friend whose style you like and judgment you trust.
- Peruse mail-order catalogs and find ones that fit your taste.
- Discover the brands that fit you well—in size and taste.
- Make a personal source guide. When you discover a store or catalog that has products you like at good prices, make a note and write down the phone number.
- When you shop, wear easy-to-slip-off garments, but also wear pantyhose, have on your usual amount of makeup and fix your hair as usual. If you're shopping for a nice dress, take a pair of heels with you. If you're looking for summer vacation clothes, take sandals.
- Make sure you can take the clothes you buy out on approval. When you get home, see how they look and feel in the comfort of your own bedroom in front of your own mirror. What else do they go with in your closet?
- When purchasing something new, consider the maintenance involved.
- Look at clothes as an investment and alterations as a part of it. If you aren't willing to hem a skirt, don't buy it.

GROCERIES

We think of food shopping as a routine, dull and necessary evil. But grocery shopping can actually be a relaxing experience, if you play your cards right and go to the store when it's not crowded and when you're not rushed. In a sense, it's a challenge: to get the choicest meats and poultry, the freshest fruits and vegetables and the healthiest dairy products for your family, all at the lowest possible price.

Shopping also gives you the chance to take a proactive role in your family's eating habits. You may not be able to control what the kids are eating in the school cafeteria or when they are at a friend's house, but you can certainly buy the nutritious, health-promoting items you want to be the basis of their diet when they eat at home. It's satisfying to fill your fridge with fresh fruits and vegetables and lean meat and dairy products, and it's somehow reassuring to know you have food in the house and readily available.

Quick Tips for Smart Supermarket Shopping

Before you go . . .

- Keep an ongoing grocery list in a central location so family members can record needs. When you open the last bottle or package of any item, add it to the grocery list.
- Keep a running shopping list. Having and sticking to a list keeps you from making a second run to the store for items you forgot and being tempted to buy extra items you don't need.
- Don't shop when you're hungry or tired. It's harder to make wise economical decisions.

In and out in less time . . .

- Create a grocery shopping routine. If you buy in bulk, shop once a month at a wholesale club. Then pick a time each week to go to the grocery store.
- Avoid long grocery store lines by shopping when others don't. When my sons were young, I shopped at 5:30 A.M. once a week. It was such a peaceful experience, I've kept up the habit through the years.
- Get in and out of the store as quickly as possible. For most people, the more time spent shopping, the more money spent as well.
- If the store offers a choice, choose a smaller cart. You'll fill it faster and be more aware of putting in items you can really do without.
- Stay on task. Many items we need to buy regularly—milk, eggs, cheese, meat—are at the back of the store and the aisles taking you there are full of eye-catching impulse items.
- For healthier shopping, spend more time around the perimeter of the store where you'll find fresh produce, breads, fish, meats and

Kids Can . . .

Let your child be in charge of saving grocery store receipts each month in a designated location. Have him total them up and compare totals from month to month. Examine the receipts together and see if you can find areas where you're spending more money than you'd like. You're both learning ways to shop smarter.

351

dairy products. With the exception of cereals, grains, pastas, herbs and some frozen foods, the inner aisles in a grocery store contain mostly processed or junk foods.

- Running from store to store to buy advertised specials can actually cost you money (and time). Buy specials at the store where you plan to shop anyway and, when possible, use manufacturer's coupons— especially on double- and triple-coupon days.
- If a clerk bags your groceries, make sure all groceries get packed and every bag is placed in your cart.
- Keep a large plastic laundry basket in the trunk of your car to cut down on trips back and forth to the car when unloading.

Stretch your grocery dollars . . .

- Don't buy health and beauty items at the grocery stores. Unless they are on sale, you can usually buy them cheaper at a discount or drugstore.
- Keep in mind what fruits and vegetables are in season as they'll be less expensive.
- Buy bagged fruit and vegetables instead of loose and save about $1 a pound. And since no two bags weigh exactly the same, use the produce scale to weigh a few bags before you choose one. You could get a few apples for free.
- Go to the farmers' market on Saturdays in the summer. Make it a family outing and enjoy fresh vegetables and fruit for dinner all week long.
- Buy bread and baked goods in bulk at day-old bread stores or bakery outlets and freeze.
- Don't assume the larger size is cheaper. Check out unit prices. A unit price is the cost for a small unit of measure, such as an ounce.
- Be careful when companion foods are on display. The chips may be discounted, but the salsa could be premium priced.
- Be aware of what foods you throw out each week. If you always waste a quart of milk or some fruit, buy less.
- Check top and bottom shelves. More expensive merchandise is often placed at eye level.

- Be aware that stores stock expensive children's cereals and candy at their eye level.

- Homemade is not always cheaper. Sometimes cake, brownie and muffin mixes can be cheaper than homemade.

- Compare prices of deli-sliced meats with packaged lunchmeats. One is not necessarily cheaper than the other.

- Try no-frills and store brands. You may discover you get the same quality as the name brands offer. Compare ingredients listed on labels to determine similarity of products. Name brands and generics are sometimes identical.

- It will take you extra time, but if you know the price of everything you put into your cart, you can save yourself money. Some supermarkets give you an item free if the cash register scans it at a higher price than is marked on the shelf. For specials, bring the newspaper ad or circular with you to the checkout and make sure the price is correct.

- If the store doesn't have the advertised special you want, ask for a rain check. In some states, you have a legal right to one. When the item is back in stock, you can buy it for the sale price.

Supermarket food safety . . .

- Check sell-by and use-by dates. Make sure you plan to use the food before expiration.

- Never buy a package that's dented, rusty or torn.

- Be careful how you toss things into your cart. If a package gets damaged, the food is vulnerable to contamination.

Extra Tips

- Buy a few frozen entrees to keep on hand for busy days. Even pricey frozen meals are usually cheaper than takeout.

- Bag your own groceries so you can put things together the way they go in your kitchen.

- Put grocery receipts in an envelope and save them for a month. You may need to return an unsatisfactory product.

- Put away groceries and prepare food for the week at the same time.

Take Note

Shop around the store for cheese. The dairy case will have staple cheeses such as Cheddar, Swiss and Monterey Jack, prepackaged. The deli and perhaps a cheese table may have the same products. Know what you want—types of cheese, state or origin, age—and shop all three areas for the best price. Usually the cheese in the dairy case is the least expensive.

We may find in the long run that tinned food is a deadlier weapon than the machine gun.

—George Orwell

- Brown as much ground meat as you'll need for the week and store in a tightly covered plastic container.
- Chop all onions and green peppers you plan to use. Put in plastic sandwich bags and freeze.
- Hard-boil eggs. Cut up veggie sticks for snacks and lunches. Make individual-size packets of raisins, chips, cookies and so on for lunches.

Smart Meat Moves

- When buying meat, an expensive lean cut may be more economical than one that requires you to throw away excess bone, gristle or fat.
- Instead of buying precut filets, buy a beef or pork strip tenderloin and cut it into filets yourself. You'll save more than 30 percent.
- Buy the freshest meat possible. Hamburger should be used within a day or two of purchase, or frozen.
- A heavier turkey will give you more meat for your money. As a general rule, a 20-pound bird has more meat per pound than one that weighs 15 pounds, and you can save up to $.30 a pound.
- Expect about a 45 percent waste if you discard the skin on chicken breasts. Boneless and skinless breasts may be a better buy.
- Put chicken in an additional plastic bag or keep it away from everything else in your cart. A wet, leaking package could contaminate other foods with salmonella.
- Either cook meat soon after you buy it, or rewrap in special freezer-quality plastic wrap before freezing. Meat displayed in the meat department is wrapped in a special kind of plastic meant for display; it breathes and helps keep the meat the red color.
- Buy a whole boneless pork loin and cut it into chops and cubes. You'll save 25 percent off the cost of presliced chops and stew meat.
- Instead of pricey center cut pork chops, buy boneless pork shoulder and tenderize it by braising.

Don't Let Catchphrases Fool You

- Does the phrase "10% More Free" tempt you to buy a product? When you see that extra-free label, look to see if it's the same size package with just a new label.

- New and improved can mean just that, or it can mean a new color, new flavor or new formula.
- Avoid "buy one, get something later" deals. Manufacturers know that few shoppers ever redeem rebates or mail-in offers.
- Watch out for nonfat products. Fat provides texture and bulking. If it's removed from a product, often it's replaced with sugar. Check the ingredients and calorie count. You may be better off with a smaller serving of the regular version.
- Beware of so-called "specials." Food displayed as "featured" or "new"—such as cookies, soda, paper towels—aren't necessarily bargains but may simply be promotions of regularly priced items.
- Don't be lured into buying something you really don't need just because a sign says, "Limit Four per Customer." Consumers tend to buy more when the stores impose a limit.
- Take cash to the store with you. You'll spend much less on food than if you pay by check or credit card.

Clip Those Coupons

If you're willing to invest a little time, and you really love to get something for nothing, coupons may be for you. Depending upon how much you want to put into it, you can save anywhere from a few cents to more than half your total weekly tab. While it may hardly seem worth the trouble to cut out a coupon just to save a few cents, you'll be pleasantly surprised at how quickly those small amounts add up. These tips will help you take advantage of coupons without getting bogged down:

- **Start small.** Try using one or two coupons per week at first. Habits always start small.
- **Establish a routine.** Set aside ten minutes every week (or twenty or thirty) to clip and file coupons. If you schedule a certain time period every week, you're more likely to do it. It's one of those jobs that can be done while sitting in front of the TV or talking on the phone.
- **Think before you clip.** Don't cut out coupons for products or brands you aren't familiar with; the savings won't make up for a less-satisfying product.

Advertising may be described as the science of arresting human intelligence long enough to get money from it.
—*Stephan Leacock*

355

Smart Bulk Buys

Rushing off to the store every time you need an item wastes time, energy and money. By purchasing nonperishable items quarterly in bulk, you will spend less unscheduled time at the store, never run out of necessities and save money since quantities usually cost less than single items. Smart bulk buys include paper products, toiletries, cleaning supplies, pet food, school supplies, batteries, videotapes and lightbulbs.

- **Be choosy.** Don't clip coupons for products you're trying to avoid, such as snack or expensive items.

- **Buyer beware.** Most food coupons are for convenience foods. Even when these items can be purchased more cheaply, consider if you're introducing your family to more expensive, less healthy items that they just might acquire a taste for. You could be potentially creating bigger grocery bills in the future.

- **Know when to say no.** Disregard coupons for larger-size portions than you usually use. You may end up wasting most of the food.

- **Mark them up.** Circle or highlight expiration dates with two different colors for easy sorting. Use one color to highlight those with a short life span (within six weeks) and another color for those that give you a year or more to use them.

- **Get organized.** Store coupons in labeled envelopes, an accordion file or a coupon organizer. Or, create a special coupon bulletin board. Create categories across the top of the board—for example, dairy, meat, baking supplies, cleaning products, snacks. Hang it in an out-of-the-way place like a laundry room. (It's a great way to be reminded regularly what coupons you have, but it's not very attractive.)

- **Weed out.** Take time at least once per month to toss outdated coupons.

- **Simplify.** Write your grocery list on an envelope, then put coupons for items on the list inside. Highlight the items on your list for which you have coupons.

- **Increase your savings.** When your store features double- and triple-coupon sales, be sure to take advantage.

- **Downsize.** Couponing experts say it's usually a better deal to use two coupons on two small sizes of an item than a single coupon for the larger size.

- **Share the wealth.** Trade coupons with friends, neighbors or coworkers. This way you can collect numerous coupons for items you use frequently while donating coupons that other people need. Once you get multiple coupons for the same item, you can stockpile and buy as many of that item as allowed when it's on sale.

- **Save smart.** Put the money you earn via coupons immediately in the bank (many stores now have branches on site). Use the money to save for something special.
- **Travel smart.** Keep fast-food coupons in your glove compartment for easy access.
- **Plan ahead.** When browsing through an entertainment book of coupons, put sticky-notes on pages with deals you want to take advantage of.
- **Rebate deals.** These are only a good deal if you are motivated to send in proofs of purchase or whatever is needed to get the rebate. Some products have instant rebates attached to the outside of the label that must be removed and redeemed immediately at the checkout.

Food Co-ops

A co-op is a group of people who combine their buying power to obtain quantity discounts. Groups can reach volume levels that sometimes individuals can't. Many kinds of co-ops exist: dairy, bread, spices, fruit and vegetable, organic and more. Buying frequency and minimum orders can vary, and some co-ops require a small membership fee. Others require that you work a specified number of hours shopping, delivering, sorting, playing cashier, handling paperwork or serving as the contact person. (Some co-ops grow so large they have full-time paid staff.)

The advantages of a co-op can include the following:

- Shopping from home. (Typically, you call in, fax or e-mail your order.)
- Deep discounts. Savings are significant even on small quantities.
- No impulse buying. You have to make thoughtful decisions about what you want and need when you preorder.
- Fresher food. Co-ops cut out several middlemen in the grocery-buying system, so food gets to you faster. In many fruit and vegetable co-ops, you buy produce straight from the farmer.
- You can join health-food co-ops and purchase organic, salt-free and sugar-free food.

357

The disadvantages of joining a co-op can include the following:

■ Quantities. They're sometimes larger than you need. You might not need 50 pounds of rice.
■ Timing. If you run out of something before pickup day, the wait may frustrate you.
■ Substitutions. Sometimes what you order is deleted from the group order because too few people want the item. In this case, usually something else is substituted and it may be something your family doesn't like.

Clothes wear out, refrigerators die and cars don't last forever. Whether you're the kind of person who likes to shop till you drop, or if, for you, shopping ranks right up there with cleaning the oven, being the personal shopper for your family is an important job.

Closing Thoughts

People often comment about how passionate I am about my work. They're right. The mission of my company, Family Manager, Inc., is to provide helpful resources and information to equip and encourage you in your valuable role as Family Manager. On every page I write and in every speech I deliver, my goal is to give you some fresh ways of looking at your home, family and life, and to help you discover strategies that will assist you in managing your myriad responsibilities, adding fun and closeness to your home life and helping you feel good about yourself and what you do.

From cook to organizer, from accountant to gardener, there are dozens of jobs a Family Manager undertakes, and within them, thousands of ways to improve home life. As you explored ways to be an effective CEO—by understanding your jobs, determining your plan, trying new ideas and delegating to your family team—you may have felt inspired, motivated and, quite possibly, overwhelmed. Don't be. No one intends that you apply every one of these tips. My goal is to help you relax, not jump-start an anxiety attack!

Because we are different—in personality, family makeup, where we live, where we work, our expectations—each of us will adapt and apply the ideas in this book in different ways. But no matter who we are, every change we are willing to make toward better managing meals, money and household tasks is worthwhile. The end result for everyone involved is a happier situation at home. I receive letters from moms every week, telling me how a few small tips really have made a big difference in their family's lives!

I encourage you to visit www.familymanager.com to learn about other resources and opportunities to help you in your role as Family Manager. After you've applied the Family Manager strategies (and hopefully have some newfound time in your day), your comments and suggestions are welcome at familymanager@familymanager.com. I would love to hear from you.

Here for you and your family,

Kathy Peel

Founder and President, Family Manager, Inc.

Index

('b' indicates boxed material)